D0725474

> *"Mother, your life certainly consists of saying goodbye most of the time to all of your sons. I hope they do a job to honor you. We try."*

Thus ends one of the many letters quoted in this remarkable book. They were written by Dr. Tom Dooley to his mother. The letters came from strange cities in foreign lands. Cities which, to Tom's mother, were little more than dots on a map. Yet, separated as they were by half a world, Tom and his mother maintained an intimate relationship which never wavered.

Out of this relationship comes the substance of this book—the story of Dr. Dooley's life. She explains why her son felt compelled to give up his chances for a career as a "society doctor" in order to become a medical missionary. She tells of his long and difficult struggle to establish a hospital, a center of healing, in the hostile jungles of Asia. She tells of his public battle against disease in others—and his private battle against the cancer that was to destroy his own young life.

Probably no one else is so uniquely qualified as Mrs. Dooley to tell the story of the man who, as he lay dying, wrote these words to a young colleague:

> *"Dedicate some of your life to others. Your dedication will not be a sacrifice. It will be an exhilarating experience because it is intense effort applied towards a meaningful end."*

Other SIGNET Books About
Dr. Tom Dooley

promises to keep

THE LIFE OF DOCTOR
THOMAS A. DOOLEY

by *Agnes W. Dooley*

The woods are lovely, dark and deep,
But I have promises to keep
And miles to go before I sleep.
                                    Robert Frost

A SIGNET BOOK
Published by **THE NEW AMERICAN LIBRARY**

Published as a SIGNET BOOK
by arrangement with Farrar, Straus and Company, Inc.,
who have authorized this softcover edition.
A hardcover edition is available from Farrar, Straus and
Company, Inc.

FIRST PRINTING, APRIL, 1964

The quotations from the following books are used with the
permission of the publishers, Farrar, Straus and Company, Inc.,
to whom acknowledgment is gratefully made:
Deliver Us from Evil, copyright © 1956 by Thomas A. Dooley;
The Edge of Tomorrow, copyright © 1958 by Thomas A. Dooley;
The Night They Burned the Mountain, copyright © 1960 by
Thomas A. Dooley; and *Before I Sleep,* edited by James Monahan,
copyright © 1961 by Farrar, Straus and Cudahy, Inc.
Grateful acknowledgment is also made to *Think,*
in which the "Letter to a Young Doctor" first appeared.

SIGNET TRADEMARK REG. U.S. PAT. OFF. AND FOREIGN COUNTRIES
REGISTERED TRADEMARK—MARCA REGISTRADA
HECHO EN CHICAGO, U.S.A.

SIGNET BOOKS are published by
The New American Library of World Literature, Inc.
501 Madison Avenue, New York, New York 10022

PRINTED IN THE UNITED STATES OF AMERICA

Contents

Illustrations

A sixteen-page photographic section, covering the major periods of Dr. Dooley's life, appears between pages 96 and 97.

one

beginnings

*I charge each of you to keep this
ever in mind...*

EARLE

My son Tom did most things with style throughout his life,
even in his earliest years. I wish there were a picture of him
at age four, sitting at piano before an audience of very
young music students and their parents in St. Louis. Not only
was Tom so small that his feet could not reach the pedals,
but his teacher was standing by in case he started to fall off
the bench. None of this cramped Tom's style in the least.
The piece he had learned was very simple, of course, but he
played it with such earnestness and ended with such a real
flourish that he brought down the house. He took the laughter
and the applause in stride, as if it could not have happened
any other way.

Tom could read musical notes before he could read
words, and his love of music never left him. A friend of
ours who taught music recognized his gift very early; she
showed him how to play on a soundless keyboard on the
floor before he ever sat at a piano. Later, during his school
years, he studied at the well-known Leo Miller Studios in
St. Louis. In his teens we enrolled him at the Juilliard School
of Music, but by this time he was quite certain that he want-

ed to be a doctor. Music was an avocation that he always loved, and he took music with him wherever he went. The famous zinc-lined piano that followed him to Laos, the story of which he tells in *The Edge of Tomorrow*, meant more to him than most people realize. But his true vocation, as he realized in his teens, was medicine. In a literal sense he was born to help people, and he knew it.

Thomas Anthony Dooley III was born at 2:30 in the morning on January 17, 1927 at St. Ann's Hospital in St. Louis. His father, Thomas A. Dooley, Jr., was an alumnus of St. Louis University and an officer of the American Car and Foundry Company. He had been a Major of Engineers and served in France with the 31st Engineers during World War I. My husband's father, Thomas A. Dooley, Sr., was the designer and builder of the first all-steel boxcar ever made. This was just before the United States entered World War I, when President Woodrow Wilson recognized the importance of this contribution to the Allied effort and personally intervened to expedite its accomplishment. Tom's Irish roots—the Dooley side—were in Limerick County, Ireland, from which Mr. Dooley the elder had emigrated.

Tom's grandfather on the other side—my father, that is —was Malcolm W. Wise, whose background was in banking. Our family came from Pennsylvania. My father's father, William W. Wise, fought in the Civil War as Captain, 15th U.S. Infantry, and was killed in the battle of Murfreesboro. His officer's commission, signed by Abraham Lincoln, is a prized family possession and now belongs to my son Malcolm. This document is reproduced on page 11.*

A very important part of Tom's story has to do with his older brother, Earle. It was Earle more than anyone else who influenced Tom, and Earle's death in World War II was one of the turning-points in Tom's life. Earle was the son of my first husband, Lieutenant Earle Manzelman, a pilot in the

---

* It reads in part as follows: "KNOW YE, that reposing special trust and confidence in the patriotism, valor, fidelity and abilities of William W. Wise, I have nominated and by and with the advice and consent of the Senate do appoint him Captain in the Fifteenth Regiment of Infantry in the service of the United States . . . And *I do strictly charge and require* . . . (Signed) Abraham Lincoln." The italics are mine for a special reason: this phrase echoes in Earle's posthumous letter to the family, and in Tom's letters from Viet Nam later. They both knew the wording of their great-grandfather's Civil War commission by heart.

THE PRESIDENT OF THE UNITED STATES OF AMERICA,

To all who shall see these presents, greeting:

KNOW YE, That reposing special trust and confidence in the patriotism, valor, fidelity, and abilities of _____ I have nominated, and by and with the advice and consent of the Senate, do appoint him _____ in the service of the United States: to rank as such from the _____ day of _____ eighteen hundred and sixty _____. He is therefore carefully and diligently to discharge the duty of _____ by doing and performing all manner of things thereunto belonging. And I do strictly charge and require all Officers and Soldiers under his command to be obedient to his orders as _____. And he is to observe and follow such orders and directions, from time to time, as he shall receive from me, or the future President of the United States of America, or the General, or other superior Officers set over him, according to the rules and discipline of War. This Commission to continue in force during the pleasure of the President of the United States for the time being.

GIVEN under my hand at the City of Washington this _____ day of _____ in the year of our Lord one thousand eight hundred and Sixty _____ and in the _____ year of the Independence of the United States.

By the President: Abraham Lincoln

_____
Secretary of War.

"Cracker Box" Air Force whom I married during World War I. He was killed in flight soon after the war, while we were living in Hawaii—we were stationed at Hickam Field—and three months later our son Earle was born. I became Mrs. Thomas A. Dooley in 1925. Two years later Tom was born, and after him our sons Malcolm and Edward arrived at two-year intervals. Neither we nor he ever considered Earle anything but a Dooley, and his legal adoption as a Dooley was completed when he was in high school.

Our house in St. Louis was attractive and roomy, and stood on an acre of ground amidst many lovely trees. My husband adored all his sons, and he was inclined to give them what they wanted, except what he thought was bad for them or foolish in itself. One foolish request, it seemed to him, was made by Tom when he was only five years old. The kindergarten our son then attended was that of St. Roch's School conducted by the Sisters of St. Joseph. One day Tom came home and proudly told his father that he had been chosen as leader of the class minuet.

"I'm going to lead the minuet," said Tom, "and I'm going to wear white shoes."

"Not if *I* have to buy them," my husband replied. "It's a great honor to lead the minuet, no doubt, but you wear out enough black shoes as it is, without going in for white ones." The idea of *white* shoes for dancing seemed so farfetched to my husband that he could not seriously believe they were a required part of the costume. He thought Tom had made this up, and Tom never mentioned it again.

To his amazement, when the gala event took place, all the boys and girls came out wearing white shoes, except his son. Young Tom was self-assured, however, as he called out his "One, two, three, *point*," to all the dancers. He made it look as if the only thing the leader could possibly wear was black shoes.

Among the many patterns of behavior that recur throughout Tom's life, self-confidence and the will to lead are evident from the beginning. He assumed he had to be first in everything he did, at almost every stage of his career. For instance, he had to sell more chances than anyone else at school to support the missionaries throughout the world. This was when he attended Barat Hall, the boys' school conducted by the nuns of the Sacred Heart. An amusing family crisis arose from these missionary efforts, when he was selling chances on a baseball catcher's mitt.

Tom had successfully persuaded his father, mother, and older brother Earle to buy chances, but he got absolutely nowhere with younger brother Malcolm. (Ed was just a baby at this time.) One evening, after we were all seated at the dinner table, Tom addressed no one in particular as follows:

"Everyone here buys chances except my brother Malcolm. What makes *him* so stingy?"

Malcolm instantly burst into tears, and sobbed out a reply which the family never forgot: "How can I buy a chance on a catcher's mitt, *when I play first base?*"

Religion was an important element in Tom's childhood, and it meant a great deal to him throughout his life. It was our practice to attend Mass as a family, and to say daily prayers at home. I tried to stress to my boys the awareness of other people's needs and the real meaning of charity. As usual, it was Tom who responded most keenly.

Tom was always passionately engaged in whatever project he undertook—whether distributing Christmas food baskets and toys, canvassing the neighborhood for contributions to charitable organizations, or whatever. He always went "all out"; no halfway effort ever satisfied Tom. I sometimes worried that he might make a nuisance of himself, and once I pointed out to him that some of the neighbors he so brashly approached for money were eminent and even famous people. His response was indignant. "Why, Mother," he said, "they're really the same as everyone else, aren't they?"

This passionate belief in the worth and dignity of every human being, regardless of his color or race or background, was deeply imbedded in Tom. This was a basic tenet of his religion, and Tom took hold of it ardently. He never let anyone forget that every soul is equal in the eyes of God. Years later, in Laos, many of the people whom he helped and to whom he administered medicine tried to make a god of him. One of the corpsmen at the clinic told me that Tom got very angry when people kow-towed before him on the roads or in the villages when he went on sick-call. Tom would always raise them to their feet, and say with great intensity: "Don't worship me or anyone else. Worship God! You're as good as I am. You're as good as anyone in the world."

It was at Barat Hall, his grade school, that Tom first learned French. He had a gift for languages which in the end even included two Chinese dialects which he acquired in Laos. French, however, was the foreign tongue he loved above all others. He studied it intensively over the years, including summer courses at the Sorbonne, until he could speak it fluently and read it easily. His knowledge of French served him in good stead at a critical moment in 1954, and altered the course of his life.

One of Tom's passing interests as a child, and an unusual one for a boy, was dolls. His father was very much against this, until he realized that to Tom the dolls were real people who needed help. They were the sickest dolls you ever saw. Tom bandaged them, gave them shots, put them in splints, and operated on them. During this phase cotton and gauze and adhesive tape were continually missing from our medicine cabinet, and I always knew where I would find them— in Tom's "hospital." In this way he played at being a doctor long before he became one. This phase was brief; suddenly the dolls all got better and they were given away.

Tom always had tremendous energy and good health, and a muscular body that could take rugged treatment. When he was very young, I would often find him up in a tree or climbing along the roof of a shed or garage while his younger brothers stood goggle-eyed, watching his feat of derring-do. He had unusual courage, for a child, and would always (often to my distress) take a dare. Tom liked to go his own way and, not unlike most children, did not wish to be restrained by anyone, including his parents. We felt that as long as he did not harm anyone—and he never did—the sudden enthusiasms and impulses of his driving nature ought not to be curbed too severely.

Tom loved horses. He developed his riding ability at Lawsonia, Green Lake, Wisconsin where he spent many boyhood summers with the family. Another sport in which he excelled was swimming. One summer the family spent its vacation at the Monmouth Hotel in Spring Lake, New Jersey. One day on the beach, Tom noticed an older man helplessly caught in a riptide. Tom was the first to reach him, and he held him up until the lifeguards arrived with a tow-line.

My son Malcolm has written his impressions of those Wisconsin summers in the late '30s and early '40s, when Tom was in his early teens.

MALCOLM DOOLEY:

Summer in the Dooley family was always a special season, one adorned not only with the beauty of Wisconsin nature, but with the fun and friendship that a family experiences on their annual holiday.

Dad was always the leader of everything in our household, but he was especially energetic and obviously excited as April turned to May and our departure for Green Lake, Wisconsin neared. As dutiful children, we at first shared his enthusiasm, then as we grew older we outpaced Dad in the annual countdown of the days until we left for Lawsonia.

Here, in our youthful garden of Eden, 175 miles north of Madison, Wisconsin, joys were experienced, loves were matured, and values were developed that later showed up in my older brothers. Sure we had fun—sailing, swimming, fishing, laughing at the folks' friends who would always find it convenient to come and visit us in our six-bedroom "cottage." In those quiet summers just before World War II, the Dooley boys had their world with vanilla icing on it.

The only member of the family who showed any real recognition of the desperate situation the world was heading towards was my brother Earle. Earle was going to Culver Military Academy at the time and had developed a very serious side to his usually happy personality. I can remember the many nights he sat beside the old Zenith radio listening to Hitler's speeches with simultaneous translations. He listened as if he knew that what was being said was going to change all our lives. A student of history, he followed these speeches with an interest that surprised us. Little did he or we know that at twenty-one a Nazi mortar shell would snuff out the life of 1/Lt. Earle H. Dooley.

Those summers in Wisconsin were the jewels that boys remember as they become men. They are the memories you hold close to your heart when faced with danger, or when you feel the terrible loneliness that comes when you try to accomplish something by unconventional or unfamiliar means, as Tom did. Later, in letters from Laos, Tom frequently referred to the good times we had had during those summers in Wisconsin, and how fresh they remained in his mind.

There was an attractive pattern of life and activity around Lawsonia for boys of our ages, and Tom plunged into that life with fervor. There was sailing; our friends and neighbors, the Bumbies, had a Class E sailboat. It wasn't long before Tom had sailed their boat across the lake, virtually out of sight, while he studied the sandstone cliffs of the opposite shore. Dad was always apologizing to the Bumbies for his foot-loose, or rather sail-loose, son who had taken over their boat.

Every Saturday night there was a dance at the hotel, which was the social center of Lawsonia. It was a shock for Dad when he first saw Tom playing the piano with the orchestra. Without the family's knowing it, Tom had become great friends with the musicians; it hadn't taken them long to appreciate Tom's real musical flair. It was a bit hard for Dad, but eventually he accepted seeing his thirteen-year-old not only friendly with the "help," but an integral part of the orchestra.

The real treat of those summers for Tom was horses. There was a stable at Lawsonia, and it was hard to keep Tom away from it. Tom and the animal known as horse became close friends. Mother was always upset when Tom was riding, and was alarmed when he would go galloping into the wooded trails without a guide or adult companion, but she could not stop him, nor did Dad want to stop him. Tom's horsemanship pleased Dad, who had been quite an equestrian in his day. He would virtually beam through his stern Victorian face, as he saw Tom speed off. Those summers were full and they were fun. They gave us a chance to be close to Father, who was a busy executive the year around, and a chance to be brothers with Earle.

We surrounded Earle with a quasi-mystic aura of adoration, for he always knew what was right, what to do, what not to do. We saw little of him in the winter months, since he was going to Culver. What Earle said, we did. What Earle wanted, we got for him if we could. We loved him with the distant love of youth for a hero. Earle appreciated this, for though we were half-brothers yet we all knew we loved each other. Earle and his example made a lasting and effective impression on young Tom Dooley that later helped him blaze his way into the minds and hearts of millions.

My son started high school in 1940. He took an accelerated course at St. Louis University High School, and finished in three years. Tom was always good in his studies if they interested him. Of course, they did not always interest him and he had his ups and downs, but he appplied himself enough to stay in the top third of his class. His father also used a bit of psychology. He told Tom that as a graduation present he could have anything within reason—except an a tomob

This whetted Tom's interest and we knew he would easily make it. As graduation neared, Tom arrived home late one afternoon with dozens of travel brochures. When his father looked up from the afternoon newspapers, Tom spilled the booklets on the floor beside him and said, "Dad, that's what I want for graduation—a trip to Mexico!"

Up to this time he had never been out of the country, and this was one of the first signs of his great interest in other parts of the world. He got his present, as promised, and he prepared for it not as a sightseer but as a student of the country. He obtained books from the library on the history, politics, and culture of Mexico, and his interest in languages encouraged him to buy a Spanish grammar. My husband and I insisted that he travel with a group of tourists under the auspices of a travel agency, and Tom reluctantly agreed. From Mexico City he wrote: "Today I went to the basilica dedicated to Our Lady of Guadalupe. It is the most beautiful church I have ever seen. All over there is pure gold-leaf work and a profusion of gargoyles, animals, and angels. All of this adds to the almost pagan opulence and creates an atmosphere of joy." After church he went to the Floating Gardens of Xochimilco where, he said, "for once in my life I had all the flowers I ever wanted." Later we learned that he sometimes broke away from the tour. He made one or two trips by burro to remote mountain villages. These side-trips, not on the itinerary, made it possible for Tom to get closer to the Mexican people.

These were very serious times. Pearl Harbor occurred while Tom was still in high school and Earle was finishing his studies at the Foreign Service School of Georgetown University. (Many years later on December 7, 1956 Tom remembered Pearl Harbor Day, and wrote me from his hospital in Laos: "Fifteen years ago this afternoon I came home from a movie at the Varsity Theater and distinctly remember walking into the entrance hall at 72 Fair Oaks where you had that white table with tile on it and the hurricane lamp. I was setting my gloves on that table when Dad told me the Japanese had bombed Pearl Harbor. How very long ago!")

It made a deep impact on Tom when, early in 1942, Earle enlisted in the Army. He had only a few months to go for his degree at Georgetown, and he was only nineteen, but Earle was determined to enlist. "Mother, I see other fellows going in and I simply can't keep my mind on studies. Foreign Service will be pointless anyway, if we don't win this war." After completing his training, Earle was commissioned a Second Lieutenant. Soon he was assigned to overseas duty and sailed for England. We never saw him again.

Tom was sixteen when he entered college during these war years. It should be remembered that in those years colleges and high schools all had accelerated programs, with classes right through the summer months. Tom wanted to take the pre-medical course at Notre Dame. His father and I were not really convinced that he knew his own mind. My husband thought that Tom did not have the patience to be a doctor.

It is true that at this time Tom had a very full social life. After all, he was a teen-ager. He dated many girls, and though he saw two or three more frequently than others, I do not believe they were steady. I have the autograph album from this period which Tom kept with enthusiasm. He often took his dates to concerts and the theatre. After the show they would go backstage and Tom would ask the artist to sign the program. Some of his mementoes include the autographs of Judith Anderson and Maurice Evans, on their wartime tour in *Macbeth;* Irving Berlin, conducting his show, *This Is the Army,* at the St. Louis Municipal Auditorium; pianists Serge Rachmaninoff, Artur Rubinstein, Robert Casadesus, and William Kapell; singers Lily Pons and Ezio Pinza; violinists Jascha Heifetz and Joseph Szigeti; ballet dancers Irina Baronova and Alicia Markova; and he even saved a card to the visitors' gallery of the U. S. Senate Chamber, signed by Bennett Champ Clark on August 8, 1942, during a weekend trip to the Capitol. At the very end of this album his father wrote, "To a wonderful son of whom I am very proud. His Dad."

At Notre Dame Tom seemed to be the most carefree freshman on the campus. There were football games, parties, girls, and lots of friends. Two of his favorite young friends at South Bend were Patricia Christensen and John W. McCarthy Jr., both from neighboring La Porte, Indiana. Pat, who later became Mrs. McCarthy, has written of these days when all three were only sixteen years old: "Tom was a student at Notre Dame then, but he often spent his weekends in La Porte. He was tall and slender, with dark wavy hair, cool blue eyes and devastating lashes. He won the heart of every girl present on that quiet Sunday afternoon when we met him. . . .

"He played the piano marvelously, with six or eight of

the girls hanging on every note. He could jitterbug like a professional, and he had an easy way of flipping his partner over his back—something we hadn't seen done anywhere but in the movies . . . We also found it exciting when he talked of his plans to be a 'society doctor' and specialize in obstetrics. If anyone had told us then that Tom would one day devote his life to the sick people in the underdeveloped nations of Southeast Asia, I am sure we all would have laughed out loud.

"But those lazy, fun-filled Sunday afternoons in La Porte ended all too soon. Most of the boys went into the Army, Navy or Air Force."

Overseas, Earle was assigned to the Fourth Division under General Eisenhower's command, preparing for an unknown D-Day. At zero-hour on June 6, 1944, Earle "went over" on one of the first waves landing on Utah Beach.

When Tom learned that Earle had been wounded during the battle of Saint Lo, he was beside himself with a complicated mixture of emotions—pride and joy at his brother's bravery; a sense of awe that someone close to him was actually involved in the real thing; anxiety and concern over Earle's well-being and safety. The whole family was, of course, involved in similar feelings, and like mothers the world over during those days I prayed that God would spare my oldest son.

It is said that war ages men, and I believe this to be so. Though Tom would not be twenty-one for four years, he really "came of age" during 1943 and 1944. Everything was speeded up and hastened by the war, and Tom's growing-up was not spared this process.

He finished two semesters between January and November, 1944, in Notre Dame's accelerated pre-medical course. Then came the surprise. "I can't go on at Notre Dame while Earle is fighting in Europe," Tom announced. "I've got a duty to the country too." He said he could not wait until he reached the draft age of 18 in January, 1945.

He now asked our permission to enlist as a U. S. Navy medical corpsman, where he could take care of the sick. My husband and I thought the Navy program might provide a good way for Tom to find out whether his desire to be a doctor was real or not. So we agreed, and he enlisted as a Navy corpsman and went to the Great Lakes Naval Training Station.

While he was there, the news of Earle's death in Germany came to us. Earle, after being wounded at Saint Lo, was treated in a Field Hospital and rejoined his organization; he was wounded a second time late in July and was sent to a hospital in England. After his recovery he again crossed the Channel and was assigned as a First Lieutenant to the 8th Division, which was one of the first divisions to reach the Rhine. On November 18, 1944 he was killed in the battle of Hürtgen Forest. He was awarded the Bronze Star and the Silver Star posthumously. Some weeks later we received the letter he had written to be delivered in case of death:

16 August 1944
England

Dearest clan:

You should receive this only in case of my being killed in action, as it should be forwarded to you along with my personal belongings.

I have a distinct feeling that I shall not return from France this time. At any rate I do not feel totally immune from death, as I once did. This is probably because I have seen so many of my comrades go down. The idea of being fatally hit does not in any way terrify me, though I do feel that I have everything to live for. I have firmly resolved to go forward and do what is expected of me to the very best of my ability regardless of the physical consequences. My leaving you is important to you, I know, but in the overall picture it is not so important. If ever a man was prepared for departure, *I am*.

What *is* important, and I charge each of you to keep this *ever* in mind, is that this shall *never* happen again. You must see to it that any attempt to begin this slaughter anew is crushed *at once*, by force of arms if necessary! Never again must you allow human stupidity to look idly aside while this scourge is permitted to fester and spring out on such a scale. We can never get rid of war entirely, but it must be limited!

Now don't take this too hard. I am truly happy now, and I have gone out in the most manly fashion. If you all, Mother, Dad, Tom, Malc, and Ed, carry out the spirit of this note, everything is worth while. Life is short and there are many things I wish I could do—but for my meager 21 years I have become a man. You made me that and I thank you.

Chin up
EARLE

"Chin up" was our family expression for times of trouble. It did not mean that we shed no tears or showed no grief; it

was our way of telling each other to have courage and remember our faith in God in dark moments. We all needed
that faith when Earle died. The words which Earle had written to each of us ("*I charge you . . .*") were most literally
taken to heart by Tom. He carried that letter with him always. It was in the far-off villages of Laos that Tom paid his
tribute to Earle.

two

from medical corpsman to m.d.

"Sir, I've been ordered to Japan."
TOM TO DR. CASBERG.

After completing his "boot" training at the Great Lakes Naval Training Station, Tom was assigned to the U.S. Navy Hospital at St. Albans, Long Island. One Saturday, just before he left on an overnight pass for New York City, he asked the patients in his ward if there was anything he could bring back for them.

One of the sailors yelled: "Yes, Hildegarde!" He meant the lovely *chanteuse* appearing at the Persian Room of the Hotel Plaza. Others jokingly took up the cry: "Hildegarde! Hildegarde!" They did not know Tom.

That night after Hildegarde's performance, Corpsman Dooley barged into her dressing-room and in a torrent of words told her that her presence was so urgently and enthusiastically demanded at St. Albans Hospital that she could not possibly let them down, no matter what other commitments she might have, especially in time of war. He, Corpsman Dooley, would be on duty the following afternoon. Would she come? Hildegarde calmly told him she would see, and he left not really knowing whether he could count on her or not.

The next afternoon Corpsman Dooley was ordered to report to the Commanding Officer of the hospital on the double. Hildegarde had arrived on schedule, all right, but she refused to budge unless Corpsman Dooley personally escorted her through the hospital. Followed by all the Navy brass— "It was the first time in my life I preceded anyone of rank," Tom wrote—Hildegarde took Tom's arm, went into Tom's ward, entertained Tom's patients, and then toured the entire hospital.

As a result of the shortage of experienced medical corpsmen in the U. S. Marines, Tom, who by this time had become head corpsman in the operating room at St. Albans, was transferred to the Marine Base at Quantico, Virginia. He found that he had to go through training camp all over again, in Marine style this time.

After six weeks, he was transferred to the Marine Hospital at San Diego. Because combat casualties were still arriving from the Pacific theatre of war, he received patients in battle dress. At the end of 1945, a few months after V-J Day, Tom was released from the service due to the fact that he was a pre-medical student and the shortage of doctors was acute. He returned to Notre Dame in 1946.

Malcolm entered Notre Dame the following year, 1947. By this time Tom had begun to accumulate almost enough credits to enter medical school without a college degree. The war-time acceleration was still in being, and Tom felt he would be ready for St. Louis University School of Medicine by the fall of 1948.

His father did not like the idea of Tom starting medical school without his B.A. degree from Notre Dame, which was possible under the wartime system. My husband's point was that Tom might later decide he did not want to be a doctor and drop out of medical school, and then he would have neither an M.D. nor a B.A. Tom's argument was that he very much wanted to be a doctor as soon as possible, and it would be wasteful of time not to enter medical school now, if they would take him. He also promised that if for any reason he did not win his M.D., he would return to college for the bachelor's degree. In the spring of 1948, he was notified by the St. Louis University School of Medicine that he had been accepted. My husband was pleased that Tom had passed the entrance exams, and I was glad that the matter was settled. My husband died two months after Tom started his medical courses.

Tom's last year at Notre Dame, 1947 to 1948, was Malcolm's first year. He describes this period at college with his brother.

MALCOLM DOOLEY:

An Indiana snowfall covers the Notre Dame campus. Walking the student paths at two in the morning is something Notre Dame men never forget. The statue of Mary atop the illuminated golden dome; the tall, erect steeple on the main church; the hush of Our Lady's Grotto; the crunch of the snow underfoot—these are a few of the beauties of Notre Dame, and this was the setting as Tom and I walked from the main entrance to our residence hall early one January morning in 1948. Christmas vacation had ended, and we were returning to classes. That Christmas was something Tom and I frequently spoke of in later years, our last carefree Christmas: We were doing well in school, we were maturing, and we had friends—friends who in later years would seldom be seen and enjoyed by Tom because of goals and accomplishments he set out to attain.

It was the last Christmas when Tom and I as young men would have the wonderful feeling all young people have of knowing that "Dad is there"—Dad, who gives us the money we need to buy flowers for the girls we are taking to the parties, Dad who lends us the car, Dad who picks up the bill for our education, Dad who is busy planning a happy summer for us. That Christmas of 1947 in St. Louis was full of fun, activity, friends, parties, gifts and the wonderful feeling that comes from being a member of a "real" family. Tom and I were college men now, and Dad was becoming more of a companion and confidant. We were older, could talk his language, and he was proud of us. It was all ended eleven months later. While stepping out of his car in front of church, on Thanksgiving weekend of 1948, Dad collapsed and died.

The previous January, as we walked to our residence halls, we recapped the activities of the past fifteen days and relived the high points of the holidays. It was Tom who finally turned serious and said, "We have a lot to be thankful for." Like a four-year-old boy I followed him to a favorite campus spot, the Grotto of Our Lady, where thanks for the many things we had were properly expressed in prayer.

Notre Dame meant much to Tom. I believe it was here

that he gained the strength his later life demanded. It is impossible to write of Tom and Notre Dame without thinking of the letter which he wrote many years later to Father Hesburgh, President of the University. Before leaving Asia for his last trip home, Tom wrote to Father Hesburgh from his bed in St. Teresa's Hospital in Hong Kong. His letter tells, so much better than I can, exactly what Notre Dame and Our Lady's Grotto meant to him*:

Hong Kong
December 2, 1960

Dear Father Hesburgh:

They've got me down. Flat on the back, with plaster, sand bags, and hot water bottles. I've contrived a way of pumping the bed up a bit so that, with a long reach, I can get to my typewriter, my mind, my brain, my fingers.

Two things prompt this note to you, Father. The first is that whenever my cancer acts up a bit, and it is certainly "acting up" now, I turn inward a bit. Less do I think of my hospitals around the world, or of 94 doctors, fundraisers, and the like. More do I think of one Divine Doctor and my personal fund of grace. Is it enough?

It has become pretty definite that the cancer has spread to the lumbar vertebra, accounting for all the back problems over the last two months. I have monstrous phantoms, all men do. But I try to exorcise them with all the fury of the middle ages. And inside and outside the wind blows.

But when the time comes, like now, then the storm around me does not matter. The winds within me do not matter. Nothing human or earthly can touch me. A milder storm of peace gathers in my heart. What seems unpossessable, I can possess. What seems unfathomable, I fathom. What is unutterable, I can utter. Because I can pray. I can communicate. How do people endure anything on earth if they cannot have God?

I realize the external symbols that surround one when he prays are not important. The stark wooden cross on an altar of boxes in Haiphong with a tortured priest, the magnificence of the Sacred Heart Bernini altar at Notre Dame—they are essentially the same. Both are symbols. It is the something else there that counts.

But just now, and just so many times, how I long for

* The University of Notre Dame has made a memorial of Tom's letter to Father Hesburgh. The complete text, engraved on a plaque, has been set up on a stand at Our Lady's Grotto.

the Grotto. Away from the Grotto, Dooley just prays.
But at the Grotto, especially now when there must be snow
everywhere and the lake is ice glass, and that triangular
fountain on the left is frozen solid, and all the priests are
bundled in their too-large, too-long old black coats and the
students wear snow boots... If I could go to the Grotto
now, then I think I could sing inside. I could be full of
faith and poetry and loveliness and know more beauty,
tenderness and compassion. This is soggy sentimentalism, I
know. (Old prayers from a hospital bed are just as pleasing to God as more youthful prayers from a Grotto on the
lid of night.)

But like telling a mother in labor, "It's okay, millions
have endured the labor pains and survived happy, you will
too." It's consoling, but doesn't lessen the pain. Accordingly, knowing prayers from here are just as good as from the
Grotto doesn't lessen my gnawing, yearning passion to be
there.

I don't mean to ramble. Yes, I do.

The second reason I write to you just now is that I
have in front of me the Notre Dame *Alumnus* of September, 1960. And herein is a story. This is a Chinese hospital
run by a Chinese division of the Sisters of Charity (I
think). Though my doctors are British, the hospital is as
Chinese as shark's-fin soup. Each orderly, companion, nurse
and nun knows of my work in Asia, and each has taken it
upon himself to "give" personally to the man they feel
has given to their Asia. As a consequence, I'm a bit
smothered in tender, loving care.

With a triumphant smile this morning, one of the nuns
brought me some American magazines (which are limp
with age and which I must hold horizontal above my head
to read)—an old *National Geographic*, two older copies of
Time, and that unfortunate edition of *Life*, and with
these, a copy of the Notre Dame *Alumnus*. How did it ever
get here?

So, Father Hesburgh, Notre Dame is twice on my mind,
and always in my heart. That Grotto is the rock to which
my life is anchored. Do the students ever appreciate what
they have, while they have it? I know I never did. Spent
most of my time being angry at the clergy at school: 10
P.M. bed check, absurd for a 19-year-old veteran, etc., etc.,
etc.

Won't take any more of your time, did just want to communicate for a moment, and again offer my thanks to my
beloved Notre Dame. Though I lack a certain buoyancy in
my bones just now, I lack none in my spirit. I must return

to the states soon, and I hope to sneak into that Grotto—
before the snow has melted.

TOM DOOLEY

Tom took of the many things that Notre Dame had to
offer with the selectivity of a painter preparing his colors.
In addition to his regular required pre-medical courses and
French, Tom on the side studied the organ. Frequently,
when I couldn't find him in his room, he would be high in
the balcony of the Main Church playing the organ. Brother
Boniface, charged with taking care of the Main Church,
would frequently find people sitting in the pews at four in
the afternoon just listening to the beautiful organ music.
They didn't even know who was playing, but they knew
that someone played the organ in the afternoons and, if
you were lucky, you might catch a session.

Of the many wonderful men on the faculty at Notre
Dame, perhaps no one was more important to Tom in 1946-
48 than Father Broughal—a priest who was later to play a
very important part in my life. Father Broughal was a young
seventy, white-haired, short and a little heavy in the middle.
He had a wonderful sense of humor and a mind like a
mousetrap. He was the man who was to show Tom the many
marvels of Notre Dame, and he was the one who so helped
Tom develop his love of his Maker, and a deep and undy-
ing concern for his fellow man.

Father Broughal was not an instructor of Tom's. In fact,
Tom met him in the cafeteria over a cup of coffee. It wasn't
long before Tom was serving his six a.m. Mass every morning and seeking him out during free time. They became
close friends, the kind of adult friend that most young men
of destiny have, who so definitely helps the younger man
shape and form his philosophy and sense of values. A friendship where the older one hopes the younger one will "do"
something with his life. To Father Broughal, who is now enjoying his reward in heaven, the Dooleys owe many thanks.

Any man who cherishes something wants to share it with
those he loves. This was the relationship that existed between Tom and me as I was about to enter Notre Dame. At
first I had wanted to go to Holy Cross, but later changed
my mind and selected Notre Dame. Tom had never tried to
sell me Notre Dame. He just sat back waiting to see what I
would do. But once I made my choice, he went into action.
My first five days on campus I met every friend of his, visited

every corner of the campus, and pretty much was told what to do, how to do it, and when.

Then as Tom saw me taking to campus life and values, which was to his satisfaction, he introduced me to Father Broughal. This was the first of many friendships I would have and develop because I was Tom's brother. Father Broughal immediately recognized the difference between us and constantly asked me what it was like to be the brother of such a fireball. As my years at Notre Dame lengthened, Father Broughal became a "root of my tree," a friend, a confessor, and a self-appointed member of the Malcolm Dooley fan club. This occurred when I was flying combat missions in Korea in 1951. I had been expressing my great fear of being killed or maimed to Father Broughal in letters, and he took it upon himself to encourage me, and then set up my fan club of which, he said, he was immediately closing the membership. There would only be one member; that was he. It was only his final illness that prevented him from performing the marriage service for my wife and me in 1953.

It was with mixed emotions that Tom left Notre Dame in the late spring of 1948. He had applied to and had been accepted by St. Louis University School of Medicine for the term beginning that fall. I will never forget Dad's concern when Tom made this decision in 1948. He was worried that Tom might not successfully complete his medical training, and would be without a basic Bachelor's degree. Dad was still convinced that Tom was not the "type" to be a doctor. He felt that Tom had too much drive, not enough patience, and was far too artistic to be a doctor. Dad was right, but he did not know how young Dr. Tom Dooley later was to use precisely those qualities, along with his medical talents, to start a reawakening among thousands of Americans of our great human responsibilities abroad.

As soon as my son knew that he would begin his medical training in the fall, he asked his father and me if he could make his first trip to Europe during the summer vacation period. It wouldn't be all vacation, Tom pointed out, because he had enrolled at the Sorbonne for a special course in French. Also he was now 21. My husband and I agreed.

On June 14, 1948, Tom sailed from New York on the *S. S. Marine Marlin.* On this trip he developed the fortunate habit of recording his experiences in letters almost every day.

Between the evening of his first night at sea and the day on which he boarded ship for his return voyage, Tom wrote over forty letters to the family. This habit was more important than any of us, including Tom, realized at the time. Because of it, he was later able to document his first book, *Deliver Us from Evil,* with great accuracy. Without all the letters he had written to us almost daily from Viet Nam, he probably could not have recalled the wealth of detail which his letters yielded. As soon as he began working on that first book, he wrote and asked me if any of his letters were still around. I was able to send him every one he had sent us. Similarly, when I was compiling this book, the publishers asked if there were any letters from this earlier period of Tom's life. In the bottom of a trunk stored in the basement were packets of letters, some slightly faded and a few a bit water-logged, but all completely legible.

The first group of letters, written at sea, were mailed in a bunch when the ship touched Ireland.

FIRST NIGHT ABOARD—This ship is just full of young people. One person said that 95% of the passenger list is under 30. There is a contingent of Boy Scouts, and the Princeton rowing team. We have a great number of American students who are of French origin—I mean they have been in the U. S. studying English for the year and are returning home. I have been talking to them a good deal. I can say all I want to say, but can't always understand what they answer. *Mais donnez-moi du temps.*

AT SEA, JUNE 17—There are some kids aboard, and they have adopted me. They follow me around as though they were the rats and I the Pied Piper. Whenever my friends want to know where I am, they just listen for the children screaming, and they know Dooley is in the middle of them. A school of porpoises followed us yesterday. They are beautiful animals and cut graceful arcs in the air with their leaps. They came to the stern of the ship and tried to rub their backs. It reminded me of the way Chummy used to rub his back on the stair railing.

AT SEA, JUNE 21—Yesterday was Sunday, and a Rosary service was held in the D-deck lounge. This is where the dances are usually held, as on the other evening when we had a lot of fun and did Irish jigs, square dances à l'Américaine, and the famous Avignon dance where they sing: *On y danse, on y danse, sur lepont d'Avignon.* Hey, hey, hey I just found out that I can get this mailed (and four previous letters) from

Ireland, so I'm sticking it in the box tonight. There will be lots more from Paris.

When he arrived in Paris, Tom went to the Latin Quarter of the city where he had taken a room in the *pension* of Madame Potel on the Avenue du Maine, not far from the Sorbonne and readily accessible to his classes.

PARIS, JUNE 28—Yesterday I went to high mass at Notre Dame. It was magnificent. The organ music was superb, and the choir was made up entirely of children. Although their voices had a high and angelic timbre, the sound echoed from the depths of the nave. . . . I was very fortunate in being able to get two tickets for Lily Pons at the Paris Opera House in the only European performance of the summer, *Lakmé*. Madame Potel just called me to dinner, and said *"Donnez mes bonnes chances à votre famille,"* so I'm giving her best wishes to you.

PARIS, JUNE 29—In preparation for tonight's opera date, I desired a bath. For the last five months, however, something has been wrong with the water pressure in the top floor of this apartment. The faucet spits, and then expires with a long puff. Just around the corner are "Bains" where I can rent a shower, soap, and a clean towel for a few hundred francs. With my typewriter case full of the needed utensils, I departed for the baths only to encounter a sign I had not noticed before. The baths are opened only on Friday, Saturday and Sunday. The French don't bathe during the rest of the week. So Madame Potel is fixing me a big pot of hot water, and I am going to take a bath IN THE SINK. Not having running hot water is somehow very French, as French as my beret. It is the custom along the Boul' Miche or Boulevard Saint Michel, the students' street in the Latin Quarter where the Sorbonne, the Beaux Arts and the Lycée are located, to wear the beret of your college. For example, the Swedish, Finns and other Scandinavians wear small white caps, some of the Indians wear a kind of turban, the Egyptians wear a fez, and the French and Americans wear berets. I bought mine yesterday and felt quite French. Madame Potel walked in during the last sentence with a large pot of water, so I can wash now and go to hear Lily Pons without (pardon the expression) stinking to the roof.

PARIS, JUNE 30—It seems unbelievable that I have been in Paris for nearly a week. This afternoon I'm going to the Pantheon to spend the afternoon reading the life of Saint Geneviève, *la maîtresse de Paris*. This morning I met four fellows from Ohio, in Paris to study art. They came here for lunch; Mme. Potel loves my bringing in guests and the terrific boost of 300 francs in her bill means one dollar extra. The opera last night was wonderful. Lily Pons was incomparable. In the intermissions we strolled through the galleries and drank champagne (thirty cents a glass for fine vintages). During one intermission Charles Boyer was presented with the rosette of the Légion d'Honneur.

PARIS, JULY 1—I haven't been able to spend much time on the balcony of my apartment, because we have been having so much rain. After school this morning, I spent two hours hiking around the Sorbonne. Voltaire walked beside me, and I saw Montaigne on a corner. Louis Pasteur was working in the chemistry labs and Madame Curie was sitting at the foot of the statue of Socrates in the chapel. I stopped and talked to Victor Hugo: *Les Misérables* is coming along fine. The school is laid out around a chapel dedicated, as so many are, to St. Denis, the legendary saviour of Paris. The hill on which he was beheaded (he is supposed to have picked up his head and walked away) is called the Mountain of the Martyr or, in shortcut French, Montmartre. Crowning Montmartre today is a truly great church. Sacre Coeur, built around 1875 to thank God for the departure of the Germans. During World War II eleven bombs were dropped on it. The miracle of it was that the bombs missed, and not a soul was injured. There is a plaque in the church commemorating this incident.

The time now is three in the afternoon and we are leaving for the Louvre. . . . Last night was *la grande nuit de Paris,* a celebration for charity. Everything was illuminated and all the fountains of the city were playing. We walked all the way up the Champs Elysées, from the Place de la Concorde to l'Arc de Triomphe, and then back again. With our backs to the Egyptian obelisk in the center of Concorde, the Arc looked as if it were suspended on a long river of jewels. Then I watched the fountains playing before the golden gates of the Tuileries, the Gardens of the Kings. Paris is indeed the City of Lights.

In his letter dated July 4th, Tom related that through a St. Louis friend, Mary Anne Sell, whose father had been in the diplomatic service, he was introduced to the Haizet family, who invited him to tea at their elegant apartment "right on the Seine near the Tour Eiffel." While Tom was there, some Chopin scores were delivered to Madame Haizet. "She asked me," wrote Tom, "whether I could play what she had and, by sheer accident, I could. Nor could I have had a better setting for Chopin. I just let myself go and played Chopin for nearly an hour. They are leaving Paris and going to their summer villa in Brittany. I have been invited to spend a few days there in August."

PARIS, JULY 6—I have conversation classes on Mondays, Wednesdays, and Fridays, plus reading from texts. Then for another hour with another teacher we have *explication des textes,* which means reading something and dissecting it. For homework I am given twenty French nouns to change into verbs. Such as *fleur,* flower, which becomes *effleurer,* to blossom. On the other two days of the week, for an hour and fifteen minutes, we have grammar. Ugh. It's the funniest class you ever heard. Ten of us grunt and groan and spit out those French nasalities until we sound as if we are all sick. Sunday night Patrice Haizet and I went to the opera and heard *Carmen.* It was excellent.

PARIS, JULY 7—I went to a place high on Montmartre quite close to the Place Pigalle. It's an old building called Auxiliatrices du Purgatoires. Here in the year 1534 a man named Ignace de Loyola hid with some colleagues in the crypt of this ancient building, hiding from enemies of the church. In this place Loyola and his six companions formed an organization which received apostolic approbation ten years later. It was called *le Société de Jésus,* in short the Jebbies. Although I am sure Ignace de Loyola intended his order to teach all nations, I don't think he specifically intended to build St. Louis University High School. Maybe if he had known that there would be four Dooleys clamoring through said halls of knowledge, one of them stumbling a bit, he would never have asked for approbation.

An amusing incident happened with my landlady, who does my laundry. I noticed that all my shirts were without starch, so after looking up in the dictionary all the words for starch, collars, cuffs, white, stiff and so on, I bought a box of American starch and proceeded to explain to her how we do shirts at home. She understood and kept saying "*Ça va, bien entendu,*" until I was sure it was all right. When I came home next day, she was nearly in tears. She had starched the *entire* shirt and ironed it. It stood up on the floor like a board. Whenever she tried holding it, white powder shot out over everything. The bosom was like a full-dress shirt, and the cuffs were like wood. It seems that American starch is much tougher than French!

Americans are accosted on the streets by men operating on the *marché noir* (black market) all the time. The lawful exchange rate is 300 francs for the dollar, but I have been offered 360 and even 380. When they approach me, I have a little French phrase which means, 'Shove off, Mac,' only a bit stronger.

PARIS, JULY 10—Glory, glory, glory, I have found another bath. This one, nicer than the first, is open Thursday. Now if I can only find one for Tuesdays, I'll be completely clean. My dinner last night at the Haizets was delightful. Pat has three sisters, Florence, Odée, and Beatrix, ages 15, 17 and 19. Also a little brother, age 10, who is crazy about Notre Dame and college *futbal*. I have a date with Beatrix for the opera tomorrow night. In French fashion, I had to ask the mother's permission first. They are really a lovely family. The grandfather, who is very old, is from Brittany. I remembered the stories of Alphonse Daudet who wrote of Brittany and Mont St. Michel. Daudet is the old gentleman's favorite author. He was astonished that an American existed who had *heard* of Daudet!

PARIS, JULY 11—I took Pat's sister, Beatrix, to the opera last night. We heard *La Traviata*, which was wonderful, and afterwards stopped at a small café near the Opéra Comique for our cognac. Mme. Haizet's father is the Comte de Marchena. That's a Spanish title, and this is how the family got it. Back in 1491, when Queen Isabella was raising a fund for an expedition by a young explorer, Señor Marchena of Spain went to the shipbuilders and ordered a ship which was named the *Santa Maria*. The explorer turned out to be none other than Christopher Columbus. Because of this, the King of Spain granted the family their title. In 1600 they moved to France, kept the Spanish title, and still have it. I went to Notre Dame this morning and lit a candle for my family.

PARIS, JULY 15—Yesterday was the famous Quatorze Juillet or Bastille Day. There was a great parade with all the military of many lands participating. The U.S.A. surely did top them all when the Marines marched by; that outfit really knows how to march. The famous Garde Républicaine pranced by on spirited mounts, wearing the identical uniform they wore in the days of Napoléon I—highboots, red velvet pantaloons, a cuirass breast armor, a high shiny helmet with a long horse-hair tail, and large blue capes that hang over the horses. In the evening Jay Meier and I went all around the city looking at the lights. We ended our hike at midnight on top of the Butte de Montmartre, where St. Denis was martyred, and where Sacre Coeur stands. I am sure Mother and Dad know it well. We stood there with our backs to the church looking down, as if we held Paris in our hands. It was all glistening with thousands of lights, and looked like a sea of jewels. There were lights of three different colors, the *tricouleurs* of France. We then stopped at the fair at the Place Pigalle. Someone started a conga chain which grew nearly six blocks long; we joined in. We finally made it home just in time to see dawn creeping over Paris. I no sooner got in bed than the bells started ringing as they do every morning at five. I then understood what the author Bragmardo meant when he said, "I wish that the bells of Paris were made of feathers and their clappers of foxtails."

PARIS, JULY 16—This letters begins a new series "writ by hand." I have a long and sad tale to relate, and I have learned a hard lesson. This afternoon my typewriter was stolen. This is how it happened. There is a Paris newspaper, *Le Figaro*, which has an exchange to which I went to find a buyer for my typewriter. A nice fellow came up and said he would buy it for a friend, but would not pay *marché noir* prices. I said I would not sell it on the black market; it is not only immoral but highly illegal and dangerous. I agreed with him on $100, which is about the regular market value. This individual had friends who needed a typewriter so I planned to meet them after lunch. At the proper time two well-dressed Frenchmen came up to me (I had the typewriter in my hand), and asked me to walk with them to the St. Augustine Boulevard nearby. They seemed very nice (I can hear Mother say, "Oh, they always are") and finally we reached the hotel. One fellow took the machine upstairs to the apartment, while I went with the other to the cashier's window. There was quite a queue, and he asked me very amiably to sit down in the lobby and wait. So I sat down, picked up a magazine, and glanced at it. I looked up many times and saw the fellow looking at me always. The next time I looked up, he was not there. I immediately looked around, without success. I called a page girl and had him paged; no response. I checked the registry and neither name was on the books. Only then did it dawn on me that I had been duped by a centuries' old trick. What a fool I am for not keeping the typewriter in my hands all the time.

It is really a great world. If I had illegally tried to sell on the black market to one of the dozen operators who approach Americans daily, I would have got more than my asking price, but I tried to do it in what I thought was the honest way. Of course the man at *Le Figaro* knew nothing when I went back there. Yes, he had taken my name, but had not given it to anyone. Someone standing in that jammed room must have heard it, according to him. Well, that is the story.

I was a sucker again. I have been taking every precaution about locks aboard ship, coats, etc., but I let someone walk away with my typewriter. How easy it was! It is very late, and I must go to bed. I am awful sorry about my typewriter, Dad.

PARIS, JULY 17—I have finished school. Monday, there are exams, but as I do not want a *degré*, I am not taking them. I am meeting Jack O'Hara on July 24th; he is in Italy now. We are going to the Riviera, Carcassonne, and Lourdes and return here on August 1st. Perhaps Switzerland, certainly Holland, and then more of France. Bernice Bowman phoned me today; she and Lee Mofit—both St. Louis girls—are in town. It will be nice to see them. Aside from *marché noir* operators and typewriter thieves, I find the French very likable. As far as I can see here, the Communists are unpopular. They had a section in the Bastille Day parade and were jeered. Yet the Communists do a *wonderful* propaganda job and the Red newspapers are defending the Berlin blockade which starves people.

MARSEILLES, JULY 29—Our train stopped at the Marseilles station, where I am writing this. We are on our way to Lourdes, and will arrive tomorrow. Then we return to Paris on the 1st. Jack O'Hara must leave on the 3rd to sail home. It seems wonderful to know that I still have nearly a month abroad. I am really quite proud of my progress with French and people comment on how well I speak it. My courses at the Sorbonne were excellent; they employed means and methods that the French Department of Notre Dame should look into (yes, I've written my former teacher). I want so much to master this language, to be able to read the papers, and to feel with and know the French people well. I can truthfully say that I have put myself well on the road to that achievement.

Perhaps the most important single experience of that summer for Tom was his visit to Lourdes. In a literal sense, it shocked him—not the shrine, but the sight of suffering. Perhaps it was his first real experience of what Dr. Schweitzer calls "the Fellowship of Pain." Perhaps it was his first realization, in a physical sense, of what a doctor's work involves. In the light of Tom's future career, this short letter is a significant revelation of the deep compassion which was to mark his whole life.

PARIS, AUGUST 1—The best thing about returning to Paris was to find so much mail waiting. First, I want to thank you for the swell way you took my stupidity with the typewriter.

My trip to Lourdes was a strange one. It has an odd fascination; I was shocked, but I loved it too. It's rather difficult to explain. To see so much sheer hopelessness, so much dreadful deformity, such weeping. It was intensely difficult to kneel and meditate on the beauty and loveliness of the miracle of Bernadette at Massabielle. Beautiful while one kept looking *up*, but one must look down too.

I joined in the candlelight procession, Mass, Communion, litanies, songs, flowers, Stations of the Cross, and Benediction, because I wanted to be a *pilgrim*, not just a tourist. But for me the last four letters of that word will always apply to Lourdes, "grim."

I did have a sort of peaceful feeling while looking up, but was torn apart when looking around me. My emotions will have to be conquered. A doctor must, to a certain extent, be cold and calculating. I do not yet possess those attributes. To acquire them will be the hardest part of my medical studies.

Then Tom went on to the little town of Aubel, outside Liège, to thank the Belgian family who had been kind to us at the time of Earle's death and written us about his burial in the military cemetery nearby, from which his body, after the war, had been sent home to St. Louis. He first made a side trip to the Netherlands with a letter of introduction from Eugene and Elizabeth Kormendy, the sculptor and painter who had befriended him at college. "I met and stayed with the Vissers," he explained, "great friends of the Kormendys and really grand people. Mrs. Visser studied under and lived with them in Budapest ten years ago. On Thursday Bé (Mrs. Visser) and I drove completely across the country to Amsterdam."

AUGUST 4—At Liège I got up early and decided to try the Army for transportation. A young first lieutenant from New Jersey took me under his bars and gave me a big truck and a Polish D.P. driver. First, I went to the Cemetery Henri Chappelle, quite an hour's drive out of Liège. You certainly did the right thing in bringing Earle home where he belongs. Of the original 18,490 there are only 9,330 left. Then we drove on to Aubel and visited Maria Thérèse's family. She is a very sweet little girl. I thanked the whole family in person for all they had done. I think they were stunned to see an American come all this way, an impossible distance in their minds, to thank them.

Back at Liège I had dinner with the lieutenant. It took two years of military service, two more of college, a voyage across the ocean and numerous train hops finally *to eat at an officers' mess!*

Again Tom's choice of a career in medicine was put to the test by a casual encounter in his hotel: "I had dinner last night with a venerable old octogenarian, and when he heard I was a student of science, he sort of lit into me. He blamed science for bringing such scourges onto the earth, and I countered with medicine, a science which has brought so much relief. He came back with that famous right jab to the chin, the liberal arts education. He was astonished to learn that I never studied Greek, knew little of early Latin civilization, and could speak only two modern languages. By brandy I was asserting that the liberally educated man, probably a product of the Jesuits, forgets most of what he learns. He answered that it is better to know the vagaries of 'servus, servi' than those of a new poison gas; better to forget Greek conjugations than to learn and remember experimental atomic chemistry. Then he sort of looked in the distance and said: 'Better by far we should forget and smile, than remember and be sad.' When I got up from that table, I felt as though I had been ground up into powder. Now I have some real new, fresh thoughts to chew on."

The next letter we received from Tom was postmarked Switzerland. It began with the startling news that he was writing "about two-thirds the way up the Matterhorn." This was the way-station named Hornli Hutte, an eight-hour journey up (only half that time going down) from the town of Zermatt, at the foot of the mountain. Tom explained that this was the point from which real Alpinists *started*, and I was relieved to learn that this is where he intended to stop.

"I arrived at Zermatt yesterday," he wrote, "and at the hotel they all said the best climb, the most beautiful, and the easiest for a novice, was to Hornli Hutte. Most people leave Zermatt at dawn, arrive here for lunch, and return for dinner. I preferred to do it more slowly, so I will stay here overnight. This morning I rented shoes, bought a spiffy windbreaker, an iron-pointed cane, and put my red sweater and things in a knapsack and left Zermatt at 9 a.m. The trail to Schwarzsee, the first stop, was well marked and well travelled. It was just steep hiking; I talked to an English couple, he

50 and she 49, who come to Zermatt four times a year 'to keep jolly fit.' The valley we came through had a raging stream whose water was white with froth as it tore down the mountainside. I felt a fear of nature, at just how powerful she can get. Reaching Schwarzsee at noon, the clouds moved and we had a really majestic view. Zermatt is 4,800 feet and Schwarzsee is 5,100. Hornli Hutte is 10,200 feet. The tip of the Matterhorn is 13,500 feet but those 3,000 feet from here on up are absolutely *perpendicular!* Beyond Schwarzsee there was hardly anything to see as I was in clouds all the way up. Occasionally the sun shyly peeped through for a few seconds. The last hour was done very slowly in a terrific high wind and driving hail. My face is now as red as my sweater and I feel as if I won't be able to shave for a week. I rested five minutes every twenty. I passed some burros coming down and I made up my mind, for it was faltering, that if God's asses could make it, I certainly could. I stumbled in here about five, and as is the custom everybody helps you off with the spikes, then the boots, then the heavy woolen socks, and you drink wonderful coffee for an hour. The air is very thin at this height and you breathe twice as fast. The temperature is far below freezing, and this big fire feels fine. After dinner I am going straight to bed. They give you hot bricks wrapped in newspaper to put in bed with you. For slippers I have some wonderful sheep's wool which come way up my legs and whose soles are wood. I think I'll wear them to bed. I will continue this letter tomorrow after my descent."

At 8:30 the next morning, Tom resumed his account sitting on a rock half-way down from Hornli. "It is a glorious day," he wrote. "The sky is a brilliant blue and all the mountains (including me) are completely covered with snow. In many corners of the trail there are great banks of snow and sometimes you can't skirt them and must dig through, and get snow nearly to the thighs."

An hour later he stopped again to write, and this is what he recorded: "Here we are really off the Matterhorn. From here on it is no longer really steep. I realize my system of letter-writing from mountainsides is far from orthodox, but the reason I write this way is that I like to think my whole family is at my side. Eddie and his poison-ivy adventure spirit would love this climb so much, Dad would be enthralled at the views, Mother would love the mountain flowers, Malc would enjoy the descent because the best Swiss beer would await him at Zermatt. I know I'm the fortunate son, and I want to share my good fortune and thrilling experiences with my family.

"Last night," he continued, "I did not sleep too well. There was a terrible blizzard and all the windows banged and though I was fully dressed and under tons of blankets, I froze. I tried to think of big bonfires and of St. Louis in July, but I still had snow in my bloodstream. Somehow dawn came. The sight of the Matterhorn with the sun climbing up it was one that warmed me. It made my head nearly dizzy with a flooded feeling. The Matterhorn seems to shout in a course jagged voice, 'Conquer me, if you dare!' I wondered how men could stand at its tip, or how they breathed at all 3,500 feet higher when breathing is so difficult here. I saw the snow fall in an avalanche on one side, and wondered what fear men must feel near the top when they see the trail brushed away and rocks and jutting cliffs sheared off by that same soft, delicate snow that we fall in, laughing, at Notre Dame."

Tom concluded his long Matterhorn letter very briefly, when he reached his hotel at Zermatt. "It was just a nice walk down," he wrote at 1:30 p.m. "The little boy (me) who used to pick dandelions for his mother picked some wild mountain flowers this time. My train leaves for Lausanne at five. Love to all from your Alpine relative."

Tom arrived back in Paris on August 15th. He would have ten more days in France, before sailing for New York on August 26th, and he told us he expected to spend a few days in Brittany as the guest of the Haizets. His address there would be an interesting one, Villa Ty-al-Lanneck, Trebeurden, Côte-du-Nord, and his next letter bore this postmark.

AUGUST 18—Nothing but peace here, an enormous amount of quiet, and the sea. The town is very quaint and colorful. Many of the inhabitants wear their native costumes, and all are shod in the provincial wooden shoes. The villa is really quite lovely, high on a hill at the foot of which is a marvelous beach. There is a terrace in front of the house and then the hill drops suddenly. The beach is very long and wide and the sand is far superior to Cannes. All the Haizets are spending the summer here, summer for them being August 15th to September 30th. Yet the house is so immense that I have been given a large suite complete with bath. I am enjoying myself immensely. We swam and sunbathed this morning, tennis after lunch, and then to the ocean again. I am returning to Paris for one day, then on to Belgium and my departure from Antwerp.

At the last moment in Brussels, Tom took time out to sum up as follows: "My heart is a little heavy in leaving Sorbonne days, Paris nights, Geneva fêtes, Lucerne music festivals, Matterhorn heights, Brittany hospitality and all, but I shall be so glad, so very glad to see that Lady of Liberty and all she stands for." He had a leisurely voyage home, and reached New York in early September. Tom's first trip to Europe was over.

He started his first year of medical school immediately on his arrival in St. Louis. Then, in November, his father died. Malcolm describes this period and its effects on all our lives.

MALCOLM DOOLEY:

The first year Tom put in at St. Louis University School of Medicine was a tough one. This was due, in my opinion, to one major cause: Dad died the November after he entered. The death of a father is unlike any other experience a man can have. Suddenly the son is older. He is now the senior, and has to try to step into his father's shoes. Tom, as the eldest son, felt this very strongly and I think he also felt lost without Dad. Tom tried feverishly to fill this void of security and to make life as happy as possible for Mother. On top of it all he had to complete his medical training successfully. The weight of this responsibility lay heavily on him and he could never really dispose of it.

One of the high points in Tom's life at this time was my graduation from Notre Dame in August, 1950. I had accelerated my courses after Dad's death, and thereby graduated at the end of the summer session of 1950. I received a telegram from California that must have cost Tom twenty dollars, loaded with "well-dones" and "congratulations." He could not attend the commencement because he was with the Army Reserve Officers Training Corps at Letterman General Hospital in San Francisco. There was a regulation that all medical students had to serve in the R.O.T.C. and spend a month after their second year in a military hospital. Tom was doing his "turn" that August. That is how he came to serve in three branches of the military—Navy, Marines, and Army.

It was while on this duty tour that the hospital ship *Benevolence* sank in San Francisco Bay, with hundreds aboard. Tom was at the hospital but off duty at the time of the tragedy and immediately joined in the rescue effort. People in California still talk of the young man who went out into the fog-shrouded bay in a small boat and time after time dove into the water to pull out survivors. Tom himself was hospitalized after this exploit and was later commended by the Army for his selfless display of courage. Many times I have wondered if people who saw him in action then realize that this was the young man who later became famous through the exercise of the same kind of courage on the international scene.

The extent of Tom's brotherly love and the degree to which he had taken on the responsibility for the welfare of the family and Mother's peace of mind were most dramatically expressed when I returned from Korea in mid-January 1952. I had just finished a combat tour as a B-26 navigator and arrived at Lambert Field, St. Louis, on a cold crisp January morning. Mother met me at the airport with her closest friend, Lucille Sullivan. Sully came along just in case Mother got a little weak from the excitement and emotional stress. I was the first son Mother ever had come safely back from combat. It was difficult for her to realize that it was really true.

When we got to the house, we sat down to have coffee and talk. Tom was on duty at St. Mary's Hospital as an extern and wouldn't be free until evening. Mother had no sooner told me this when Tom raced the car into the driveway and bounded into the house. He stood there in disbelief, just looking at me. Then he reached out and touched me. Finally his usual exuberance broke out and he spent the next five minutes pounding my back and shaking my hand.

Tom had been convinced that I would be killed in Korea, and he now revealed this to me. He had worried about Mother and how she would take such a loss. Earle had been killed in 1944, Dad had died in 1948, and here I was in combat in 1951-52. My safe return gave Tom a long-deserved relief from the many family worries heaped on his shoulders, and allowed him to concentrate more on his studies which were now entering their critical stage. I sometimes wonder how he ever finished Medical School. He ran into difficulties with some members of the faculty.

One of the people who helped him most at this crucial

juncture, and the man who knew him best at Medical School, was Dr. Melvin A. Casberg, the Dean. He has described his first meeting with Tom, which occurred at the dinner held in honor of his inauguration as Dean in the ballroom of the Jefferson Hotel in St. Louis. Dr. Casberg writes:

"Barely audible in the chatter of a thousand voices and the clattering of dishes, an informal piano recital was being given on the stage at the end of the big ballroom. The pianist was Tom Dooley.

"Tom, as a medical student, showed evidence of his dynamic energy in ways which were not always appreciated by those responsible for the administration of the university. Schedules of clinics and class attendance are a necessary part of organized instruction; but Tom chafed under certain of these rigid restrictions to the extent that instead of attending required classes he often became absorbed in unscheduled medical activities. The faculty reaction to such unorthodoxy made it necessary for Tom to meet me occasionally in the Dean's office.

"Even at this stage of his development I recognized a heart which could not be restrained within the boundaries of the routine things of life. These early meetings of Tom Dooley, the student, with me the Dean developed into a friendship which continued to draw us closer through the ensuing years."

Tom had loved the Navy from the time he was a corpsman, and he now planned to apply for a Navy commission. A few weeks after my marriage to Gabrielle De Pirro in February, 1953, at which he was my best man, he received his M. D. from St. Louis University School of Medicine. His diploma was dated March 15, 1953.

On April 9, 1953 the U. S. Navy appointed him Lieutenant (junior grade), Medical Corps, with his commission dating from March 23rd. He then plunged into his Navy life full steam, with the desire to be the best doctor in the fleet. His first assignment was the naval hospital at Camp Pendleton, California. He was moving swiftly toward the fateful moment of his life.

Among my son's papers is a full account of this period of internship at the U. S. Naval Hospital, Camp Pendleton, California, from April, 1953 to April, 1954. According to the record of this busy year, he attended 153 operations in the operating room, and assisted at 61 surgical operations. He also attended in his capacity as intern 50 obstetrical cases and 50 autopsies. The record shows that in addition he served 15 weeks in the general medicine department, including contagion; 13 weeks in general surgery; 9 weeks in orthopedics, 2 in urology, 7 in obstetrics, 4 in pediatrics, and 2 in eye, ear, nose and throat. He also received 83 hours of lectures and demonstrations in pathology, and 51½ hours of lectures and demonstrations in roentgenological technique and interpretation. The intern record concludes by certifying him as "a person of good moral character who has proven himself worthy of his profession."

This is the formal record, but somehow a letter which he received from the Veterans Administration Hospital at Long Beach, where he volunteered to entertain their paraplegic patients in January, 1954 tells us a great deal more about Tom's character:

"Since as a doctor you are so well acquainted with patients, you realize that there are some things they can take and some things they can leave. Confidentially, classical music falls into this latter category. You will be pleased to know that your warm personality, combined with your unusual talent, made classical and semi-classical music really live for our paraplegics. Some of our patients are still chuckling over your doing the 'Dragnet' theme when the G. U. technician went trekking through with his equipment, and when the attendant came through with the laundry truck. They figure that anyone who had nerves good enough to withstand those confusions must really be a swell guy as well as a good artist. We are certainly looking forward to having you return at your convenience, and will make frantic overtures to date you for an auditorium appearance when the structure is completed."

Dr. Casberg, his Dean at medical school, also throws interesting light on the Camp Pendleton period of Tom's career:

"The next stage of our friendship came about with Tom's graduation from Medical College and his desire to serve his country. In the interim my duties changed from St. Louis to Washington, D. C., where I had been appointed Assistant Secretary of Defense (Health and Medical). Tom then was in the Navy and on one of my trips to the West Coast I stopped at the Naval Hospital at Camp Pendleton, California, on a routine inspection of the personnel and facilities.

"At the hospital over a cup of coffee I asked the commanding officer how Tom Dooley was doing as a member of his staff. 'Dooley is certainly *different*,' he said cautiously. 'He has boundless energy, but I must say that he utilizes his energy in the most unorthodox ways. This relates not to a willful desire to upset routine but rather to his becoming completely absorbed in a project to the loss of his sense of responsibility to other related areas.' Obviously, time, experience, and discipline had not changed him."

In the summer of 1953 Tom shipped a wedding present from Camp Pendleton to his newly married brother Malcolm, stationed at an Air Force Base in Texas.

MALCOLM DOOLEY:

While Tom was at Camp Pendleton, he did a typically Dooley-like thing. He wrote my wife from California: "I've found a lovely present for your mantel." I was stationed at Bryan Air Force Base in Texas, and we lived in the officers' family quarters just off the campus area of Texas A. and M. We had only been married a few months and we didn't have much furniture, and we wondered what Tom's present could be. One day in August I was notified at flight operations that the Base Material officer had a large package for me at the warehouse. After duty I drove over in my new station wagon, and asked for my package.

"Do you think you can manage it?" the officer in charge asked.

"Well, I have my station wagon. What on earth is it?"

"I don't know, but I can tell you that it's seven feet long and has a gross weight of 425 pounds."

I took a look at the large wooden crate, which revealed nothing of its contents, except that the sender was clearly marked as Lt. (jg) T. A. Dooley, Camp Pendleton. I had to hire a commercial moving company to come to the base the next day. Gay and I were dying of curiosity. We decided that instead of a present for our mantel Tom had sent us a living-room sofa. The weight was no doubt explained by the fact that he had wrangled Navy packing and shipping; they are famous for over-efficiency.

Next day in front of our house all the children in the neighborhood stood around to watch the uncrating of our enormous package. Their eyes widened (and so did Gay's) as a colorful and very large object emerged. It was a life-size cigar-store Indian in full regalia. All the Air Force wives knew about it in a matter of minutes. We stood the Indian on his pedestal in the middle of our almost empty living-room, and when our neighbors came by and asked "What's with the Dooleys?" we told them that my nutty brother in California had sent us an ash-tray.

Naturally we phoned Tom that evening to express our sincere thanks for his thoughtfulness; as young marrieds we were sure we would find his gift useful. I can still hear him laughing now.

There's a sequel to the story of Sam, as we named our Indian. In October we were transferred to Bergstrom Air Force Base in Austin. We were now able to claim Sam as a "household possession," and this time the Air Force moved him. That Christmas at a celebration in honor of Father Miller, our Chaplain, we gave him Sam as a present. I have been told that today Sam stands in the men's room of the officer's club at the base, a gift to the club from Father Miller, who in 1955 was transferred to Africa.

Late in 1953 Malcolm was ordered overseas to the Pacific, and was stationed at Anderson Air Force Base in Guam. As Tom's internship at Camp Pendleton Hospital was nearing completion, he put in for "change of duty" orders overseas. He was assigned to the U. S. Naval Hospital in Yokosuka, Japan. As soon as he received his orders, he called on Dr. Casberg, who recalls the visit:

"When I had retired from the Defense Department, and was settled in California as a practicing surgeon, Tom drove up to our home one afternoon, unbuckled the seat belt and jumped out of his flashy red convertible without even opening the door. The gleam in his eye told me that he was off on some new adventure.

" 'Sir, I've been ordered to Japan,' he said standing erect before me, his face wreathed in that captivating Irish smile. Tom always addressed me as 'Sir,' a hangover from the days when I was his Dean. Following that brief visit, he drove north to San Francisco, where he embarked for duty in the Far East.

"Letters began to arrive from across the Pacific. As the correspondence focused on his activities in North Viet Nam, it was evident that Tom had been shaken to the very

depths of his being. There came an awakening to the desperate needs of people in that part of the world. I knew
then that Tom would never be the same carefree young
man again."

This turning-point in Tom's life was drawing close. As he
left for Japan, he arranged air transportation so that a stop-
over in Guam would make a reunion with his brother possible.

MALCOLM DOOLEY:

Guam is not an interesting place and certainly not a
tourist spot. The rain virtually takes the oxygen out of the air
and the heat gets into your bed linens. However, at night
(when you need a jacket) Guam becomes a beautiful lady,
the queen of the Marianas, spangled by her coral beaches. On
her northern tip is a place known as Anderson Air Force
Base, where the Strategic Air Command stages one of her
forward retaliatory strike forces, and from which planes operated for the many activities that surrounded the "H Bomb"
test of that spring. In 1954 I was a 1/Lt. finishing his four-
year tour with the Air Force as navigator of a KB-29, better known as a "flying gas-station."

On a hot May afternoon, I received a military cable that
Tom would be coming through Agana Naval Air Station on
a C-54 of MATS en route to Japan. "PLEASE MEET IF POSSI-
BLE," the message read. Agana was eighteen miles south of
Anderson, and it made a dusty and hot jeep trip. I knew that
Tom was being assigned to Yokosuka in Japan, but what the
heck was he doing coming through Guam? This certainly was
not the normal MATS route. But off I went in my jeep to
Agana Naval Air Station, and there I observed the triumphant arrival of Lt. (jg) Thomas A. Dooley. The orange and
white Naval MATS C-54 taxied up to the ramp, and out
dropped the young "Doc," clean and crisp in his uniform,
blinking from our Pacific sun. As he spotted me, I suddenly felt very dirty and unsanitary. Just a few hours
before I had returned from a nineteen-hour mission into the
"Zone," and I certainly was not an ad for an enlistment
poster. Tom greeted me with an exuberance; he was thrilled
to be in the South Pacific for the first time. He got in my
jeep and off we drove to Anderson. Tom had a twelve-

hour layover until his C-54 was due to leave and he had many things to tell me.

When we got to my quonset hut at Anderson, I went to shower and shave. Tom continued with his rapid-fire conversation causing me to stick a wet head out of the shower curtain many times to pick up the train of thought of his excited speech. We went over to the Officers' Club for dinner, and while I sucked on a double martini I stared in awe at my brother. Tom was telling me of the wonders of a Navy career for doctors, how he planned to stay in the Navy, how exciting and wonderful Japan would be, how pleased Dad would be now that he, Tom, had made the Navy his life. Then in hushed tones he told me of a special briefing he had had at Camp Pendleton in California before leaving, which suggested that he might be sent with a Military Advisory Group into Viet Nam to help in the fight against the Ho Chi Minh forces. Now I was really alert and Tom was silent, for suddenly he realized that he might be in combat—a situation that can quickly remove the romance of the South Pacific or the Orient. I was amazed by his knowledge of the military-political situation in Viet Nam. Dien Bien Phu was under siege at the time. I knew that Tom spoke French fluently and that he could be of enormous value with a U. S. MAG group. But though the younger, I felt very old. I had lucked my way through a fifty-seven-mission combat tour in Korea, and was about to return to a "normal" stateside civilian life. Why was Tom now coming along with all this enthusiasm for "activity"? He was the shining and artistic one—the musician, the traveler, the polished, cultured member of the family. Surely, he should not be concerned with the methods and manners of warfare. Our short but serious talk ended as quickly as it started when a few of my Air Force friends came to our table and joined the party. For the next three hours the young Navy "Doc" played the piano while the SAC pilot and navigators sang lusty songs. I'll never forget my Commanding Officer, Colonel Brusk, saying to me, "Who in hell is that seabee? He can really play the piano." I straightened and said. "That is my brother, sir, Lt. (jg) Thomas A. Dooley." I felt a twinge of pride as I said that, a twinge I would feel again many times in the future.

When I next saw Tom, it was in Japan that very month. To show you how it happened, let me take you inside the flying gas-station in which so many vivid hours of my life were spent.

It takes power, noise, dust and prayers to get a loaded B-29 off the runway, but once airborne this plane is warm and throbbing, smooth, swift and reliable. John Addington slid his seat back as we started our planned climbout and let young Bill DeWeese, the co-pilot, take over. John came back to my navigator's desk and re-checked with me our Flight Plan which was to take us from Guam to Japan with an intermittent aerial refueling of some B-50's we were to rendezvous with up the line. This was a standard proficiency exercise in SAC, yet this trip was something special to the whole crew. We were going to Japan—and we would have thirty-six hours free time when we got there. As the only member of the crew who had been to Japan before, I was under constant inquiry as to where to go and what to see. These were the things John and I discussed until Guam disappeared from my radar scope, and I had to go to work with my celestial navigation to make sure we "found" Japan.

Eight and a half hours later we picked up Tokyo Airways and John brought the ship into Haneda Air Force Base with the ease of an executive turning his car into his driveway. The crew took off for the city, while I caught a train for Yokosuka Naval Base. It is a little over an hour on the train from the Tokyo area to Yokosuka, and I was filled with memories as I watched the rice paddies slip past the train window. It seemed so long ago when I was last here, yet it had been only two and a half years. Then I was the frightened young man who was flying combat missions in Korea. After every fifteen missions, we were given a five-day pass to Japan for rest and relaxation, and I plunged into those five-day periods as a professional soldier very much aware that "tomorrow we die." Memories of Korea, combat, dead and maimed friends, passed through my mind but were quickly removed for I was happy this May afternoon. I knew that next month I would be back in America with my wife, and that in less than an hour I would be with Tom.

The Officers' Club at Yokosuka was certainly no exception to the Navy's reputation for smoothness. I sat at the bar waiting for Tom. When I had reported at the gate, the Medical Officer of the Day had advised me that Tom was operating and that he would be finished in an hour; meanwhile he suggested it might be more comfortable if I were to wait in the Club.

A little after five the Club started to fill up with the usual evening visitors, and the place was alive by the time Tom arrived, just before six. There he was in whites, clean, tall and confident. He stopped to talk to many friends before he made his way to the bar. He greeted me with renewed enthusiasm, as if we had not seen each other in years. Yet just three short weeks before we had been together in Guam.

The war in Viet Nam was over and a truce had been signed in Geneva between the French and the forces of Ho Chi Minh. Tom appeared disappointed that he would not get to Viet Nam, as he had thought he might a few weeks earlier. Yet he was happy in his work at Yokosuka and was obviously very popular with all his fellow officers.

Finally Tom said, "Come on outside, want to show you something." There parked in front of the Officers' Club was his Chevrolet convertible that he had bought in St. Louis a year before. By working a "deal" he had had his car shipped to Japan. You can drive from Yokosuka Naval Base to the Shrine of Kamakura in less than forty-five minutes. Tom never stopped talking as we sped over the narrow road, and he never revealed to me where we were headed. But he kept remarking how happy he was that it was a clear night and that we should have a full moon.

The shrine of Buddha at Kamakura is a magnificent thing, and to see it in early moonlight is something not easily forgotten. From the parking area we walked slowly the several hundred feet toward the base of the edifice. I marveled at Tom's complete preoccupation with the magnificence of the huge statue and the pagan beauty of the shrine. Here we were, both young Catholics, and both feeling a sense of awe in the presence of this memorial. We stood in silence, the silence of men at prayer, then suddenly Tom spoke up with authority and said, "Let's get a drink."

There is a tea house a few hundred yards from the Shrine of Kamakura and here we sipped sake, ate eel, rice and shrimp, taking more than two hours for the meal. It was during this Japanese dinner that I realized how deeply preoccupied Tom was with the Oriental mind, customs and religion. By talking privately with the owner when Tom was out of the room, I learned that he came here often, asked many questions, and spoke better Japanese after each visit.

As the night progressed and the conversation extended, it was obvious that Tom had become completely entranced by everything Oriental, and had acquired a deep understanding of the strength and quality of Asian convictions and beliefs, without in any way compromising his own faith. He kept saying, "If we, the Western world, could only learn more of these people, if we could only present our ways, our government, our convictions about freedom to them more successfully. We in America have so much, yet we are gradually becoming hated by the Eastern world because of our actions abroad. Yet we really want to help all people everywhere." Tom then said one thing I have never forgotten: "We must make our American dreams Asian realities."

I was rather surprised by all this. Later I realized I had witnessed the early stages of the international education of Dr. Tom Dooley. When matured a few years later, it would cause kings, presidents and statesmen to marvel at this young man's inspiring role on the world scene, a role that would make Tom Dooley beloved by the masses of Southeast Asia, and would cause him to be the target of daily anti-American propaganda from radio Hanoi and radio Peking.

The trip back to Yokosuka that night was a slow one. Tom wanted to talk, and he appreciated having me as a listener. He knew that if I disagreed I would say so, yet he knew I would not take offense at anything he said and that he could let go his deep religious feelings without the embarrassment that causes so many men not even to mention God, just when they feel Him most strongly.

He also let me have a few good slams, for Tom was very disappointed that I was getting out of the Air Force. The idea of my going to St. Louis and becoming a stock broker was nothing less than revolting to him—and he told me so.

As we parted the next morning at the Main Gate, Tom said, "So long, civilian." Then with all the snap of an Annapolis cadet he saluted, and I returned the salute. The flight back to Guam was routine. I left feeling that some kind of transformation was going on in Tom's character. What I could not foresee (nor could he) was that he was now destined for a historic rendezvous with fate in the very place he thought he was all through with—Viet Nam. In one sense, his whole life up to now was a preparation for this moment.

three

passage to freedom

I have to get it across to our sailors that these people are not a stinking mass of humanity, but a great people, distressed.

The whole thing started very casually. The word that dominates this entire period is "temporary," and a more ironic word for it could not be imagined. On July 14, 1954 Tom received what the Navy Calls TAD orders. As he later wrote: "Those letters mean Temporary Additional Duty, and they also happen to be the initials of my name, Thomas A. Dooley. We were to take part in amphibious exercises, and practice landings on the Philippine beaches. The duty seemed so 'temporary' that I allowed a Navy nurse at Yokosuka to drive my new convertible while I was gone, and I told my roommate that he could wear my brand new civilian suit. When I got back to Japan, eleven months later, there were 20,000 additional miles on the speedometer and as for the new suit—well, I couldn't have worn it anyway. I had lost 60 of my 180 pounds."

Tom's orders were as follows: "Proceed and report to the U.S.S. *Montague* for TAD in connection with medical matters. Period of temporary duty will cover approximately fourteen (14) days. Upon completion thereof, return to your duty station and resume your regular duties." They were the longest fourteen days in history.

The first letter of this series from my son was written at anchor in Subic Bay, Philippines, on Sunday, August 8, 1954. They were expecting to stay there two weeks, he said, "before departing for Hong Kong." The tone and contents of his letter indicated that he was concerned wholly with medical and moral problems on shipboard and expected to be back in Yokosuka soon. "The heat is pretty bad," he wrote, "and the humidity worse. I now know what tropical *ennui, malaise,* and fatigue are. It is about 105° most of the time, and heavy; no one attempts to keep starched or pressed. There is a large swimming pool about two blocks from this pier and we can take off for a quick dip before each meal, so it is not too bad.

"I certainly am enjoying this trip," he went on. "I organized a 'Happy Hour' on the voyage down, a sort of amateur hour of entertainment, with a skit about the officers, songs, and a lot of nonsense. We have a piano aboard. The Captain and all the crew and officers attended, and a great time was had by all. Such things the crew is direly in need of, from the viewpoint of morale.

"Even though I step on some officers' toes to get things done, they think I am OK and appreciate what I am doing. For example, the heat in the engine-room is about 110° all the time. The doors to the crew's living compartments do not fit tightly enough, and as a consequence much of that awfully hot air leaks into the crew's quarters, making it hotter. I have had them all repaired; two had to be completely replaced. Also much of the ventilation system needed cleaning and repairing; this has now been done. The roach problem is tremendous. But by many small changes, even in so small a matter as the potato bins, things are improving . . .

"I know it is hard for you not getting much mail. I'll send a wire from Hong Kong when we arrive, and when I return to Yokosuka another wire. Duties such as these are good for me and show me the various problems of medical officers. There are a great many things a good medical officer has to do besides simple doctoring. I am learning them, and winning friends also. Love to all for now, and I'll write again soon, Mother. Don't worry, I am healthy and happy."

It was the very next day that the surprise orders came. Tom's ship was given two days' notice to take part in the evacuation of North Viet Nam, the operation which came to be known as the "Passage to Freedom."

The Treaty of Geneva which ended the war in Indo-China, after Dien Bien Phu fell to the communists, stipulated that the area north of the 17th parallel was to be communist and the area south was to be free. It also stipulated that anyone wishing to transfer from one zone to the other could do so up until May, 1955. When the treaty was signed by France in July, 1954, Secretary of State John Foster Dulles refused to sign, stating that the United States would not be party to an agreement which handed half a country over to a totalitarian government. Early in August, there started a trickle of refugees from the Tonkin delta in the north into Hanoi and Haiphong, transfer points for the south. At once South Vietnamese and French officials asked the U. S. to assist them in evacuating all the refugees who wanted to go south. The United States instantly agreed, Navy Task Force 90 received its orders, and within a few days the great exodus was in swing. No one, least of all Tom, had any idea it would assume the proportions it did, involving nearly half a million people.

"We were in Subic Bay," Tom wrote to Dr. Casberg, "when the word came that we were to take part in the evacuation. We had to leave in two days, and there was no Operations Order out yet. So we had to whip our imaginations to figure out what would be needed. By the time we arrived here in Haiphong four and a half days later, we were ready. When the order arrived we found we had anticipated every point, and had a few more ideas which Task Force 90 received most willingly."

From Clark Field in the Philippines he and his men got 2,000 pounds of DDT "through channels and by cumshawing." Tom explained how they rigged four dusters: "Through a boatswain's ingenuity, a large compressed-air Venturi wind-tunnel hopper machine was made with several hoses. This we hang over the side of the ship; it blows the powder down the refugees' shirts and pants.

"In our holds," his letter to Dr. Casberg went on, "living spaces were made, with Lister bags for drinking water and half oil drums for wash water, and with portable honey buckets. On the deck six ten-seater latrines were made out of oil drums split lengthwise and welded together, with a hose in the forward end and a pipe going overboard on the after end—a continuous stream of salt water. The tops were constructed Chinese fashion with long boards. Remember the Japanese bengo? This is its sister equivalent.

"I lectured to all the crew twice daily for four days on the diseases that would be brought aboard by these poor miserable refugees, and I didn't spare the punches. I believe my 300 men know all the layman can ever hope to know about dysentery, typhoid, typhus, intestinal parasites, malaria and TB. Especially, they understand the infectiousness. They were inoculated (I had to beg serums from the sick-bay at Subic as there were none left in the warehouse) and anti-malarial treatment was started. We set the machine-shop to work making screens for *every* porthole on the ship.

"All the plans for messing had to be made, six tons of rice were acquired, plus sardines, olive oil, corned beef, etc. The medical officer was involved in this because I have been in this part of the world and know what they eat. Pie tins and chop sticks were bought and made. Sawdust for the honey buckets was acquired. The carpenters made ladders for the whole ship—four levels to each cargo hold, and five holds. That takes a lot of ladders. The Captain had conferences late at night to get the triage set up.

"When we first arrived at this bay, just outside of the seaport of Haiphong, three other ships were loaded with refugees first. I went over to observe the U.S.S. *Mernard,* and the skipper was having a very difficult time with the French Captain of the LSM that brought the refugees down the river. He could not get across how he wanted the LSM tied alongside, Chinese fashion, etc. So I went on the bridge, saluted good line-officer fashion, and introduced myself. He bellowed, 'What the devil do you want?' I meekly explained that I spoke French as well as I did English and perhaps I could help him. With that he said, 'Speak then, man, speak.' I took the loudspeaker and in my best sotto voice asked the skipper of the French ship to back away, turn around, etc. He replied with a broad smile and gentle *'merci bien'* and backed away. From that time on I scarcely left the Captain's side. I helped him handle the whole thing, speaking French to the French officers, helping the unloading of the 1,000 refugees from the LSM up to the AKA. I know enough Vietnamese to tell the people to walk up, down, carefully, etc., so I was able to earn my pay there too.

"Evidently the word got to the Captains of the other vessels, because each morning a dispatch comes to our ship requesting that I go over. This is good because not only is the collateral duty of an interpreter good training, but I was able to spy on the things they had set up on their ship, what went well and poorly. I would return to my ship in the late afternoon and get the changes made accordingly. I helped in the loading of five ships before ours.

"Yesterday we loaded, and we did it in record time, with little or no trouble. We had to stop only long enough to have a baby on the deck of the LSM. But a Stokes was lowered over the side and the mother and child brought to sick bay. The delivery was fast, because it was her ninth child and there wasn't too much resistance from the pelvic floor, nor was an episiotomy needed. I should say not

"We are enroute to Saigon now, a total of a 2-day trip. We have 2,217 aboard, and all is going well. The stench is pretty terrible, and it seems these poor people devour tons of rice a day. Medically there are a great assortment of things to be seen. Some I treat and many I do not, because the mission is the transportation.

"There are a lot of staph infections of the scalp, that seem to be superimposed on a subdermatitis of the scalp. There are two full blown cases of roseola. All the aged have varieties of arthritis, and several good illustrations of that Marie Strumpell spine. Trachoma and other eye maladies are numerous. They seem to be completely free of fungus. Their feet, in spite or perhaps because of standing all their lives in rice paddies are in excellent condition. One very severe old asthmatic I am just keeping alive on epinephrine q4h until he debarks. All their teeth are blackened with this betel-nut lacquer. All these you have seen in India I know, but you don't find them in every clinic in the States. Many of the unexplained fevers I suppose fall into the typhoid and perhaps the typhus group. One looks like it is Rickettsial for sure. There are no lice left on them because they were thoroughly dusted, nearly bombed, when they came aboard.

"Doctor Casberg, this letter is running into epistle length, but I thought you would be interested. The most pleasing thing to me is that we were able to figure out all the requirements that we needed, prior to the Op order coming out. I think the Navy should make a policy of not telling anybody anything about their task for three days, thereby forcing the officers to search in the foggy cerebral recesses for situations that may arise.

"I feel even more strongly about the Navy as a career

than I did before. I believe they will allow me to continue my TAD after it runs out next month. I am sure they will. This Medical Corps is still tops in my mind.

"Please give my very best regards to Mrs. Casberg and all the younger ones. By now that hot-rod should be running well. Send it on over; we can use it for the evacuation. At Haiphong I saw the famous Route Number 5 that runs from Hanoi where all the citizens are milling to the sea. That hot-rod would be great on the road. You can hardly see the pavement for the solid block of people the whole way from Hanoi to Haiphong."

Tom concluded this long letter, which Doctor Casberg later printed in full in the U. S. Navy *Medical Newsletter,* with a joke: "I assure you some day about 22 years from now, I'll invite you to my dinner when I am made the Surgeon General." Dr. Casberg showed the letter to Rear Admiral Lamont Pugh, Surgeon General of the Navy, who wrote Tom:

"If you haven't spoken an eloquent piece in support of my contention that military medicine is a specialty *sui generis,* and one that requires a special breed of man for its practice, I must conclude it is simply no use. But, however that may be, Doctor, I can promise you one thing as a reward for your sedulity, and that is the satisfaction which singularly can come from a personal realization that you did your level best in the interest of a just cause. That kind of a reward in my book is transcended in sublimity by nothing else. After reading your letter I feel disposed to beseech: 'More and more power to you, Doctor.' It is my earnest hope that good health and good fortune will continue to march with you along tomorrow's road and that some day you may become the Surgeon General of the Navy, not merely because you say that is what you want to be, but because I will leave that office soon with a sense of contentment that it will be in most worthy and 'can do' hands if it ever reaches yours. I envy you, in that your career and a lot of fun are still ahead of you."

Admiral Pugh's letter, a source of much pride and joy to Tom, is reproduced in full on page 57.

The complete story of Tom's role in the "Passage to Freedom" has never, to this date, been told. For security reasons, it was not possible for Tom to give the full background of his last days in Haiphong, when he came to write his book,

THE SURGEON GENERAL OF THE NAVY
WASHINGTON

20 September 1954

Dear Doctor Dooley:

Doctor Casberg has been kind enough to make available to me your letter written to him under the heading of Haiphong, Indochina, and date of 21 August.

I have just read it and I want to say it is a most interesting and heartening letter. It is gratifying to know that there remains at least one service doctor who appreciates the opportunity of going places and doing things. I want to commend you, Doctor Dooley, in all the sincerity and depth of appreciation at my command, for the manner in which you have manifested the attributes of enterprise, ingenuity, versatility, psychological agility, and seriousness of purpose in connection with providing for your prospective logistical needs while you were still in the Philippines and for the devotion to duty which was inherent in the lectures you gave to those accountable to you while en route, or at least prior to your arrival at Haiphong, and lastly, for the demonstration on your part of a willingness to make yourself useful in a sphere entirely foreign to the conventional practice of medicine. I refer to your performance in the role of interpreter. If you haven't spoken an eloquent piece in support of my contention that military medicine is a specialty sui generis, and one that requires a special breed of man for its practice, I must conclude it is simply no use.

But, however that may be, Doctor, I can promise you one thing as a reward for your sedulity, and that is the satisfaction which singularly can come from a personal realization that you did your level best in the interest of a just cause. That kind of a reward in my book is transcended in sublimity by nothing else.

After reading your letter I feel disposed to beseech: "More and more power to you, Doctor." It is my earnest hope that good health and good fortune will continue to march with you a long tomorrow's road and that some day you may become the Surgeon General of the Navy, not merely because you say that is what you want to be, but because I will leave that office soon with a sense of contentment that it will be in most worthy and "can do" hands if it ever reaches yours. I envy you in that your career and a lot of fun are still ahead of you.

With kindest regards and much gratitude,

Sincerely yours,

LAMONT PUGH
Rear Admiral, (MC) USN

Deliver Us from Evil. However, his letters to me after he returned to Japan told the whole story.

Tom wrote me 116 letters during these eleven months. His amazing narrative divides into several phases. First, the transportation of refugees by U. S. Navy ships from Haiphong in the north to the free port of Saigon, in the south. Second, the setting up of a medical processing camp within Haiphong itself, as the flood of refugees from northern outposts and villages poured in at such an accelerated rate that transportation could not keep up with them and a backlog developed. Three, the gradual withdrawal of military and naval personnel and vessels from the northern area. Four, the final evacuation by plane of the few persons remaining behind with ship-to-shore contact by radio and walkie-talkie only. It is this last phase about which Tom was not able to write freely. At the very end Tom was "detained," his letters reveal, as a prisoner of the communists.

The important thing to keep in mind is that Haiphong was *within* communist territory. The small crescent-shaped area around Hanoi and Haiphong was to remain "free" until May, 1955, according to treaty; however, the free area started shrinking before this date. "When people ask me when the heart of Haiphong stopped beating," Tom has written, "the date I give them is the fourth of May. On that day an advance echelon, the Viet Minh Committee of Experts, was allowed to enter the city . . . The committee arrived, 480 strong, in brand new Russian-made Molotova trucks. (This) was not bad in itself. But trouble arose because, when they arrived, they brought several thousand armed bodyguards with them (not provided for by treaty)."

We shall come to Tom's detailed account of this final period, but let us start at the beginning with his letter of August 15, 1954. He was writing from a port in south, or free, Viet Nam:

FEAST OF THE ASSUMPTION—At this very minute (it is about 1600) I am sitting at my desk on the ship in the harbor of Tourane just south of Hue, in Viet Nam south. We pulled in here late last night. We received no recognition from any other ships in the harbor, or from the port authorities, much as though we were not very welcome.

This morning two other ships from the group doing the evacuation mission also arrived, and there was a meeting of the CO, the execs, and the medical officers. We showed our plans for putting some 500 persons and their baggage

—whatever miserable loads they will have—in the various holds. It will total somewhere around 2,500 people each trip, poor refugee Vietnamese who are trying to escape from the Communists, to whom their country has been turned over.

Since there was no contact with the beach, it was decided that a party composed of certain officers (and an interpreter, *me*) would go ashore. And we did. We landed, found the French, and said hello, sort of paying our respects. We were coldly received, and then departed in an effort to find some American around the place. The French did give us a jeep, which took only the two Captains and myself. We found the airport, which was about 3 miles from the town of Tourane, that not being much at all. However on the airport there were literally hundreds of American Flying Boxcars, built by us, and given to the French. We then finally found the American contingent. There were some 200 of them. This is the group that lost four men a few months ago; they were swimming on a beach, and were captured by the Viet Minh. When we asked had they any news, the Colonel in charge (we were standing in a hangar where they were playing volleyball) said that they had heard nothing. One of our Captains wondered aloud why they had been out of bounds. The Colonel pointed to a beach some mile and a half to our right and said, "That is where they were . . ." The Communists (Viet Minh) have conquered all of this state of Viet Nam right down to the northern part of Saigon. However, a thin seaboard strip running from Hue to Tourane (16 miles) was not ever captured, though there had been many attempts. All the hills are scorched with napalm bombs. The airport is a mess from bombing. And we are literally surrounded by the Viet Minh. However, the war is over, France has abandoned some 3 million people, and no more shots are being fired.

Tomorrow we leave for Haiphong which, as you know, is the seaport town of Hanoi. There we will pick up the refugees and carry them either down here to Hue or Tourane, or south to Saigon. We do not know for sure, but will find out when we reach Haiphong and contact the Military Advisory Group there. It is anticipated that we will load over 2000 people on this ship.

Mother, you can't imagine what a load like that will be on a relatively small ship like this. We are about 8 tons. Imagine 2000 refugees with their little miserable bundles and large straw hats, their lice, typhus, typhoid, tuberculosis, dysentery and intestinal worms. I am in good health, and am anticipating a good deal of education from this evacuation. After our first load, I'll send you a detailed account, because

I want to keep one for the record. We shall make some 6 or 8 runs like this one planned for tomorrow.

My French is coming in as a great aid. I get to know what is going on, and see how the powers work. Love to all. Malcolm's baby should be coming soon, is it September or October?

Five days later he wrote from Haiphong:

20 AUGUST—We have been laying off here in a small bay 30 miles south of the main seaport of the Tonkin Red River Delta area for the past four days. The staff of the Transport Force has given the collateral duty of interpreter to me. So each day around ten in the morning I am taken to the ship in this bay which is due to load the refugees aboard. There I report to the captain and stand with him on the bridge. The refugees are put aboard a large craft called an LSM which is about 100 yards long, with a large well deck and a mouth which opens up. Malc will explain; they were used during the war to land machinery on the beaches. There are about 700 refugees crammed on the tank deck of this LSM. Then they start up—milling, miserable, filthy, lame, blind, crippled, and war-wounded come aboard. I am sure you have seen the newsreels. Eighty percent are very old men and women, and the others are infants, all swollen with malnutrition and starvation, and literally dozens without limbs. They carry yokes or _balanceurs_ with two paltry bags on each end. This is all they have left in the way of possessions, and we try to get them into the holds of the vessels. Of course the refugees are reluctant to do this, because they don't always understand our intentions or trust our explanations. Most of the Vietnamese understand French because the French have ruled them for so long, but I can't always understand them when they speak back. Getting them into their holds and compartments, explaining that they are not to wash in the urinals, nor use the decks for toilets and all that, is the job of the translator. I am finished only when each ship is loaded and ready to leave. Then around six every evening I am taken by small boat and returned to my own ship, the _Montague_.

You can see that they keep me busy, but I couldn't be more content. I am getting to see and learn a great deal from this whole thing.

They will live deep in the holds of the ship, their food and water being passed down on dumb-waiters, enormous garbage-can-like arrangements with rice, chopped fish and corned beef, and the like. We intend to feed to them two large meals per day, but must keep them off our decks. Even with the delousing that we do as they come up the ladder, they are laden with disease. Although we have to treat them much like animals in a cage, they don't seem to mind, because they realize that we are carrying them from slavery to a free world.

It is about a two-and-a-half-day run down to Saigon, where we will pull all the way up the 76-mile river to the city. Certainly I shall get ample opportunity to go ashore. The only other French-speaking officer in the area is down there now, and he is due up here tomorrow to take over my job, and I'll do his at the other end.

I am benefitting a great deal from this. Not all medicine or epidemiology or rodent control, but especially human nature and human suffering. All the pictures and descriptions in the world cannot give you the true account, the stench, the fatigue, the swollen bellies, the nausea, the filth, and the maggot-ridden wounds of these people.

Don't plan on it, but I may be home at the end of this operation which will be some time in November. This ship is due to return then and I may ride it back.

These illusions of an early return from his "temporary" duty persisted. Tom did not, of course, leave the area until after the treaty deadline of mid-May, the following year. His next letter contained his first view of the southern capital, Saigon:

1 SEPTEMBER—The debarking phase went smoothly. The trip was hectic with a great many sick aboard, though luckily no death. I delivered one baby, and took care of a thousand different skin diseases, mostly staphylococci infections, and old-fashioned cradle-cap, etc. Five cases of measles, much typhus, and two that I am sure had the famous rose spots of typhoid. We had a hard time getting the people to come up out of the holds to use the deck plumbing, and as a consequence had to have a lot of buckets beneath in the holds. These had then to be emptied by hand.

Saigon was a lot of fun, much like being in Paris. All is completely French, and three blocks from the docks (which is like the river is to St. Louis) I was sitting in sidewalk cafés listening to new French music, watching people pass by, and with no apparent cognizance of the horrible load of miserable refugees that we had just debarked. I did a lot of sightseeing, the Hindu temples, the Mohammedan mosques, the Catholic churches. Saigon is called, and rightly so, the Paris of the East. Beautifully manicured and gardened, it is almost breathtaking after the LSM. The heat is pretty awful, but at night it cools and the trees sway gently. Mimosa, bougainvillaea, gardenias and other lush tropical flowers everywhere. It was a good break after the terrible preceding days. I had good champagne and lobster thermidor.

My present hopes are these. This ship is due to go back to the states around the end of September. I am now due to go back to Yokosuka at the end of October. However the man passing out the TADs in Yokosuka told me that if I did want to extend for another month on this ship in order to get stateside, he could arrange it. Around a week before this ship is due to go, I shall take a feel of the situation. So we will see. There is a good chance that I'll be home for a 14-day leave around the first week of October.

You can't imagine how awful the heat is here. We are near the Equator, and even the ocean's breezes are like oven-air. I have had all my shirts and trousers cut to make them shorts. That is the uniform of the day. My nose is consistently red from the sun. I am using French all day every day. The French liaison officer assigned speaks no English whatsoever, and I am continuously doing his interpreting. Certainly hope we receive mail; haven't had any for a long time. The baby should be coming soon.

The first big change in Tom's existence occurred with his being detached from the *Montague* and "offered" new duties. He explained what they were:

2 SEPTEMBER—Received lots of mail yesterday when we arrived in Saigon. Rear Admiral Lorenzo S. Sabin is the commanding officer of the whole task force. The Admiral called me to the flagship when we arrived in Saigon, and with the Captain who is in charge of all the medicine of this mission, offered me a new job—and a new challenge. This ship, the *Montague,* is due for one more load, leaving September 4th, arriving on the 7th, and then the ship will return to Yokosuka, and then head on to the states. My tentative plans were to go with it, but the staff of CTF 90 wants me to become a member of a team of three doctors and a dozen enlisted men, severing all connections with the surgical team and do preventative medicine studies, and epidemiology work in Haiphong, and in Laos, high in the mountains.

Now get up off the floor and read the rest. We have found that a tremendous amount of contagious diseases are coming aboard these vessels with the refugees, and I am to set up, on shore at Haiphong, the same setup that I made on the ship and start into operation a DDT decontamination and screening-for-disease station. That way all the refugees will be screened prior to being put on the LSMs. After it is set up, I am to turn it over to the French public health authorities for them to continue. One of the doctors is Commander Amberson, an expert in the logistics department who can get all the equipment, etc. The other is a good man in epidemiology. And apparently I am the one who can get things done. So it should make a pretty good team.

But that is only part of the job. We will also make an exhaustive study and catalogue of the diseases of importance in this area of the world, Indo-China (that small part not yet Red for 200 days), Laos and perhaps Thailand. The Admiral said, "We want to know everything there is to know about the diseases in this area." It was not given to me as an order, but rather, an offer. But when the Admiral of the outfit makes a JG an "offer" it behooves him to accept it. It will be very interesting to learn about this phase of medicine. And many other facets are good. Laos in the Himalayas should be most interesting. Malcolm, we will have our own helicopter assigned to us. Just about 15 men and a private helicopter. And then butterfly nets, rat traps, roach powders, and mosquito netting.

I am to make the last run on the *Montague,* and then on the 7th will be detached, and flown back to Haiphong to join the rest of the team. So I am now to be on a second team, only not surgical, this one is Preventive Medicine and Epidemiology. From the tone of this letter I hope you can see how pleased I am.

Seven days later Tom was in for another surprise on his own ship:

BAIE D'ALONG—When the news came to the ship about my orders, many of the crew were really sort of upset. I had mixed emotions about leaving the ship which was my first and, of course, my best ship. Well, this morning out of a clear sky, just leaving Saigon after dropping our last load of refugees, the captain called an All Hands meeting on the number three hatch. About 300 crew appeared and on the quarter deck about 25 officers including yours truly, wondering what it was all about. The captain then proceeded to talk over the mike about the ship going to the states and how happy he was and all, but there was one sad note to the whole thing. The Doc wasn't to go with us. You could have knocked me over. He then spoke for ten minutes with very wonderful adjectives about the job I had done, from the circumcisions to being chaplain's assistant. At the end he read a letter of recommendation that was being put into my service record, with a copy being sent to D.C. I don't have to tell you how thrilled I was. But that wasn't all.

The mike was turned over to one of the enlisted men who

then awarded to me, the first officer in the history of the ship, the Good Shipmate award. This is given monthly to the enlisted man who has been the best shipmate for that month. It is only an enlisted man's award, and no officer has ever gotten one. The sailors said that they couldn't give me a letter of recommendation or a promotion, but they would give me what they held closest and most prized. So I was given the scroll and the boys really let out with some whoops. I had a hell of a time to keep from crying all over the place. When they yelled "Speech, speech," I told them that I really was at a loss for words. Someone yelled, "That's hard to believe!" I was really very very pleased, Mother. It is gratifying to be appreciated. Tonight at dinner there was a large cake that the bakers had made for me. (I had sandpapered one's pock-marked face, circumcised two others, and appeared as defense counsel in the fourth's court-martial.) It was a two-layer job, with a large copy of my oak-leaf medical corps insignia.

The other ships in this Task Force have begun to learn my name. At various times I am called for various things—every-thing, even a near-riot on one of the LST's that passed us during the night. We stopped, I was called for and sent over in a small boat to board the LST and talk in French to the refugees to quiet them down. There have been many episodes, obviously the result of Viet Minh infiltration amongst the refugees. They start riots over the lack of drinking water or, as on this ship, let the people think that they are being taken to Hainan, which they fear. We have found several hand-grenades planted around the ship so that, when the ship is empty and rolls considerably with the waves, they break loose and later explode.

I am used for all kinds of odd jobs. Last night at 0200 I was called out to go to a smaller non-medical staffed ship for a possible appendicitis. It was that, I found. Although they did not have a doctor aboard, they did have a pretty good little sick-bay and plenty of instruments, etc. I took my own operating-room technician, gave a spinal, and had no trouble whatsoever. (My first shipboard appendectomy, by the way.) This was in the Saigon River, about 20 miles up. When I asked the Captain of the other ship why he called for me, instead of some of the doctors on two other ships in the vicinity, he re-plied, "Well, I've heard of you, Dooley . . ." So this Task Force knows me.

11 SEPTEMBER, BAIE D'ALONG—As my boat pulled away from the *Montague*, almost all of the 300-man crew were manning the rails, and I felt real upset leaving the old tub. But a new job now, and new acquaintances. I remember that Malc,

with the wisdom of a sage, once said all you do in the service is say goodbye to friends. As I left the ship in Tourane, I went to a command ship and got me transportation on this LST to Haiphong. Only the LST has a last-minute change in orders and instead of going right up the river to Haiphong, stopped here in the Baie d'Along. We will stay here tonight, and in the morning will go to a staging area. The *Estes*, the flagship, has helicopter service, so I can get it tomorrow at Haiphong. This LST is the smallest I've ever been in. Only four officers, and my bunk is the size of a small pullman berth.

Just before I left Tourane I received your letter of the 18th, with Eddie's enclosed. How strange this delay in time is. For three weeks now I've been on this Evacuation mission, but no letter of yours has acknowledged that you even know what I'm doing, although I am sure that you now do. I think Ed has done the right thing absolutely, and nothing is so tough (boot camp, etc.) that he can't take it. On the contrary, he will probably wallow in it, if it is sweat and hard work. It must be desperately hard for you to say goodbye to a fourth son into the service. Mother, your life certainly consists of saying goodbye most of the time to all of your sons. I hope they do a job to honor you. We try.

14 SEPTEMBER, HAIPHONG—I have arrived on the new assignment, and am living with three other American Navy officers. One of them is my chief, Commander Amberson of the Medical Corps, and two other Navy men connected with the Military Advisory and Assistance Group (from now on referred to as MAAG). We are the only Americans living in Tonkin. All of Hanoi has been emptied, as they have only another three weeks before Ho Chi Minh moves in. The enlisted men who work for us, 12 of them in total, are not allowed to live on the land, so they live on an LST that is about one hour up the river. This is hard on them as they have a one-hour boat ride twice a day.

We are doing the medical processing of the refugees who are here in such large numbers, awaiting their French LSMs to the Navy transports down at Baie d'Along. The large camps have no facilities whatsoever, just tents thrown together. We are installing a water purification plant today, making 30 gallons per minute. I spent six hours working on it yesterday, and today it will start operating. The enlisted men handle the DDT dusting at the embarkation site, down on the waterfront.

We are also setting up a lab that has been sent down from Yokosuka. It is a complete Epidemiological lab, that includes Bacteriology and Parasitology. We will collect all the types of intestinal parasites, blood parasites, samples of the contaminants of the water and food; and then all of the various insects, mosquitoes, rats, etc. These will be catalogued and sent on to the Bureau of Medicine and Surgery.

It is now anticipated that we shall be here about one month before moving elsewhere. The *Knudson* is laying off about one hour away, and it is sort of an office. We have a helicopter assigned to us, with a pilot, and use it like a taxi. I came out here to the ship this morning to get some equipment, and just wrote this. And now I'll have to close. Love to all.

15 SEPTEMBER—Haiphong is a strange city. It is not as turbulent as I expected it to be, yet uneasiness is definitely evident. There is antagonism bordering on fanaticism against the French; every day trucks are overturned and barracks blown up. Are these the Viet Minh, or are they Viet Nam who are mad at the French? No one really knows. So far antagonism to Americans is not evident. I've seen none of it personally. All the Vietnamese treat me well and seem grateful. On the 10th or 11th of next month, Hanoi is turned over. That will certainly make a change in the conditions here, and I am a bit fearful of this time.

It is just after dawn, and the ship will be arriving any minute. I was up most of the night setting up and learning how to run a machine. Tell Malc that I am getting a tremendous amount of flight time in. Yesterday the helicopter ride took almost four hours.

17 SEPTEMBER—Camp de la Pagode is the large 14,000-refugee camp where we have set up a water purification plant, and many other things such as latrines, slit trenches, and the like. We also have a medical tent there which we use as a collecting tent. At night, we have fly traps and rat traps out to catch some of those, and comb the rats for their fleas, which carry plague and such. So far none of this bothers me, but one thing the Commander has in mind upsets me. He wants to keep his eyes open for a large cave, then we will put a mosquito net across the mouth, and go in deep into the cave, release an aerosol bomb, and all the bats (and there are an enormous number of them, vampire and otherwise) will attempt to fly out, and will be caught by their wing claws in the mosquito netting. We shall then gas them, and mount them.

Interesting work, to say the least. It is new and unusual. The French yesterday gave us all new clothes. So now I wear French boots, high stockings, shorts (which would never be allowed on the Country Club grounds) and my uniform shirt, with a pith helmet or one of those elephant hats.

Living ashore is strange. The town is a mixture of bustle and fear and evacuation, with long lines of trucks and equipment clogging all the roads for a few hours, then absolute still and quiet for the rest of the day. Many have no intention of leaving until the very last minute. The Chinese people collect all their debts on 1 January, and they intend to stay at least until then. Hanoi falls on the 10th of next month, but Haiphong has several more months. Don't worry about me, I am in the best of health, extremely busy, and very happy.

21 SEPTEMBER—Things are progressing very well here. Living on the beach has its ups and downs. The hotel, although one of the better, is simply awful. The French evidently aren't leaving until January or perhaps February. Many believe we shall be in an all-out war by that time.

Tell Malc that I am becoming a radio operator. We have the large type walkie-talkie in the lab, and we can call the station ship for a boat, and other things. "This is Cockroach calling . . ." Tell Dr. Vincent Jones that if I ever see another case of trachoma it will be my 10,000th. It is the greatest cause of blindness in the world, and a good 15% of the population of all ages here are blind with it, while about 80% seem to have it. We are really doing great things, Mother, in helping these people, and they realize it. Bac Sy My in Viet means "Good American doctor" and the people keep saying that. No one ever seems to have treated their eyes, no one ever set up living improvements for them, no one ever chlorinated their water. Now the USA is doing it, and they are appreciative. The Viets always thought of America as an extension of France. Now the people are seeing Americans for themselves, and they find that we are a gentle people, and a people who want to aid them. They are confused and grateful.

This morning I went to the Cat-Bi which is the hospital in Haiphong where the Dien Bien Phu death-march patients are living. It would take a book to describe the abject horror of these boys. They had to march 400 miles barefoot, for one month. They were fed one peanut and a handful of brown rice daily. If they fell out, they were buried alive. They are suffering from all the vitamin deficiencies known to man, and their feet are about the size of small hams; the ulcers on their bodies are of the indolent type, which cannot heal because the body has no regenerative powers. Many are still unable to hold food on their stomach. Almost 100% have infectious hepatitis and 100% have dysentery. They are really in miserable condition. They are almost all legionnaires, the young movie type of swashbuckling lad full of sound and fury. Only, unlike the quotation, these signify much.

I have sent some pictures home also, so you should be getting a pretty good idea of this whole thing. Pass on the word to as many of our friends as you can, because I would like to see an awareness of this situation. The luxuries of America seem very far away. I am learning a great deal about misery, and appreciate a great many things I used to consider common.

22 SEPTEMBER—The refugees in the camps yesterday told me that there are thousands and thousands who would like to get out of these towns, especially the towns of Nam Dinh and of Phuly (look them up on the map, they are south of the city of Hanoi and Haiphong) and that the Communists will not allow them to leave. These people are forced to sneak out at night and many of them bear the scars and the marks of this attempt. Not that we ever expected the Reds to hold to the clauses of the treaty of Geneva, but the clause definitely states that those who want to go south will be allowed to do so. The Reds are not "allowing" them.

I wonder what America is saying about this whole thing. I would appreciate it, if you would cut out articles concerning this "Passage to Freedom" and mail them to me. Living so close, really right in the thing, it reaches gigantic proportions, and is all-consuming, but in America it may well just be another item in the newspaper.

A disappointment came for me last evening in the form of a dispatch relieving Commander Amberson of his command. He is due for promotion to Captain and a decoration and is to go to Washington. Doctor Amberson is one of the finest men I have ever known and the type of Navy doctor that makes younger officers want to stay in. One excellent type like this makes up for all the half-baked ones.

When I take care of these Viets, Mother, I feel like packing them all up in my suitcase and sending them to Thomas Dunn Memorial. The kids are so cute and sweet and honest, and try to help each other so. This eye-disease, trachoma, affects the kids first. After I arrive in the field near the camp sites (where there is a constant turnover to the ships) the kids swarm around me, and hand me things from my box, and generally just get in my way. But they are trying so. Then after they catch on that I am treating their eyes and leg ulcers and the like, a little five-year-old will disappear and come back with a two-year-old on his back, to the "Bac Sy My" or American doctor, to have his eyes treated too. This caring for each other marks the Viet Nam character. They have had such a hell of a hard time for so many years that they realize the only people they can depend on to help them is themselves.

That is about all I have time for now. I hope these letters are getting through to you all right. All is very well with my health, and still I am so pleased with the job. I wish you could see me with my head shaven close because of the heat, clad in British shorts and long socks, and then a *chapeau brossé*, which is that elephant hat that all people wear in the tropics, not the pith helmet but a large fedora hat, with a wide brim, one side pinned up and the other side hanging down. That brim hides my nose from the sun. Believe it or not my legs and arms are tanned, but my nose is constantly burned. Hope Malc is well set, and the baby coming soon, and love to all of you always.

29 SEPTEMBER—I go out daily to the Dien Bien Phu Hospital where all the returned prisoners are. The exchange is still taking place, you know, the last group of 30 came about eight days ago. These boys are Dachau all over again. Horribly undernourished, enormous swollen bellies, knees and ankles. They have had no shoes for months, and have had to make forced marches, etc. They are racked with dysentery, all types of intestinal parasites, and of course the haunting, recurring malaria falciparum, the scourge of this part of the world. The boys are a wealth of medical information, and although I dislike sticking the end of their fingers for malaria slides, I know it is for the protection of my own brothers.

The French have good medical equipment here, but they have no terramycin, one of the bulwarks of treatment for amoeba. As a consequence, my coming with a box of 1,000 bottles was a panacea for the French, and a door-opener for me. Now I have full run of the hospital. This particular hospital is way out in the country, in the middle of a beautiful calm rice field, really about ten square miles of rice fields, and it sets up high on a hill with a gentle breeze at all times. Each room with about 20 beds is well ventilated (it needs it, as all the boys have fecal incontinence) bright, cheerful and pleasant. The mental attitude of these men is strange and requires peace and serenity. A great number are French foreign legionnaires, ages averaging about 21, and they are really not fighting for anything, no country in particular, no group of people, no idea, just fighting. As a consequence of this strange mental attitude, when they are taken prisoner and tortured, and starved, and neglected, and marched, there seems to be no reason. It is better and easier to endure something when you understand firmly and believe wholeheartedly the cause, whatever it may be. These legionnaires have no cause. So their general mental attitude is, *why?* Confusion and anguish.

Right now there is a sort of revolution brewing in Saigon between the fine and independent Ngo Dinh Diem, and two army generals who are refusing to recognize his authority. These two generals are pawns of the French, who do not want Viet Nam to have full independence. They are causing all sorts of strikes and the like. The news today was that the city was surrounded by French troops who would not permit people to enter or leave without certain papers. Part of my job here is to get the papers that certain military people need to get down there. I am using French all day, so much that I actually think in it. With the reading of the newspapers and the translating of statistics and medical journals, I am getting quite proficient in it. It is an invaluable tool. I am so grateful that you and Dad were willing to give me that time in Paris. Little did I realize in what good stead it would stand me.

1 October 1954, 0710 HOURS, 1,550 FEET OVER HUODUONG— For Malc: I'm sitting at this moment in the radio seat behind the pilot and co-pilot of this C-47. We are heading straight W on the compass, the RPM says 17, and next dial is 30 manifold pressure, air speed is 170, and oil pressure is 75. Will I make it? Flying over this Tonkin Delta it is understandable why they call it the Rice Basket of the Far East. It is green and fertile. (Just felt the wheels go down. I'll stop here and resume when we leave Hanoi.)

Later. They have just loaded 72 refugees aboard. There are 30 bucket seats; the rest squat on the floor. The pilots are reading some sort of laundry list prior to taxiing. In the air now, over Hanoi, and it looks like a phantom city. Very little traffic, no large convoys of military, like Haiphong. No masses of refugees scattered around. Little smoke from the factory chimneys, most of the paddies seem deserted. The newspapers say Emperor Mao of China, Chou En Lai and Ho Chi Minh are having a great meeting in the resort on the Lake of Hanoi, which I can easily see. I suppose they will divide up the sections of Viet Nam for individual deglutition.

Over 350,000 so far have been evacuated by combined air and sea lift. We have DDTed over 100,000 ourselves. That is quite a few and when this is over I don't want to see DDT again. CAT (Civilian Air Transport): this group of civilians has proved to be a very handy bunch of boys. They are flying the Hanoi-Saigon airlift. Because Hanoi is closed to foreigners now (in 11 days, according to the Treaty, the Communists legally take over), the pilots live in my hotel at Haiphong, 30 minutes by air. Each morning 5 planes leave for Hanoi, stop long enough to load refugees, then head to Saigon, four hours away by air.

It is getting a little bumpy, so I'll close off here and mail this in Saigon. Little did I realize a month or so ago, when the old *Montague* pulled into the quay at Saigon, that I'd be flying down here later from Hanoi on a plague statistics mission!

4 OCTOBER—The weather in Haiphong is clearing a little. The monsoon season is almost over. Some days it rains in torrents for as long as eight and ten hours. You actually hurt on the top of the head and shoulders from the rain beating on you. Yet the sun shines brightly during all this. The river swells and the current gets very swift and dangerous. No lightning or thunder, no storm, just rain and rain. I am constantly wet, but never cold as the temperature remains so high.

It is about time to leave and take the next boat into town. I have a luncheon engagement with the Indian who is the chief of the Mixed Team of the International Commission of the Geneva Conference. I am supposed to tell him some things that I have learned about the refugee problem. The flagship is using me as one of the U. S. representatives in all this muddling that has happened with the refugees. The camps in Saigon are awful. Under water, filthy, and like the slums of St. Louis. The French are supposed to keep them up, but they do not. As a consequence, the news is filtering back north not to go south as the conditions there are so poor. It is the job of the International Commission to insist that the French do a better job. They are not keeping my camp up, but I get my own sailors and shovels in the hands of the kids, and keep it in pretty good condition.

Another great fear here is that all the Communists who are south and supposed to be going north are not doing so. Very few are appearing in the north, and hardly any on the roads. There are no Communist ships evacuating north, as we are evacuating south. The fear is that these people are going into the small towns and villages to do underground work, and assure the country of going Communistic by the elections in 1956.

Another change now occurred in Tom's situation. He learned that only one doctor and several corpsmen would remain at Haiphong, now that collecting of the epidemic and other medical data was completed.

Tom recorded this reaction to the news that he was to be the lucky doctor: "The epidemiological work of our group is complete, and a request went to the command ship (the *Estes* at Saigon) to have the team sent home. The remainder, the medical aid group to the few Navy ships up the river here and the MSTS ships in Haiphong can be done by one doctor and a couple of corpsmen. It seems that I shall be the one to stay here.

"I am not too displeased with it, as there is still a wealth of things to do for the refugees. I shall have to continue to have the water plant running (the mechanical setup is handled by an enlisted man) and I shall continue to give treatment to the refugees at Camp de la Pagode.

"There are always opportunities to lecture on the various ships that come up the river in the afternoon, spend the night, then load refugees. I enjoy telling them the history of our country, and of the war, and how things came about, and attempt to explain to the white hats what the future of this situation may be, and how it will affect many of them. I am always completely amazed at the questions that some of the men ask me after one of these talks (and I have given many). The level of intelligence of the average white hat is higher than statistics and officers give credit.

"To be on these ships, participating in the evacuation, seeing the misery, smelling the people, hearing rumors of plague and other things, precipitates an intense interest in the situation. I answered so many questions that I decided I would organize a history of this whole thing, dating back to when the French occupied this country in the 18th century. I looked up a lot of things, read a lot, and sort of organized a speech. The first time I gave it it was so well received, especially by the officers in the group, that a dispatch went out on it, and I was called to some other ships in the area to give the same talk again. So this lecture by Dooley is getting to be the expected thing when a ship comes up the river. I enjoy giving it, it behooves me to learn how to lecture, it behooves me period. Am I an uncle of a boy or a girl? I wonder, I wonder, I wonder."

13 OCTOBER—I have spent many hours with the International Commission of Geneva for the Peace Treaty of Indo-China. They are a group of four Indians, four Poles, and four Canadians who are in charge of what their title says they are in charge of. They are to investigate the problems that the refugees say exist, such as inability to get out of the small towns, the Viet Minh taking away their sampans, and so on. The few who do escape travel by night in small junks and tubs and tell me many others can't get out. As a result I inform the Navy and then the International Commission. I then take such refugees there and they are questioned, etc. It is all very interesting and heart-rending.

From the *Montague* through devious means I received a letter that I am copying and sending on to you. I delivered many babies during the trips on that ship, but received only one letter from a parent. It is enough. I think it is eloquent and poignant.

"Dear Sirs:
    I come in the name of my wife, my new born, my family and myself to present my sincerely respects, appreciation and thanks.
    All of you have given much help in the birth of my little daughter. We have brought you many troubles while you have brought us great help.
    You and your doctor lost sleep in order to render service to us.
    I was working in American Medical Section for four years, but I did not understand the American language well. In the days that we lived on your ship we have understood you and your ways. From the Captain to the last sailor, you have hearts of gold.
    And my family and myself, we thank you very much and wish to all you Americans, many victories in your fight against communism."

Isn't that wonderful? Now that I have this letter I read it at the end of my talks, and I think the white hats are really taken aback. The other day on one of the LSTs when I finished and read this letter, there was just silence from the 60 guys sitting on the deck in front of me. Finally one man raised his hand and said, "Doc, what can a bunch of white hats do in America to make the people realize how wonderful these people really are?"

Previously many of the sailors were angered with the refugees. They smell bad, have awful-looking diseases, don't understand English, and the like. I tried to show the boys that they are really a fine and noble people and that they are undergoing tribulations that many of us Americans could never endure. They have to sell and give up all their possessions, save those they can carry on their *balenceurs*. They have to run and hide and travel in darkness, they are cold and wet and sick. Then they are herded into large tent camps in Haiphong which they don't understand. Then onto American vessels which frighten them. They have heard Vietminh-born rumors that they will be gassed and tortured by Americans. So they come to us like frightened children. They squat the minute they find a square foot, and are often very hard to budge. Then after four horrible days on the ship, stifling for lack of air in the holds, they arrive in Saigon, and are again herded into a tent camp, this one being a morass of stink and filth. Here they wait patiently for redistribution to the rice fields of the Mekong Delta, never knowing what will become of them, their *balanceurs,* and their children. I have to get it across to our sailors that these people are not a stinking mass of humanity, but a great people, distressed.

25 OCTOBER—Well, again, many things have happened. Number one, and most important, is that a complete change has been made by Admiral Sabin, the Commander of this Task Force 90 and head of all the ships in this area concerned with the Evacuation of Tonkin. A new unit has been formed. Its name, The Preventive Medicine Unit, CTU (Task Unit) 90.8.6. And your son is the "C" of this TU, or the Commander of Task Unit 90.8.6. The Admiral told me that I had done an excellent job and asked me if I would like to stay on and continue this job. I said yes very much, assuming that I would get a new commander, hoping that it would be like the first one, Amberson. He then said that he considered that volunteering, and I said that it was just that, I was so wrapped up in my refugees and in the whole situation here that I did not want to leave, even to go back to Yokosuka. If there was still to be an evacuation I should like to stay. He then told me that pleased him. The staff then had a conference, and they decided to break precedence in my case and make *me* commander.

I am to be appointed CTU 90.8.6, to have five corpsmen assigned to me, and to continue ALL the functions of the previous unit, except the research, and the collecting of specimens, etc. I am literally REPLACING commanders Amberson and Britten. Secondly, they told me I could have any corpsmen I wanted in the Far East. Immediately I sent dispatches off to some top corpsmen in Yokosuka and on my old ship who had worked for me, and whom I knew to be excellent. All replied affirmatively, and in four days (today) they all arrived, two from Yokosuka, one from Hawaii, and one from a ship here. CTU 90.8.6 had its formal change of command ceremony today and I now rate staff gangway. All units are headed by a Commander or a Lt. Commander. Having a JG head a unit is unheard of, and unprecedented in this Command.

The Admiral said that I was doing a good job, and he had recommended me for the position, as no new man brought down could be so well acquainted with the situation, could speak French, and the smattering of Vietnamese that I know, etc., etc. So I have the job, and am delighted with it. The authorizing dispatch read, "Authority granted you to extend temporary additional medical duties to Lt. (jg) Dooley as necessary." So you see, I am still on temporary duty.

27 OCTOBER—All is going very well here. The new unit and its new CO are doing well. We are doing all that is asked of us and doing it well, I believe. Some new things concerning the refugees however. As you very well know, we have been running a daily census of about 4,000 in the camp. We load them into ships about every other day, which means that they are escaping from the reds at a rate of 2,000 per day. And we are shipping them out equally fast. The Camp de la Pagode, where I treat them, keep them, and have them processed, inoculated, where I make their potable water, and keep their sanitation somewhat decent—this camp has a daily census of about 4,000, changing every other day.

Well, just lately, the last three nights the following has happened. Through a system which no one will explain, the people around Phat Diem and Nam Dinh and Nam Binh and Bui Chu (south of Haiphong) are getting out on small rafts and extremely small boats to the seaport village of Van Ly. From here, at an exact time they paddle out beyond the 3 mile continental limit and are met by French LSMs and small craft which bring them up 77 miles to Haiphong and to my camp. This is the first time that we are actually picking them up.

How long we will be able to do this, we don't know. However, we now have 12,000 people in the refugee camp (almost at maximum capacity). One night 2,650 came up, arriving at 0300. I was called down to the camp to direct traffic, and again and again.

I made a run on one of the fast French corvettes which we use to pick these people up. I was a very thrilling sight. We left at ten in the evening, and got to a spot three and one-quarter miles off the coast at Van Ly. Not a thing in sight at 0300. We went below, had some cognac and coffee and talked until we were called up. There, coming out to the boat, was a solid mass of rafts and bum boats, and little tubs, with 1,800 refugees, complete with their pigs, and chickens, and three had water-buffalo on the rafts. The rafts were made of bamboo about four inches in diameter, and lashed together with line. They were about ten by ten, with perhaps 30 people squatting on them. You could not even see the rafts as the weight kept them submerged about half a foot. Not a sound was made, you couldn't hear a paddle touch the water. They got to the boat, most of them. When the final count was over, the old man with a goatee said that over 2,000 had started, but many drowned on the way out. I personally through the glasses saw one raft tip over, and many people unable to get pulled up on other rafts. So when he said 300 drowned I believe him, because I saw a group sink myself.

These old men and women have been beaten. Some are full of black and blue marks, and have many broken collar bones and upper arms. These are from being hit with gun butts by the Viet Minh. These aren't young and hardy soldiers, but old debilitated people. This is the kind of war it is. We loaded them all around the decks, and brought them back up the coastline, up the river, and into the usual embarkation site. We radioed the number and the Viet Nam officials at the refugee camp started the rice kettles going. When they were trucked from the embarkation site to the camp (three miles) they were received and fed and given hot tea.

This has been done three times now. The last one was last night, and I was at the site at 0200 when they arrived last night. At the camp site there is a road that is just a dirt trail from the main paved highway to the camps themselves. This is about 800 yards long. The large trucks are unable to drive on this road, so the people are put off the trucks on the paved road, and they walk down the wide path to the tents. This morning I was there, there were several thousand people lining that road on both sides in perfect column formation, with candles and lanterns. As the new arrivals from the sea arrived, and were disgorged from the trucks, they walked down between those long lines, down this living corridor. In this way people looking for relatives or for friends, could see them. As a relative would spot someone dear, she would cry out and they would get together, help carry each other, and walk on down the end of the line to the tents where I would direct them into the various camps.

You just can't picture nor feel the scene, Mother, unless you are here. It is so pitiful you want to weep, yet so tender and fine and noble that you feel humble before these refugees. We are unable to get them all to leave on our ships now, because so many are waiting for relatives. However, with such a large census of 12,000 there are usually some 2,000 willing to leave.

29 OCTOBER—I have just returned from sick call at the city orphanage. It's called An-Lac or Peace. There are over 1,000 mutilated little kids from the war. They have lost their parents, and have been collected around the Tonkin Delta area and brought here by Madame Ngai, a very intelligent woman who runs the place. Many of the kids are very ill, mostly with malnourishment, and cholera and upper respiratory infection. Under Viet Nam Medical Liaison, I take care of them with the richness and opulence of American Navy medical supplies.

1 NOVEMBER—I am in excellent health today, as I have always been, but somehow I feel a little better than usual today. It has been a long one. My refugees invited me to High Mass this morning at the refugee camp. It was an important invitation (written in Viet, no less) because it shows that strong anti-American feelings are dwindling as refugees learn that we are not all monsters who drown their babies. To have them invite me to the highest thing in their lives, a Mass, is an important thing.

They had the altar on the little mid-point of the camp, and thousands of refugees gathered around. They had a wooden *prie-dieu* out for me, which put me about five feet over the little altar boys, and directly in the middle of the altar so that when the priest would turn around to say *Dominus vobiscum,* he would have to lean a little to the side because he was absolutely face to face with me. But I tried to do as I should. The refugees sang the Mass in sort of a monotone, and the sun rose during the Introit. It was truly magnificent in its simplicity and humility. Then they gave me a breakfast of Chinese soup, which I ate. Then I came home and took some terramycin, just in case.

So perhaps the good start makes this day a good day. Strangely enough, I have always been in good health here. Many others have come down with a touch of diarrhea, and the like, but never your son. I am extremely cautious of what I eat, and of my health, and though there be cholera and plague rampant around here, I am fit as a fiddle. I have inoculated myself against everything in the book.

One of the men in the Viet Nam Army who is an important contact for us has a son with polio and with residual paralysis. I have been giving the boy some help, and he has now departed for Saigon with a letter to a U. S. ship's physician down south. The father today came to my office with a gift. It is an enormous solid bronze elephant, very, very old, and about two feet in height. It must weigh about 50 pounds. I don't know what I'll do with it, but I'll try to send it home. Don't be too frightened if it arrives.

22 OCTOBER—Today I received a beautiful letter from the Surgeon General of the Navy.* I hope you let Dr. McMahon see this. Evidently Dr. Casberg showed Admiral Pugh my letter of last August. He was the one that Dr. McMahon spoke to personally, pleading that I be allowed into the Navy when my slate at medical school was so messed up. Now Dr. McMahon can feel that he was justified in recommending me. Not only does this letter please me a great deal, but it should make Dr.

* This letter appears on page 57.

McMahon feel that he supported somebody who was not a total loss. I am keeping the original because I want to have something to read when I get to feeling a little low.

5 NOVEMBER—I received a letter yesterday from Malc, dated 16 October, in which he gave me a detailed account (complete with time-interval between pains) of the birth of his first child. I am happy that Mother is now a grandmother, which is what I think she wanted most. What is my niece's name?

Get out your old maps, and 88 miles or so south of Haiphong you will find the city of Van Ly. This is the coastal margin of the province of Bui Chu. Of the 2 million Catholics in Indo-China, three-fourths of them live in Bui Chu. This story is a beautiful example of how successfully a well organized underground can work. At certain hours late at night, on the most desolate parts of the Van Ly beaches, French ships would pull in to the very limit of the continental line of 3 miles. Then the escapees got into rafts, small junks, and anything that floats, and went out to the 3-mile limit. There they got into the French landing craft with their mouth-like bows opened, the stern heavily weighted to keep the bows out of the water. The escapees literally floated into the bows of the ships on their rafts, and these ships then turned around when loaded and sailed another three miles to the large *General Brewster,* a 6,000-man transport ship, and there they climbed up ladders hung over all the sides of the ship. This would continue for several hours until daylight intervened. Then they stopped and the French ships left. No one got suspicious. The next evening the same pattern would be repeated until the *General Brewster* had almost 8,000 people aboard her, in the troop compartments, on the decks, and even on the bridge.

Then the *General Brewster* pulled in to the Baie d'Along here and the reverse of the usual procedure was carried out and the escapees were brought to my refugee camp. There they were treated for everything from immersion foot to beri-beri, inoculated, dusted with DDT and reloaded in a few days for further transfer to Saigon.

This is just one of the methods used to get the refugees out. It shows the excellent cooperation and timing carried out by the underground, the French and us. The French cooperated wholeheartedly and did a superb job, I am glad to say.

8 NOVEMBER—The *Balduck* pulled up from Tourane for a day, and tomorrow it goes on down to Saigon. Unfortunately, I must remain here in Haiphong, but I don't really mind. The work continues in the same intensity, and the refugees have completely won me over, so I don't mind staying at all. It has

turned quite cool here the last few weeks, and I now have to wear a jacket. The change was quick. Everyone around caught cold last week, except me. I must be in good fettle. Never felt better. Never a touch of malaria or of any dysenteries. Don't know about my weight, however.

11 NOVEMBER —The CIC (the International Control Commission) set up by Geneva to investigate the carrying out of the clauses of the treaty has mobile teams that investigate various cities in Indo-China. The underground here in Haiphong was able to find out that the CIC was anticipating going to Phat Diem early in November, and sent word out to the surrounding areas to gather in Phat Diem to celebrate All Souls' and All Saints' Days, and, when the commission arrived, to present their complaints. Some 35,000 people came to Phat Diem for the religious occasion. Catholicism has not been erased from this Red area yet, just suppressed. Daily meetings for Communists' propaganda usually conflict with Mass schedule. The enforced labor is for priests, too, which interferes with the caring of their churches. The Reds say that religion is 'interior" and does not require priests and churches. Barracks for soldiers are needed and the "exigencies" of the situation have required the Viet Minh to take over many large missions. And so on.

The 35,000 people gathered. They brought with them a little to eat. This is all. The VM smelled a rat, so forbade the people to leave the churches and missions to buy food. They said, "You are here to pray, then pray . . ." The CIC did not go down on the 1st, nor the 2nd. We were informed of this, and of the growing shortage of food within the missions. So a few more days the people would be forced by starvation to leave and return to the villages, and when the CIC finally arrived, there would be few to complain. As a result of Admiral Sabin's urging, the French high command urging, and General J. Lawton Collins' urging, the CIC went to Phat Diem on the 7th. Yesterday word came that CIC had instructed the Viet Minh to allow some 25,000 people to leave, and that they be allowed to leave on the beaches (as they have been doing for months).

With the arrival of General J. Lawton Collins, there was much pleasure, because we felt that America was dismally unaware of the seriousness of the situation here. We feel deeply of the propaganda importance of American aid (NOT INTERVENTION) here. To show the free world that the U.S. is willing to help a young and newly free country get on its feet, this is a good and an important thing.

14 NOVEMBER—We received a report today of over 1,000 people drowning on that sand bar near the mouth of the Red

River, near Phat Diem. Though the small French craft often went behind the three-mile limit to pick up refugees, the Communists have issued a warning that any ships so doing shall be fired upon. Therefore, even for the humane reason of saving those 4,000 still on the diminishing sand bar reef, no ships can go in.

Also got some more mail. Your letters are the ones that I read the most, Mother, keep writing, often. I am really out of contact with the world here. Now that all the ships are leaving, there are only about 11 Americans in all of Northern Indo-China. Mail means a lot.

16 NOVEMBER—Well, it has just been Christmas. Let me tell you what happened. I am on the ship for lunch today, as I was informed by my "agents" that they were having ice cream. I haven't had ice cream for over four months. So after three bowls of vanilla cream with chocolate sauce, I sat back in opulence and rested. Then the sergeant from the MAAG office in town came out to the ship with a mail pouch, which he said was for me. "The whole pouch?" I asked incredulously. "Yes, sir," was his answer.

In spite of all the warnings not to open until Christmas (you really didn't expect me to wait, did you?) I opened them, and was certainly pleased. You know I am intensely interested in reading anything I can get my hands on about the Orient, especially this southern area, including Burma, Malaya, Thailand, Indonesia, Java, Sumatra, and the rest of this part of the globe which is going to play such an important role in the world's future. So your book on Indonesia was well received. And *The Teahouse of the August Moon* is one of the top New York plays, so it is most welcome, as I've never read either the book or the play. Then the pen and pencil, complete with refills (which is using your head, dear Mother, as refills are unavailable here) is something that a doctor always needs. I am using a scratchy Indo-Chinese version of one now, that I truthfully believe was made out of old beer cans. Where did you find cuff-links with medical insignia? I don't have any dress shirts here, but when I return to Yokosuka (some day I shall) I can wear them with my white shirts. So thank you very very much, Mother, for my Christmas. I feel positively out of season because the temperature is around 90.

17 NOVEMBER—The refugees have again slowed down, thank God, we now have time for a breather. We are awaiting an overland transfer via Molotova trucks to the perimeter at Huiduong. The communists inform us that they are bringing to us (at the perimeter, 11 miles away) some 15,000 "insurrectionists" who want to leave. These "insurrectionists" will prob-

ably be little old women, and farmer peasants, and infants still on mother's breast. But for now it is quiet.

18 NOVEMBER—The refugee problem has come to almost a halt. There are only some 7,000 sitting around, and one ship load of 6,000 will almost take care of them.

Those released from Phat Diem are to be brought up by Viet Minh transportation. In the past four days, only 61 have arrived. The reasons are two-fold. The Viet Minh say they will keep their side of the bargain, but the miserable people have been duped and tricked so often that they don't believe the VM. Often they will not get on the large busses and trucks when the VM say, "These will take you to Haiphong," for they fear they will be taken to Than Hoa or other communist strongholds, famous for brainwashing techniques. The second reason is that the VM demand pay for the gasoline at the rate of 8,000 Ho Chi Minh piasters, or 250 Vietnam piasters. That amounts to about ten dollars per person. For the average large family this presents an impossible amount of money to raise. All in all, the situation is bleak.

P. S. Went to Mass and Communion, as today and the 16th are Earle's anniversaries.

23 NOVEMBER—Mother, would you contact Mary Virginia Roberts, and ask her to give you the name of some good books that she used in her course on the Comparative Religions of the Orient? I am finding this part of the world more and more fascinating, as everything here is in French, which I can read. For example, the Buddhists are beginning to leave Tonkin, which is considered extraordinary, as theirs is a religion of resignation, and if Buddha has sent the curse of communism to them, they must bow their heads and endure. Then, also the Taoists have recently done some amazing things in central Viet Nam in reference to a national unity movement originating in Peking. I should like to understand more about these religions. So if you could send to me some books on Buddhism, Taoism, Shintoism, and Confucianism, I would appreciate it. Mary Virginia should have a wealth of information on the subject.

28 NOVEMBER—The refugees are no longer called refugees, but escapees. The International Control Commission has done much complaining, and has successfully brought to the attention of the free world the fact that the Viet Minh are not respecting the clauses of the Geneva Treaty. As a consequence a little pressure is being put on the communists in the form of adverse propaganda. They have responded, at least in the Haiphong area, like this. They are now "aiding" in the "re-allocation" of those who wish to leave their benevolent areas

of Tonkin to go south. They do it this way. If some wish to
leave they go to the control team in their town and give it
their name. Then 100 per day are called to the Viet Minh city
hall and issued a passport (for several dollars) after filling out
the names of the relatives they are forced to leave behind
Then of the 100 who are given passports the next step is for
them to "buy" their tickets for transportation. By walk it is
only some 40 miles to freedom. But the Viet Minh has offered
the transportation, and none may refuse. 80 people a day are
put into a ferry boat that runs north and west, and after two
and a half days on the winding river, they finally arrive on the
north perimeter (really south of Haiphong) where they are
allowed to cross the river to freedom. During this voyage they
are lectured on the blessings of the People's Republic of Viet
Nam, and on the horrors of the American form of life. They
aren't fed much, and they live in great fear that they aren't
being brought to freedom at all, but are being take somewhere
deeply inland. But they are so determined to have their freedom that they are willing to risk anything.

Several times I have gone to the perimeter to watch these
people come across the river. They are still shaking with fear
and with exhaustion from the ordeal of the trip. Seeing an
American doctor is usually quite amazing to them, especially
when I don't beat them or whip them. Instead of that I give
them some penicillin and give them eye ointment for their
trachoma. Then they are helped aboard Viet Nam trucks to be
driven to the camp in Haiphong, where I see them again, and
listen to their stories.

Mother, I have seen things here that I didn't believe humans
capable of doing. Last night late I was awakened at my hotel
by a Viet Nam priest who asked me to come with him to the
outskirts of the city. First, let me say that there are very
few doctors here in Haiphong, and French doctors prefer to
have nothing to do with the Vietnamese. I am the only doctor
that takes care of the refugees here in Haiphong, save for one
female V.N. doctoress, a grand gal. So everyone in the city
knows me. This priest and I went in the jeep about four miles
from town, not too far from the perimeter. There I was asked
to see an old priest who had just escaped across the river. Two
nights before the priest had been in his village church of
Namh Giang (look it up) and the Vietminh soldiers came in
to tell him that he had been preaching lies to his people about
the Vietminh. Their leader spoke with a heavy Chinese accent,
this the priest stated firmly. The answer of the old priest was
that he was teaching only of God.

They took this old man and hung him from a beam overhead in the mission by his feet. They stripped him naked.
Then they beat him with short bamboo rods, with the emphasis on his genitals. Into his head they stuck thorns (so he

could be like the Christ of whom he spoke) and then into his ears they rammed chop sticks. When I saw him, there was hardly a square inch of flesh that was not swollen and purple, and often split, though not bloody. Being left hanging feet up all night, the vessels in his eyes ruptured, leaving him nearly blind.

The following morning at dawn the young acolytes came for Mass and found him like this. Realizing that he would be killed the next time, they began their juvenile plans for getting him out. These children left their homes, probably with their families' blessings and help, and carried the old priest through the rice paddies, for a day and a night. They hid in the rushes on the river's edge until night fall, then made a bamboo raft, put the wooden stretcher on the raft, and slipped into the water. They pushed this raft across the swift river's current, and came on the other side, several kilometers down stream. Then they walked to this mission of Kien An, where I was called for to see the priest.

There was little I could do for him. Few of the marks had broken the skin. The stout bamboo rods would bruise the skin rather than puncture it. He was a mass of hematomata, black and blue, and purple and bruised all over. His scalp, where the children had removed the thorns, was just a mass of matted blood. His ear drums were both punctured, and the canal of the external ear was torn from having sticks of greater diameter than the canal itself rammed into it. I gave him antibiotics against impending infection, and washed him as best I could. He was in tremendous pain from the beating, and the hideous condition of his groin. I can't even write of these things without getting filled with emotion.

I am not writing this to you to nauseate you or make you feel bad, as I know it does, but in hopes that you will let others read this, and understand the nature of what we are fighting. The conditions here in Indo-China directly affect us at home. Again my letters are not a cheerful thing. I write to you, Mother, as though you were sitting across from the typewriter. I don't reread what I write, and I don't go back and correct my spelling or typewritten errors. I write it as it comes from me, just as though I were speaking to you. Tell the McDonalds and the McMahons and the Bittings and everyone how we, who are here, feel.

30 NOVEMBER, THANKSGIVING—I loved your description of Eddie buying the baby (now I know her name) her christening present. Glad that Eddie is reading my letters. Hope you can forward them to him from time to time. I receive mail from Malc in spurts, and it is always good to receive. Mail is my only contact with the outside world. When the ship is not here, I live and spend my whole day and night in town,

seldom seeing any other Americans (save my four corpsmen).
I have a horrible feeling of complete lack of contact, as though
I was severed. Sometimes this is almost frightening. You know
that the only Americans north of the parallel are the six in
Hanoi, who are behind the bamboo curtain protected only by
American policy and diplomacy, which has failed considerably
in Poland, Hungary, etc.

Then there are the equivalent embassy team at MAAG here
in Haiphong, about ten in total, and my four corpsmen and
myself. We are of course in free territory, this sort of island,
like Berlin is in Germany. The exact perimeter covers all of
the sea to our east to the island of Hainan, save a little bottleneck three miles wide through which our ships can pass. And
the Americans have that helicopter sitting at the airport. That
is our passport for a hurry.

Broken glasses are a family tradition. When I broke mine,
I wired a friend of mine at Yokosuka Naval Hospital, the
oculist. Now I have three pairs of sturdy Navy circular steel
glasses. They make me think of those safety goggles that Dad
had all the men wear at the plant, they are that sturdy.

As for my getting to Japan, I have no idea whatsoever
when that will be. I know it can be no later than May, as that
is when the communists take over Haiphong. The Navy policy
is no leaves from an overseas base, unless emergency. However, as I will have been in Indo-China for such a long time,
relatively speaking, and as I am the ONLY Navy man who
started here the day the evacuation did (all the others have
been relieved) and since all tell me I am doing a good job;
when the whole thing is over I am going to Admiral Sabin
and request that he give me leave to the states. He has the
power to do this.

Don't start holding dinner, however. I shall give plenty of
advance notice, as it will take weeks to get home after he says
OK. But it is something nice to think about. Another thing
for the file: the Navy has now a new program concerning
residencies. Now they will give residencies to reserves, who
extend for one year for each year of residency training. That
means that I can extend for two years, and get one year's residency in. Orthopedics still interests me, and the U. S. Naval
Hospital at Oakland is the orthopedic training center. So I
am babying with the idea of applying for this around June
1955. Just a plan now. I know that if I do apply I will get it.

By now you have heard of the letter in the Navy publication. I saw it when one of the transports was in. I am a little
amazed. I received a dispatch several weeks ago requesting
permission to publish, but I thought they were referring to
that article about the ship that I had sent to you. Instead they
published the personal letter to Dr. Casberg. I am getting a lot

of ribbing. Some older officers have commented on the fact that it is refreshing to hear someone who isn't complaining about the Navy's policies.

My lecturing has reached quite a scale, and often consumes a lot of time. I received instructions from the Admiral to talk to every ship in the task force when it came through Haiphong. Many ships have a podium and loudspeakers rigged up. Several ships have made wire recordings of the things that I have said. When a sailor really understands what he is working for, he does a wonderful job.

General O'Daniel and General J. Lawton Collins were in Haiphong last week and I had dinner with them. General Collins is more like a benevolent old uncle than a tough Army General. He is intensely interested, and almost youthful in his enthusiasm. My health is grand, and though it certainly doesn't seem like Thanksgiving here in the tropics, I know it is. I am thankful for things that now seem very close at hand, and before were only words—like freedom, liberty, and Catholicism. They are now very real things that walk beside us, and whose absence is markedly noticed when their warmth is taken away. It is good to have a wonderful family, and wonderful memories of Dad, and all the fine things you have given us. We love you very much, Mother, though sometimes we hurt you. Remember most of all that we love you.

1 DECEMBER—I received a long letter from Eddie yesterday with his latest address at Chaffee. I was pleased by his intelligent letter, with the interesting news and all. I know that it is true that Eddie only writes seldom, but he writes a good letter. His basic training sounded tough, and his interview tougher. Got a kick out of his description of my niece. According to him she isn't nearly as interesting a sight as her father, strutting around, not allowing anyone to touch her, and himself oo-ing and coo-ing at the baby.

General J. Lawton Collins yesterday flew through for an inspection trip. He did not remember having met me, because I was in a white surgical gown, really quite dirty and bloody, standing knee-high in kids at the medical tent at Camp de la Pagode. I had no hat on and the gown covered my Navy collar. General Collins turned to one of his aides and said, "I know this guy's an American," I hadn't opened my mouth. Something about some kind of map being on my face.

Weather has turned quite cool here lately in the wake of a typhoon that hit the south. My beaten little old priest is doing very well now. The kids are all right, and I am in the best of health.

7 DECEMBER—I have found a great new friend, my typewriter.

In the evenings now I write. I have literally hundreds of type-written sheets about this operation—individual stories of what is going on, declarations from the refugees. One story a week is mimeographed and sent to the two ships now in the area. I have several histories of Indo-China on my table now and I am working on a *précis* of the history of this war. About six pages done, four to go. This will also be mimeographed for the crew. So my evenings are not as drab as you fear. I am so terribly tired at the end of the day that a long dinner with a good book, then an hour at my typewriter, and I am ready for the sack. This is the way I like it, you know. Never did like to have too much free time. Before the *Balduck* went to Saigon I wrote a long article about all the places to visit, and the interesting historic sights, etc. I want to keep the boys out of the low-down bars and opium dens. The very last thing many of the sailors said as their ship pulled out of Haiphong last week was, "Don't worry, Doc, we'll be careful."

Concerning a request for transfer, I couldn't do it in a million years. Everyone knows me here, and feels free to come and see me. The shoe-shine kids on the street and the newly arrived refugees all look for the "Bac Sy My" when they need a doctor. I feel that, aside from the medicine, I am doing good sociologically and politically. Previously they associated Americans with the colonial mismanagement of the French. Now they are learning that Americans at heart are really rather good and charitable. I have learned to speak the Viet language quite well. It is easy, hardly any grammar, and the people are tremendously pleased when they hear an American "wrestling" with their language. I represent to the people the softer hand of democracy, not the pugilistic one. So I will stay until Uncle Ho comes in. This is not a burden, but a privilege.

8 DECEMBER—Today is Pearl Harbor Day here. I am very disturbed that you are going to have such a lonesome Christmas. If we could work it out, I'd send you some money and have you come to Haiphong. You could help me hold sick-call with the refugees. Bet you would be quite good at it. Next Christmas it will be different. So far I have received many Christmas presents from you. The other night before the *Balduck* left we had a lot of laughs playing the games you sent. It took mental calculations that I have not been doing lately. Malc sent me an instruction note for the Christmas present that is not here.

The pictures of the baby are fine, what I can see of her. Just the nostrils, and a wee bit of the mouth. Please strip her down raw, and take angle shots so I can see if her navel is healing, if her legs are straight, if she has diaper rash, how round her head is, etc. Uncle Tom.

9 DECEMBER—We have had a rough day. This morning when we went out to Camp de la Pagode we found that the one rice paddy from which we draw the water which goes through our chlorination machines for the manufacture of potable water, had completely black water. All the surrounding little ones were clear, as usual, but this one was black. None of the people knew what the cause was. It was definitely not tidal, and had nothing to do with sewerage, etc., because all of the paddies would have been so affected. That leaves just one alternative. The Viet Minh underground purposely poisoned the water.

We moved the entire water-making apparatus, and three large 3,000-gallon rubber storage tanks to another paddy on the other side of the camp. All the hoses, connections, filters, the sand and the pumps were moved. It was a large undertaking, and took us most of the day, but by evening I was able to wire the Commodore in Saigon that it worked. I had wired him at 0800 about the findings at the camp. He wired back, "Correct it." We couldn't "correct" the condition of the water, so we just moved the whole plant and I wired at 1900 "Difficulty overcome, potable water processed at Camp." It makes us uneasy to know that the Commies will use such tactics to terrorize the people. Thank the Lord it turned the water black. If it was a clear poison, we might have killed hundreds. We know the Viet Minh are looking for something to create an anti-U.S. feeling and poisoned water would be a good one.

Sent a wire on to Japan today, and asked for my winter uniforms. It has become quite cold. Not really cold, but cooler than usual, a penetrating type of dampness.

10 DECEMBER—The Viet Minh are playing a two-faced game. In Hanoi, where they are being watched by the world, the CIC, the press, India, and all they are ruling with a velvet glove. We receive trainloads of refugees every day who have decided to leave, but for economic reasons. No beating, no arrests, no repression. The velvet glove. While on the other hand in the areas around Phat Diem, Thai Binh, Bui Chu, and Nam Dinh they are ruling in the typical horror we know so well. The refugees from these areas are really escapees, usually beaten and exhausted when they arrive, by their devious means.

As you know, this area is completely surrounded, save for an air lane five miles wide, and a sea lane five miles wide. Fearful of missing the air lane the planes of our embassy (two a week), the French air-lift and official planes all fly straight east outside of the continental limits, and then on down to Saigon. You realize the area immediately south of us all the way to the 17th is Viet Minh, and the air above it. That explains why no civilian lines, mail, etc. can come in. For emergencies General J. Lawton Collins has instructed our small group here to utilize the American Embassy in Saigon, Attention Haiphong. He says that we are not to feel isolated at all (hah!) and that daily radio contact is to be made with him. At the slightest indication of trouble, we are to leave. He has sent up detailed Evacuation plans A, B, C and D. Having him down there, a military man, makes us a good deal more comfortable. So don't fear, Mother, he will not let anything happen. Saigon is only four air hours away.

14 DECEMBER—I don't think I would leave now on anything except direct orders. This is a fascinating job, and I am eager to watch the closing months. The city is dying a little every day. Not in the throes of agony, just slipping off little by little. The butcher shops and bread shops are closing. For the non-military, things are hard to get. The only civilian filling-station and garage in town is closed, which stops civilian traffic, not that there ever was much. The Indian shops are all on sale and are closing one by one; the city water works have cut production one-half, so that the whole city is on water hours—the French ships are loading on a 24-hour basis down on the docks, in a frantic effort to get their material out.

It is strange to watch a city die like this. I want to see the end. I will stay here until there are no more refugees to put aboard U.S. vessels, probably until April. The city has informed all civilians who are going south to be out of the city by the end of January. It is the military who are transporting them and they say that they will transport no one after the end of January. We will still take refugees, of course, but we have never transported the small shopkeepers, etc. I won't even be able to buy a Paris newspaper in two weeks. I don't want to leave. Who would take care of the refugees, who are still in need of much?

Believe it or not, I am freezing to death. It has gotten quite chilly this last week, and the dampness here makes a penetrating chill. These hotels have absolutely no preparation for cold weather. There never was any hot water, and now I really miss it. I have bought a couple of heaters which I keep on all day. Also a hot plate, which at this very minute is heating a pan of water so I can shave. It is 0700 just now, and while waiting for the water I thought I would get this note off. My hands are so cold that it hurts to hit the machine.

We were trying to figure why it is so miserable here. The

decision was that in the states you get cold but can go in somewhere and warm up. Here you just stay slightly cold the whole time. We have given the refugees blankets by the droves, but they are accustomed to this type of weather and endure it easily. My system: as soon as the water warms to shave, I put my coffee pot on it. I can make the best instant coffee in the Orient. The sugar comes in a blue box, an import from France, and the company that manufactures it is named St. Louis. The box bears a picture of that famous statue of St. Louis on Art Hill, so I feel quite at home.

15 DECEMBER—Last night I dreamed up another way to wish you a Merry Christmas. I am perhaps taking some of the surprise out of it, but when it arrives I want you to be all ready for it. Through the United States Information Service in Saigon I am having a tape recording sent up. The chief of the outfit was here in Haiphong making lots of films and tapes. During this time I helped him a good deal. So the tape recorder is coming with a 15-minute blank tape. I intend to talk to you directly, Mother. Don't know just what I can talk about for 15 minutes, but I'll manage. It will be fun, and should help you know your son is in good health.

I heard from Pfizer Laboratories in connection with my letter to them. They are sending me 100 bottles each containing 100 pills of terramycin as their contribution to the work here. Also, you know, the other day the vitamin company answered, and said they were sending a lot of vitamins. If this keeps up, I shall have a lot to treat my people with. American Economic Aid has a lot of medicines here, or had, but was never prepared for the influx of half a million refugees in four months. They have pretty general stuff—worm medicine, aspirin, APCs, vaseline—nothing really expensive, for obvious reasons. So I am very pleased with the contributions made. Americans are quick to cooperate when they understand the situation.

18 DECEMBER—Shades of Malc at Notre Dame, you should see my room. Malc's old cafeteria at Notre Dame was a piker compared to Room 4, Hotel du Commerce, Demilitarized Zone, Haiphong, Viet Nam du Nord, Indo-China.

Since there is no heat whatsoever, I have three resistor-type heaters. Then I have two hot plates, one with a metal medical basin on it (I heat water from the faucet to shave and wash with) and the other with a water kettle on it, with a half dozen bottles of water (have to buy the bottled stuff here as the city water is not potable). The sugar is now in a large glass container, and the label "St. Louis" is pasted to the sides with bandaids. Peanuts grow profusely in the regions around here, and can be bought for a few piasters the sack. As a consequence, I have become an avid peanut eater. They have a fruit much like the tangerine, called "mandarin," and I have a bowl of those on the desk. Glory, glory, the *Balduck* returns Saturday for a couple of weeks. I can eat American food at least once a day then.

When I get home from the camp, kind of dirty, always a little down in the dumps because of the misery of the people, and very very dirty-smelling, I think of Mother who always says that she is such a "homebody." I get the water cooking, the heaters going, the peanuts cracked, the coffee measured, and just revel in it. I am not telling you this to make you feel sorry for me, because there is no need to. I am really opulent compared to most. I am thoroughly enjoying this strange bit of existence, and I assure you I shall appreciate things (like a hot shower) when I get back to them. I'll never be flippant about the necessities of life again.

CHRISTMAS NIGHT, ON BOARD THE U.S.S. BALDUCK—I have had my fill of Christmas turkey just as though I were home, but I missed my home very much today. The *Balduck* is back in the Haiphong River, so I came on out here to celebrate Christmas.

On Christmas Eve, Mme. Ngai who runs the orphanage in town, had a party in my honor to which she invited all the governors, mayors, the Commodore, French Admiral Querville, and French General Cogny. I was able to raise over $200 from the crew and the officers of the *Balduck* plus innumerable other things like vitamins, medicines, the promise of the new legs from A. S. Aloe for the amputees, and my daily sick call. So Mme. Ngai, being quite a great gal, decided to make public what I was doing. She asked me over for some Chinese soup on Christmas Eve. I frequently go over for dinner there, as Mme. Ngai is sort of a social figure in town.

When I went over last night I found everyone there, and about twenty of the kids lined up on both sides of the courtyard like side-boys for an admiral. They then presented songs, a short Vietnamese play, and presented me with a beautiful gift, a solid silver cigarette case. I don't smoke, but the thought was wonderful. I was practically crying, the kids were so proud of what they were doing, and there had obviously been a lot of rehearsals. Mme. Ngai had invited all the brass to drop in for sort of a Vietnamese Open House, and then she sprung this on them. Not the French Admiral nor the French General nor the American Commodore, nor Colonels (three) of MAAG, but the Lt. (jg), the doctor is the one that she thanked in the name of the orphanage, and gave the gift to. This might have made others a little unhappy, but I don't believe it did, though. They realize how many nights I've worked over the little kids with pneumonia, with no oxygen equipment, no electricity, just basic medicaments and prayers.

So at the present time your son is floating rather high. They are all Buddhists, so having it on their Catholic doctor's Christmas Eve was touching. The Commodore immediately sent back to the ship for the photographer, so I should have some good pictures of it to send to you. I wish so much that you could have been here, Mother. It is always much more pleasing to be praised when those who love you are there. Merry Christmas and Happy New Year to you, so very far away.

27 DECEMBER—This is just two days after Christmas and I'm out in Baie d'Along for the first time in over a month. The *Balduck* has come out here to refuel and replenish from one of the large transports which came in today, and leaves tomorrow with refugees. I just rode down for the day off. I'll have you know, Mother, that I was ordered to take the day off.

Christmas Eve was a long affair, with the party in my honor, then Midnight Mass, then a coffee party on the ship ending at 0500. I had sick-call at Camp Cement, the new one, at 0930 next day (people get sick on Christmas just like any other day). The 26th also found me working and, I suppose, looking a little the worse for wear.

I came out to this ship again last night for dinner and was called to the Commodore's stateroom. He took one look at me and said: "Tomorrow you ride to the Baie with us and sleep the whole way down and back." I smilingly asked if it was an order or a command. He snapped back, "A command." So I went to bed last night around 2200 and woke up at 1300 this afternoon. It is sort of like being on a private yacht for me. I don't do a thing, just loaf around. We will get back late tonight, I'll stay aboard this night, too, and go back to work in the morning.

The 29th we will have a load of 5,000 refugees, all from the town of Vinh, which has been captured for over 9 years. These people are in pretty bad condition, and to judge from the ones already processed, are the toughest we have had. The others have escaped from several months' rule, but these people came out after many years. Their escape was a pretty heroic thing, much like the famous off-the-beach escapes at Bui Chu. I have found a lot of beri-beri in them, and the old vitamin pills work wonders. The power and efficacy of such commonplace medicines as vitamin pills, aspirin and the like. *One* aspirin tablet on the black market in Haiphong sells for five cents.

I am in the best of health, much like a rested debutante just now.

1 JANUARY—1955 already. So very long since 1954, when I

was at Pendleton. There were several little parties around the city, each consisting of large crowds of maybe three. I was at Mme. Ngai's with a group of Vietnamese. We made the tape-record for you over again, as the first one was pretty bad. I'll send it today via U.S. mail because there is a strike in the Paris Postal Services.

Mme. Ngai's home consists of a living-room about the size of your bedroom. Cushions are on the floor Oriental style, with a large Buddhist altar at one end of the room. There is a very low table about four feet in diameter in the middle of the room. You sit on the deck and use this small table. The whole center of the room is completely covered with these multi-colored cushions. You walk into the room, take your shoes off, flop down on a cushion and sit for hours like this. It is wonderfully comfortable, even if a little hard on the press in one's trousers.

We put the machine on the table, and then passed the microphone around to various people who were sitting around the table. About 100 kids were standing outside in the little courtyard that opens out of some large French doors. During the tape you will hear the kids talking, the dog barking, and hear them singing and answering when I talk to them in Vietnamese. It was a lot of fun making it, and a completely amazing thing to the kids, a minute later, to hear their own voices played back.

Nothing new in the refugee situation. We have about 12,000 in the camps, and the day before yesterday we loaded out 6,000. Another load going out on the 4th. Cardinal Spellman is arriving in Saigon on the 5th, so he will be there when the 4th arrives. Admiral Radford left for Hong Kong and had nothing but praise for the young government of Viet Nam. Seemed to be very hopeful, as opposed to some of the correspondents who are now beginning to be interested in Indo-China. Last week for two days Homer Bigart of the *Herald Tribune* was here; all we need now is Maggie Higgins to come down from Russia.

My health is fine, and it is quite chilly here now. I wear a heavy foul-weather jacket all the time. The Viet Minh are trying to show how strong they are in the city and what control they really have, so every night the city electricity goes off from about 8 to 11 P.M. It is frustrating because you can't read, can't go to a movie, or anything. I usually go out to the ship and eat dinner, see the ship's movie, and go back to the beach to sleep. That is all for now, Mother. Let the New Year be a happy one for you. And thank you for everything that you have done for me in the past year, and the past years. I love you very much.

2 JANUARY—A carrier sailed up from Saigon today and brought some mail, including your letter of December 17th. I certainly am relieved to know that you received the bracelet. I enjoyed arranging to have it made. I first had to pick a design out of a penciled book. Then with the designer I went to a place where we weighed out the gold, then to another place to buy the pieces of jade. Finally he put them all together and two weeks later I received the finished product. It seemed exquisite, all hand-made, hammered, etc. Would suggest you have your jeweler give it a check-up to make sure the clasp is strong enough, with a safety chain. I tried to match the shade as best I could remember it. Did Gay's pin arrive? And the old wooden box?

Another wonderful thing happened to me today. I was asked at 1130 this morning after Mass to come to the Governor's palace for lunch. I went and found about a dozen delegates there. They had invited another American, the fellow in charge of U.S. Information Service. We were each given a gift from the government of Viet Nam. I received a magnificent, enormous scroll, about eight feet long and four feet wide. It is one of those Oriental things that hang from the wall. This is an antique, which I am told is "priceless." The others when they saw it were amazed at its beauty and value. Mine has the four happinesses on it, *Long Life, Prosperity, Knowledge,* and *Happiness.* These are the same symbols that are on your bracelet. The scroll* is over 200 years old, and literally falling apart. It is on silk paper and is really beautiful, the colors somber, yet still brilliant. It is from China, and everyone who has seen it says it is a museum-piece. The pictures are a woman (*Happiness*), a decorated deer (*Prosperity*), an old man (*Longevity*) and a bat flying overhead (*Knowledge*).

These gifts I've received sort of take something out of me. I'm always so taken aback at their spontaneity and their thoughtfulness. I received a large bouquet of flowers from one of my refugee camps. Imagine, in this dry, barren atmosphere where the refugees bear a desolate burden of despair and disease, they give their doctor a beautiful bouquet of colorful flowers.

7 JANUARY—What a windfall! Today on the Embassy plane I received 27 letters and cards and four boxes. Both sets of Oriental religion books, the fish book, a gift from Dottie of a wallet, and a camera that I had ordered from friends in Japan. I am so glad to hear that Christmas came off all right. Having Eddie home was certainly fortunate. The books are wonderful, and exactly what I wanted. Also received some

* This scroll can now be seen in the Dooley Trophy Room at the University of Notre Dame.

eight letters and clippings from Dottie. Glad that you and I
have a friend and that she is a help to you. I am certain
that she will come the minute you call, and be advantageous as
a nurse. Meanwhile, be her good friend and let her love and
help you. She writes more information on you and your health
than you yourself do.

Just rolled with laughter over the Kormendy's going "way
out on Kingshighway." Am sorry that you missed them; they
write me all the time and are so very good. They were so
generous to me during those years at Notre Dame (which
seem so far away). I received two long letters from Malc who
seems concerned over my feelings of American complacency.
He, with a paternal pat, tells me that "all sailors and soldiers
go through this phase . . ."

11 JANUARY—Had a minor catastrophe today. Went out to the
camp this morning to find that the water tank had ruptured
and spilled out 6,000 gallons of water, nearly inundating a
small section of tents. Three tents were under a foot of water.
People were sound asleep when all of a sudden it popped,
water flowed everywhere, and they must have thought it was
the end of the world. It is going to be quite a problem to fix.
Ordinarily we would just put up another tank, but we have
no more tanks now. We want to repair it right away because
on the 13th Ambassador J. Lawton Collins will be here for
an inspection. The refugee committee has been working its
tail off to get the camps cleaned up, we have been burning all
the garbage and trash areas, spraying and dusting like mad.
Then the tank blows up.

On the 20th the *Balduck* will leave and be replaced by the
Cook, another of the same type destroyer-personnel ship. The
11 officers of the *Balduck* are all top-notch fellows and we have
had many enjoyable evenings together. Mme. Ngai, the lovely
Vietnamese woman who runs the orphanage, has had several
dinner parties, to which I have been allowed to bring six or
eight guests. She serves nothing but Vietnamese food, with
chop sticks, on a table one foot off the deck, while you lounge
Roman-style on cushions. The only thing she doesn't have,
Eddie, is opium. The fellows from the ship, have come in
town on those occasions. On the other hand, I have eaten a
great many meals on the ship. Also those hot showers. It is so
cold here that cold showers, though healthy and invigorating,
are torture. So I only shower about once a week and go out to
the ship for that.

The Embassy informs us today that there would be only
one mail plane a week from now on. All the more isolation.
Don't know how people live without mail. It is my mainstay—
that and daily Mass.

15 JANUARY—Well, the Ambassador has left. He arrived in a swirl, and left as hurriedly as he had arrived. The camps were in excellent condition and he was lavish with his praise of them. He expressed great surprise at the fact that I had learned to speak Vietnamese so well. He said that, as far as he knows, I was the only American in Viet Nam who had learned the language. It is thought a lowering of oneself to speak the language of one's colony, hence the French do not learn the Viet tongue. You know that I have never had trouble with languages, and I have an excellent teacher who comes to me three times a week. Then the refugees are very patient with me. The Ambassador really seemed more surprised and pleased with that fact than with anything at the camp.

He made a whirlwind tour of everything, was very gracious, extremely overpowering, completely ignored all the protocol that had been made out for him, much to the annoyance of many here. But he showed the typical American spirit of "hurry up, get going, get the lead out, etc." and it was well received. To those here who felt that America was backing out of Indo-China, Ambassador Collins was a steadying influence.

18 JANUARY—Mme. Ngai had a grand birthday party for me. The children gave me about a half mile of beautiful Chinese white silk to have some shirts made. I have decided to send it to Dorothy as a gift. The material is really quite fine. Some officers from the staff have given me a sort of loving cup thing, which matches exactly the soup bowls I bought you last week. So put the loving cup on the table with flowers, and you and Mrs. Carroll drink some bouillon and think of TAD. The *Balduck* is leaving tomorrow for Yokosuka so they will mail all my things. Packed in heavy wooden crates are a large bronze elephant and the famous scroll for you, and a large brass tray for Malc. This will all be shipped from Diego in May when the *Balduck* gets in. If they take until June to get to you, I may be home on leave myself. I still have every intention of requesting leave when this is over, 17 May.

21 JANUARY—The good old *Balduck* has departed. The other day the new ship, the U.S.S. *Cook,* arrived and took over as station ship. I am aboard her right now on my way down the river to Baie d'Along to visit the flagship. Admiral Sabin has come down on his flagship *Estes* to make a quick review of the situation here. He sent a dispatch to the Commodore, saying "Immediately on my arrival wish conference with you and Dooley on *Estes.*" So the Commodore called me to come aboard the *Cook* and we are on our way down to the bay now.

I received your letter dated the 6th in which you were so desperately concerned. I know that there is nothing I can do to keep you from worrying, Mother, but please don't do it for undue causes.

Everyone in this theater of operations is watching us. One day the Commodore mentioned in his situation report "Dooley and four Vietnamese in hospital for bullet wound treatment ..." or something to that effect. The fact is that I was in the hospital *treating* the bullet wounds. Within 24 hours the Commodore received a dispatch from the CNO at Yokosuka and from Admiral Sabin requesting clarification. So you can see that everyone is watching out for me. Please don't worry.

Tomorrow is Chinese New Year, and it will be so noisy in town that I am just as glad to be out in the bay. Am going to bed in a few minutes and intend to sleep until eleven tomorrow; the conference is at 1130.

23 JANUARY—Well, these last few days have certainly been fast ones. When we reported for the conference, I was invited with the Commodore to have lunch with the Admiral and his immediate staff, along with General Cogny, head of French troops in north Indo-China, and Admiral Querville, head of the French navy here. After lunch the French left and I sat in on the high-level discussions. You would be very pleased to know that many times the Admiral and members of his staff turned to this jg and said: "Well, what is your opinion on this point, Doctor?"

The Admiral was very generous with his praise, and commented that I was the only man in his whole Pacific fleet who started with the Viet Nam Evacuation on its first day, on the first ship, and was still here. He also assured me that I shall remain here until there are no more refugees being carried on U.S. ships. The present plans for that will be 17 May, 1955. This is as I want it, Mother. If I left, there would be no one here to do my work. The Admiral had heard about my knowing the native tongue, and was surprised that after my working hours I was finding time to study the language. He said, "If more Americans would learn the languages, customs and traditions of the countries in which they work, America would be better thought of."

After the meeting was over the Chief of Staff, who was the Commodore here back in September and October, called me to his office for a personal chat about the city, Mme. Ngai, and our other mutual friends here in Haiphong. He was by far the most beloved here, Commodore Walter Winn (who married one of the Behans of St. Louis). He said, "Stick this Navy out, boy, and you'll go just as far as you want to go. Don't let an occasional kick in the fantail by somebody get you down."

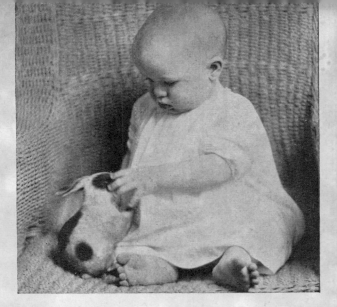

Above: Tom at six months.

Below: Tom, looking up from his sled, with his mother and grandfather, Thomas A. Dooley, Sr.

Above: Tom (age 4), with his mother and older and younger brothers Earle, (age 8), and Malcolm (age 2).

Below: Tom's first pony ride.

Left: Tom at summer camp.

Below: Tom's half-brother, Earle M. Dooley (1923-1944).

Tom as a marine.

Lieutenant (junior grade) Thomas **A.**
Dooley, M. D.

Above: Tom with two refugee children.

Below: Tom and a picturesque Viet Nam family group, spanning three generations.

Above: Lt. (jg) Dooley in Viet Nam during the
"Passage to Freedom."

Below: Girls in dancing costume, under the
tutelage of Mme. Ngai, entertain Navy personnel aboard the U.S.S. *Balduck.*

Tom after his promotion to Lieutenant early in 1956.

Above: Tom and his mother in Rome in 1957, on his return trip from Laos.

Left: Tom at St. Mary's College to receive an honorary degree; sister Madaleva is third in line.

Below: Tom at the stateroom piano on board the S. S. *Independence.*

Tom with Lao children at Nam Tha.

Tom and his mother enter the ballroom for the
Criss Award Dinner, 1959.

—*Felici*

An audience with Pope John XXIII at the Vatican in May, 1960. (Tom, center left.)

Tom with President Eisenhower at the University
of Notre Dame in June, 1960.

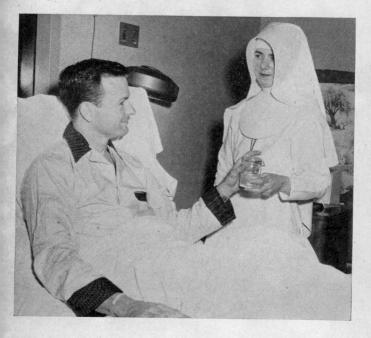

Tom as a hospital patient.

Above: The requiem Mass at St. Louis Cathedral.

Below: The tombstone at Calvary Cemetery in St. Louis.

At the White House on June 7, 1962, President Kennedy presents to Mrs. Agnes W. Dooley the Thomas A. Dooley authorized by Congress. *Center:* Malcolm, Gay and the boys, Malcolm, Jr., Michael, and Thomas Anthony IV

There are going to be some changes made. My team is being enlarged, and four more men are on their way to be assigned to me. Then I am being placed on the Admiral's staff, so that I will not have line officers between the staff and me.

That is excellent all around, and all are pleased. It is a feather in my cap. My Commodore is pleased because he doesn't have to interpret the Admiral's orders. Several times the Commodore turned a topic to me at the conference and said, "Well, the doctor's been here the longest, and he knows the Vietnamese people better than any of us. What do you think of such and such, Doctor?"

This morning I was flown back by helicopter to the city. You know, at the end of a long day of sick-call, with such despair and hopelessness, and such awful disease and filth, sometimes I come home and drop in bed and think, "Why? Why all this? I'm not denting the surface . . ." If I cured 1,000 cases of trachoma, I would still leave a million people blind. But to hear the head of the Pacific area say that he thinks I'm doing a fine job, then I begin to feel again that maybe it does make sense.

29 JANUARY—I am sorry to have missed several days since writing, but we have been going through a paralyzing period called the Chinese New Year. It lasts *en principe* three days but in practice closer to five. Nothing whatsoever is open, you can't buy anything. Nor did any refugees move in or out of the camps. We had a devil of a time trying to keep up the latrines and the dusting and the water and all the other things that must be done. No coolies, no working parties of VM nurses, nothing could be had.

It is over now, and today starting at 0500 we loaded 5,000 aboard ship; tomorrow we load another 5,000 on the *Marine Serpent* just arrived from Japan. We now have two TAPs carrying a total of 10,000 per week, and the French air-lift carries 400 per day, or 2,800 per week. Added up, you can see that a lot of refugees are leaving. We expect an influx, now that the New Year is over.

The new ship is fine, though a little less hospitable than the other. Perhaps it is just its newness. I have given several lectures which were well received. My second one started at seven o'clock on the quarter deck, and already at six some three-quarters of the crew were sitting around waiting for me to start.

We are now in the windup period. The last influx is expected in the next month. Then we will start to collect our own vehicles, our own tents, begin to dismantle the camps, and set up one new one in the abandoned area in the middle of the city. This way no trucks will be needed for transportation, and no potable water need be manufactured. They can use the city's supply, which is awful by our standards, but potable by theirs. So after the final push, things will slow down. How this place is dying!

30 JANUARY—I have just returned from dinner with the CIC (International Control Commission). As you both know, at the Geneva conference a control commission was appointed, with one Communistic country, Poland, one free country, Canada, and one neutral country, India. There are teams composed of these three nationalities distributed around Indo-China whose task it is to see that the treaty is observed. They try hard, and they send in many reports; but they are powerless because all they can do is write. Giving credit where credit is due, however, they have shown the world that the Viet Minh are not observing the truce.

Here in Haiphong the team is composed of two Indians, two Canadians, and two Polish officers. All are delightful guys, and I often dine with them. The other night the Polish showed a movie. Not a word was mentioned by the Polish officers of the nature of the movie. Finally, just before the film started one of the Indians said: "Is this another blankety-blank propaganda movie? If it is, you will never sell communism to the Doc here." We all had quite a laugh, and we were glad the film was not entirely a bore. However, I am doing what Malc says, "Keep a road map available."

Things are very quiet here, all eyes are focused on the Tachens. We only get bits of news here, but rumor on the ship has it that the *Cook* will be leaving to rejoin Admiral Stump's Seventh Fleet. My health is fine, weather still *crachat* or spittle, that is, misty and foggy.

3 FEBRUARY—Now it is going on to three weeks without any mail. I really miss it. Didn't realize what a crutch mail was.

With the new Commodore (yes, we have changed again) there have been many changes. In my department I have been assigned more men than usual, and have quite an intensive campaign going on in the camps. Daily spraying of areas, diesel oil and kerosene burning of the garbage areas, manufacturing of potable water, and never-ending sick-calls. The sickness is remarkable. The same diseases, yaws, skin diseases, childhood diseases, chickenpox, malaria, some typhoid, plenty of dysenteries of all type.

In the last letter I received from Bill Long he told me to be sure and reassure you that I was not contacting any Oriental diseases. He said that his mother was more fearful of that than battle wounds. Well, have no fear, I have been in excellent health ever since I've been here. No nose trouble whatsoever, and my intestines must be lined with lead. All others, without exception, have had remissions of acute diarrhea, but I have never had any.

The refugees are coming at about the same rate, without the expected influx following the Chinese New Year. We have around 10,000 in the camps with a daily intake of another 1,000 or so.

Haiphong dies more every day. There is no traffic on the streets, just the interminable rickshaws. There is little military traffic, as most of the 120,000 French military have gone south. There remain only 10 vehicles belonging to the city of Haiphong, and I could almost list them, the governor's car, the mayor's car, my jeep and my truck, and a few others.

A lot of long-range planning is going on, as the end draws nigh. We have only February, March and April left. All of us will probably leave the first week of May; Ho Chi Minh arrives the 15th. The camps are going to stay up until March, then they will be dropped one by one, and the equipment, the tentings, water plants, wiring, etc., flown out. Finally only one camp will remain. The cargo ships, the two that are here, shall be converted in March into passenger ships. I have been called in on all the conferences here for the rebuilding of these ships. I have to tell them how many ladders, how much rice, how many chop sticks, how much ventilation, etc.

8 FEBRUARY—The Embassy has definitely forgotten us. The mail plane was cancelled these last three weeks, so it seems forever since I last had any mail.

The city is now flooding with refugees. Not so many from the "other side" as from right here around the perimeter. We loaded 7,000 yesterday and have over 15,000 in the camps. A goodly one-half of the city is signed up to go, and another ship has been called.

After being here six months, you would think that I'd know better, but I left both my cameras in the jeep the other day for a minute to buy a bottle of water. Came back and they were both stolen. I passed the word out among my Vietnamese friends, and two days later I had my Argus returned. How they ever found it in this city of thieves I'll never know, and I am not going to ask. My health is fine, but I'm tired.

12 FEBRUARY—I am glad you agree with my idea of writing a few of the doctors in St. Louis. When I left St. Louis there were perhaps some who thought badly of me. Remember how reluctant the Navy was to accept me? Now that people seem pleased with my work, I would not mind at all if this news got back to the people who thought me incapable, etc. I hope

Doctor McMahon does not have to hide his face when he talks to other Navy men about the doctor he recommended so wholeheartedly to Admiral Pugh. Maybe this is one of the reasons I am trying so very hard to do more than an average job. Not all of those doctors in St. Louis thought poorly of me, but those who did let me know it.

Admiral Sabin got me three new water tanks in a matter of three days, by air-lift to Saigon then here by French freighter. That shows how important he considers the manufacturing of potable water. My corpsmen here are really plumbers, mechanics and medical corpsmen combined.

The books are wonderful, and I especially enjoyed the Catholic philosophy book. I had to smile at you, Mother. I can see you puzzled and concerned for fear I might become a Buddhist and join the local Order of Bonzes.

18 FEBRUARY—Remember that horribly beaten priest? Well, he has recovered very well due to a fortitude that only these Orientals seem to demonstrate in the face of the basest of tortures. There have been other cases, Mother, one so miserably beaten that I had to leave the little hut I had been taken to, and I vomited and vomited. That was the only time I ever got sick to my stomach over a medical thing. But it wasn't just medical, it was something sort of the soul and heart and the very nature of man. Besides being beaten, this priest had had the distal portions of all ten fingers crushed between stones.

Mme. Ngai just loves the bowl. She has it on her Buddhist altar heaped with myrrh (you don't burn it, just leave it there like unlit vigil lights).

At present I am taking a siesta (the whole Orient stops functioning from 1300 to 1500), a thing I have never been able to do. But I am tired today, so resting.

25 FEBRUARY—I am on the ship at this moment getting squared away with packages. You see this ship, the *Cook,* is going to the Philippines tomorrow for a week, then to Hong Kong, so I am mailing a great many packages here. There will be another APD like this one, arriving tonight, the *Bass.* I'll continue to use it as a second home.

Speaking of homes, we are planning to move. With everyone leaving, housing is easing up. It will be excellent for all the Americans to be living in the same building. After 1 March there will be only Major Ralph Walker of MAAG, Roger Ackley, head of USOM (who pays for everything), Mr. and Mrs. Austin of United States Information Service, and Major John McGowan, the Embassy's military attaché. Then my fine corpsmen Pete Kessey and Dennis Shepard, and Norman Baker, who is actually a Boatswain's Mate.

1 MARCH—These past few days we have really been swamped. The refugees are pouring in, the camps are all overloaded, the French are getting panicky, and even more uncooperative with us, and the spectre of smallpox is present. We have had several more cases of it and have increased the inoculation schedule around the clock. I often have to substitute for the Vietnamese nurses myself. I have also got working parties from the ships, instructed them in the technique, and sent them out to vaccinate throughout the city.

Now we have over 50,000 refugees living in the camps and in empty warehouses and barracks in the city. The Viet Minh have completely undermined the city now. Even semi-potable water is not available. Martial law is enforced and no one is allowed out of doors after 2200. Guards are on the streets, patrols, etc. Ho Chi Minh would not dare attempt anything now. He knows the eyes of the world are watching.

You know I am using the *Cook* for my address now. MAAG has completely folded up here, save for one officer. The consulates are gone, so it is better to rely on the USN for mail service. They fly a seaplane in from the Philippines every week or so, land in Baie d'Along and transfer the mail to the *Cook*. With the *Cook* here I am very safe, fear not.

2 MARCH—The Embassy plane came in today, finally, and it brought a great deal. I received a total of seven wonderful books, Mother. They are certainly grand. I find myself too tired at night to go out. As soon as my work is done, I eat dinner around nine, then to my room for a few hours reading. Thanks again, they are the best thing that you could send.

Received a letter from Barney Dickman, a man as busy as the Postmaster General, yet he finds time to write to me. A very fine letter; he says that all I am I owe to my great parents. I kind of agree.

I also received a long letter from Rose Gilmore full of news of horses and trips and irrelevant things which seem so solid and good somehow. How anxious I am to get back to riding a horse in the early morning, with just a little brisk fog on the ground, with everything fresh and clean.

The article in *Reader's Digest* was wonderful. The expression he used when he said, "The stench and heat of the refugee boat made me gag . . ." Sometimes the camps also do just that. Inside the sick-call tent, in hot weather, with the flies hovering over everything, it makes me gag at times.

4 MARCH—Loaded 6,000 out yesterday. Sometimes they try to take too much baggage, "too much" meaning a wee bit more than they can carry. It is a very difficult thing to say, "You

can't take it," when they have brought so pitifully little with them—a clock, a bed, a chicken, a Buddhist statue, or whatever they consider their most valued possession. We are crating the orphanage up now, beds, mats, baskets and kids. The first load will leave on the 15th of March, the second on the 15th of April.

I wrote a woman who works as secretary in the dining halls of Notre Dame, a wonderful woman, Malc knows her well, Erma Konya, of the children in the orphanage. She sent a half dozen boxes of colorful small T-shirts, socks, and underwear. It was so sweet of her, and I am so pleased by the faith and sunshine in her letter. She always signs them, "Your second favorite lady of Notre Dame." Write her for me, in care of the U.N.D. dining halls, and thank her for the inspiration of her letters, and her wonderful presents for my kids.

Glad that you spoke to the nuns at Desloge. I know they are praying like hell for me all the time. Sometimes I can feel other people's prayers directing me.

The rains are continuing. The camps are just a mire. The mosquitos are breeding larvae and even with my sleeves rolled down I still find half a dozen bites. The refugees are all going through phases of malarial fevers again. I have only so much medicine. Even if I gave out 10,000 capsules, it would only touch 3,000 people. See the futility of it all.

6 MARCH—Sick-call at the camp was the usual misery, pot-bellied starved children, beri-beri which is rampant now, and malaria which is also high. There were four people dead. Their relatives had kept them for me, fully aware that they were dead, yet with such faith in this combination American-doctor that they believed I could give a shot or a pill and perhaps bring them back.

So when all this was over, around three, I went by the mission to see a priest I've been taking care of for tetanus. He had six nails driven into his head by the Viet Minhs a month ago, escaped nevertheless, bundled up in a *cyclopousse* (see my pictures sent earlier). All the nails save one had been removed, and that I took out. They were about the size of our carpet tacks, like we had at Fair Oaks. He had developed tetanus, but now he is doing all right. Why are these atrocity cases always priests? Why do they hate priests so—because they are so near the One they really hate?

The CIC did do one good thing: I took a Canadian, an Indian and a Pole to the mission to see it, and they agreed to its barbaric hideousness and publicized the case in the

Saigon papers, for all the world, I hope. Anyway I saw the priest, and then came home.

8 MARCH—It is a little after five in the morning. I have just got up and shaved, and I'm waiting for the water to boil for my coffee. I must be at the loading area at 0600. This is a good time to get a note off about our new building.

As the city is dying, most foreign enterprises are leaving. The Bank of Hong Kong, which is staffed mostly by English and Chinese, has a fabulous building, the street floor of which is the bank, and the other stories living-quarters for officers of the bank. Now that the building has been abandoned, we have made a deal with the British for the whole blasted thing complete with furnishings. Roger Ackley, Major McGowan, Major Walker, and myself are moving in. There is an enormous high-ceilinged living-room with piano, four bedrooms, a large dining-room and kitchen. There are even a maid and a couple of house boys thrown in. It has magnificent fixtures and is really elegant. There is a high wall all around the place, typical of colonial style here, to keep the poverty and stink of the streets from over-sensitive noses. As I understand the deal, we "buy" it for $200 a month, over three months, so that it becomes American property. I have a feeling it will quickly become communist property on May 15th, and their highest ranking officers will immediately move in for the benefit of the People's Republic, of course, because after all some are more equal than others. Well, in the meantime, I am going to enjoy the luxury, cleanliness, the bath *tubs* (no plebian showers here), and hot repeat hot running water. So now for my coffee and off to the cloud of DDT.

9 MARCH—I have just finished a hot bath and feel like a million dollars. I was so tired before, soaked for 30 minutes, now feel like going out to battle. This mansion is the answer for me—at least as a respite from the camp. Think of all the people who never have *any* respite.

The smallpox scare is rising—35 cases so far this week, and it is only Wednesday. They come in small groups, and are inevitably amongst the escapees, rather than the local Haiphong people.

Over 35,000 more on the books now, about 10,000 living in the camps. One is now closed up; we are beginning to pull in our horns. Many of the empty warehouses and vacated barracks in the city have been taken over by the evacuation committee to house the refugees. Each camp has about 115 tents.

The camp that was completely closed is Camp de la Pagode. Seeing the empty camp before they tore the tents down really filled me with a strange nostalgia. How very well I remember standing in the September sun, pointing out where to set this one up, where to dig that drain and this ditch. Now the camp is empty, and the tents sort of yawning and void. How many thousands and thousands of refugees had gone through them, how much suffering and sickness. Today I went out to the place and it is now barren, just the bare ground, the ditches, and still some of the smell. We will close Camp Cement at the end of this week.

12 MARCH—I believe that I told you the magnamycin arrived. I had written the company, as I did with the vitamin and soap companies, telling them of the situation here and requesting "samples," about a year's supply. The magnamycin people sent somewhere around 10,000 capsules. I sent them a very informative letter, and pictures of their stuff being distributed that they are entitled to use if they want.

The new house is really grand. The weather is improving as the rains have slowed down. We even had some sun the other day.

I received pictures of you, Mother, from Dorothy. The colored one at the baptism is wonderful, but what were you doing in a black dress? You know very well that I much prefer you in colors. When I get home, which may well be two months from today that I depart, I don't want ever to see you in anything else except colors. And that will be spring and summertime.

18 MARCH—Indo- China is having her Spring today. It is really lovely. I'm sitting in my room looking out over the main park of the city, the only park. During the past eight months it was used as a parking area for trucks, tanks, jeeps, etc. When all that was transferred to the south, coolies moved into the park. Now it is sort of a housing area, but really doesn't look bad. The breeze is blowing the odor the other direction.

I can see the church steeple across the park. There are workmen in the steeple, taking down the cathedral bells. Ho Chi Minh has a way of turning church articles into bullets, so the mission here isn't going to accommodate him.

I was told today that the population of the free area is now less than 200,000. That is quite fantastic.

I took a roll of film yesterday and drove out to the former site of Camp Cement, Camp de la Pagode and Camp Shell. Show the old films of the camps and compare. You will see on the second roll the deadness of the town, the closed shops, etc. This set of movies should give you a pretty good history of the birth of the freedom of Indo-China and then the death of Tonkin.

Mme. Ngai has most of the orphanage packed up. Much leaves on the 28th, although the kids stay on until about the 15th of next month.

22 MARCH—The little girl's artificial leg arrived. I took it right over to the orphanage, put it on, and it fitted wonderfully. I then photographed her as she took her first steps, literally her first since her leg was torn off by a land mine eight months ago.

It did a lot for me, too. Mme. Ngai says that I am happier than the little girl. But it did my heart so much good to see the radiance in this little kid's eyes. So many of my children here are so sad and miserable. Perhaps they brighten up in Saigon, but here it is just grim and sad. With this little one, however, it was a climax. I hope the pictures come out.

This bank living is wonderful. Number One Boy is an excellent servant, and insists on giving me my breakfast in bed. Seeing as how I go to dawn Mass, I must come back, take my shoes off, and perch on the side of my bed while he wheels in this typically English cart with two big wheels on one end and legs on the other. Then he just stands there while I eat. Even puts the sugar and cream in my coffee. I am afraid to start to scratch myself, for fear he will come over and do that, too. The cook is good, his wife is the laundress, and there is someone else around cleaning up all the time. All this for so few piasters.

24 MARCH—The Philippine movie men left today. They are going to make a film in Saigon starting in May or so. It will be a story taking place during the evacuation. The Philippines have done a great thing here, you know, Mother. Their "Operation Brotherhood" brought a dozen doctors and a couple of dozen nurses out to the refugee and resettlement camps of Saigon to work around the clock for six months. Some generous man in Manila has paid privately for the planes to fly them and their equipment out. The film men were here to gather background material, look, listen, etc. It was really amusing because two of them were exact counterparts of Hollywood, with ascots, colored jackets, and spotless white shoes. Here the refugees wear a drab brownish shirt and black pants. I wear faded patched old khakis, my jeep is so dirty on the outside that you could write a book in the dirt, the city is overrun with rats, and then to see these two technicolored characters was funny. But it is good, too, because the Philippines were only a few years ago a colony, and now they have their independence. Viet Nam continuous-

ly refers to the Philippine-U.S. relationship as the kind they want with France.

27 MARCH—It is just a little after noon and I have just returned from a loading, 1,680 this morning. It is hard to get to five o'clock Mass, then out to the loading and back. Makes for a long morning. After lunch I am going to abide by the colonial (and native) custom and take a siesta.

All is quiet, no particular change. There are less escapees from the other side of the curtain, but an increase in the exodus from Haiphong. The shops and stores are closing down all around. Our cook makes the bread here, from the flour we buy from the ship. The French are pulling up stakes rapidly now, and all the troops will soon be leaving too.

20 APRIL—I have just returned from the ship, which is quite a jaunt these days. To get there I take a small boat, the Commodore's barge, first down the river two hours and then out on *high* seas for almost another hour. The reason I went today is that on the radio the Commodore said, "State your preference. Do you want your mail sent in, or do you want to come out for liver and onions and chocolate ice cream, and your mail, too?" Needless to say, I went out. In my haste to open your letter (written on your birthday) I cut it in three pieces and had to scotch-tape them in order to read it. I also received a letter from Gay with that wonderful picture of Malc, and a letter from Pat Haizet. Erma Konya sent another box of clothing. Fortunately it arrived the day before Madame Ngai left. Erma certainly used her head, plenty of useful articles like T-shirts, diapers, panties, scads of buttons, thread, needles, and little "tricote" machines, a kind of knitting affair, like a spool.

By now you know about my leave being cancelled. Hope you are not too discouraged. I am somewhat, but I am much too busy for morose thoughts. News from Saigon is bad. A sharp lad on the ship caught a radio broadcast in French, switched on the recorder, taped it and called for me. It told of the machine-gunning of the air force base and the Majestic Hotel right in Saigon. We feel safer right here.

Some time ago I sent home a set of seven small stone horses. They are based on an old Chinese legend about the Princess who never laughed. The Emperor offered a reward for her cure, and finally one day a man arrived with seven multi-colored horses, and said he wished to try. The Emperor warned him that if he failed he would be rent asunder by these very horses. The Princess came to the courtyard and the horses, with their bizarre coloring, assumed such outlandish poses that the Princess laughed. The man (he was, of course, a mandarin) then waved his hand and the horses turned to stone, in the very positions they had taken at that moment. The Princess was delighted, the Emperor was so overjoyed that he gave her in marriage to the mandarin, and they lived happily ever after. Any home that keeps these statues of the Horses of Happiness will know good fortune always. As an equinophile from way back, this story is especially appealing to me. When I do get home, at change of duty time (on the completion of 18 months overseas), it will again be winter.

22 APRIL— I love the little picture of Maureen, and feel like the proud poppa myself, and show it to everyone. The refugees just look and look at it, and can't get over how *dop lam*, or "clean and shining" she looks. It is almost a novelty now for me to see a baby without cradle cap and some horrible fungus all over its scalp. Tell Mrs. Carroll to leave her china to me. I won't always be a bachelor. I'm feeling very, very old these days, and more and more in need of some old-fashioned loving, with home, fireplace, wife, and, if you don't mind, horse.

The ship is taking a quick run to the Philippines today and will be back on the 28th. The International Control Commission is now requesting the signatories to the Geneva Convention to open up three areas along the coastline at Vinh, Van Ly and Phat Diem to French and American ships, and to extend the date so that the escapees can get out without going north through the bottleneck here. It is well worth the request, but somehow I can't see Emperor Chou En Lai signing.

27 APRIL—Today's mail brought your letters of the 12th and the 16th. I was so delighted to hear that you have received the statues. Sorry about the broken Chinese god's staff. Confucius is one of my favorites, especially the way he lists to the port. Take him to the laundry and see if you can find out what the Chinese characters mean. The elephant should be there. Hope you don't attempt to lift it; it must weigh a small ton. I think you will like it the best.

Received a nice letter from McCarthy Hanger about the artificial leg for little Nia. If you can, invite him over to see the movies of the little girl. How did they come out?

Today "info" was sent from General Collins to Admiral Sabin (we get a copy because it concerns us) requesting that I be sent to Saigon for several days of "debriefing" and "summation" concerning the evacuation, the political, intelligence and medical situation in the Tonkin. Just when this will occur, I don't yet know. It will please you to know that I am moving onto the ship around 1st of May. The ship will be back here on the edge of town (the *Cook* leaves the 1st, the *Diachenko* will be here) and though I shall spend the whole day ashore, at night I will sleep in the security of the U.S. Navy. I'll come ashore every morning at 0600 (still can get to Mass daily), will eat in the house, etc., but return to the ship on the 2200 boat at night. I am pleased with that arrangement. I have to get a special pass from General Cogny to be on the streets at 2200 when leaving the house for the docks, but that will be easy. I will feel better on the ship and I'm sure you will too.

You ask me if I am very "weary." One gets weary with boredom, not with a meaningful job that keeps you going all day. Today for example (now it is the 28th, started this letter yesterday) I loaded 6,300 refugees from 0600 until about 1130. Then had to get a working party from the ship to go over to the LST landing area where we are loading the radio equipment on a French ship to go out to the American LSTs in Baie d'Along. After that I came back for a 1400 lunch (Number One Boy can fix a meal any time; he feeds the other three officers in the "boarding house" from 1700 to 0100. After lunch I went to the camps to hold sick-calls, finishing around 1900. Then a hot shower (ahhh, that hot water) and ate dinner at 2030. Thought I'd get this letter off, remembering that I started it yesterday, so I am sitting in my skivvies finishing this. It is exactly 2145. There is my day. "Weary," perhaps, but not from boredom. Exhaustion is a better word. But it is a healthy feeling, with the satisfaction of a job done as well as one can.

1 MAY—It is evening time, the first of May. Contrary to expectations it has been a very quiet day. We loaded refugees this morning, only 1,855. Fear prevails so much that it alone succeeds. Without it, some people would probably *never* leave.

I drove out to Kien An yesterday as this area goes to the Viet Minh on Tuesday. Took movies of rice workers transferring water from one level of paddies to another with baskets, shots of the now-vacated airstrip and storage dump (I have an earlier picture of this storage area, filled with vehicles, now it is completely empty). Then pictures of the rice fields showing again the richness of the green Tonkin Delta. A visiting U.S. big shot and his party made a quick cruise through town, arriving and leaving in the same day. Of all things, the V.I.P. brought his wife, who wanted to go "shopping" in a dying city.

2 MAY—Just time for a note. All still calm. Not many refu-

gees, sort of piddling out. Don't know the exact day I shall leave here. Situation in Saigon looks grim. It is reflecting itself here by the *decreased* numbers who now want to go south. I guess it is pretty much all over.

Suddenly there was a break in the flow of mail. Not until much later did I fully understand my son's predicament.

9 MAY—Quite a jump in time since my last. We have been so desperately busy. There has been one riot after another. We had to close off the house the other afternoon, because the tear gas the French had used to break up a riot down the street was drifting in. I've not got time just now to give you all the particulars.

How right you were to remain pessimistic about my getting out before the last moment. The French would say, *vous avez l'habitude de la tristesse*. This is all for now. Remember, I am in good health, and the danger will be all over by the time you receive this. Right now I'm sweating a little.

The Viet Minh already have several large areas, like having Forest Park, East St. Louis, and the North Side. They are driving around the city in big Russian-made Molotova trucks. Their uniforms are everywhere. The people in the city (many VM sympathizers) have hauled out the red flag.

Haiphong was over. The most crucial event in the life of Thomas A. Dooley was over.

Again and again in the months to come Tom would say: "How can I make people see that things will never be the same?" Even I did not fully realize what he meant. Of course I knew he had had a tremendous experience. Following it with him through his own eyes all these months, worrying and hoping and praying, I felt as if I had almost been there.

When I finally heard that Tom had been flown out of North Viet Nam, I wept with joy. He and the American officers with whom he lived in the bank building were ordered to Saigon on May 12th. At 1 P.M. they left Cat Bi airport on the last American plane out. "The airport was formally turned over to the Viet Minh at 1700," Tom wrote later. There were two extra things on the plane with them, he said, "our Number One Boy and the statue."

The story of the statue has been told, but it belongs here too. A group of Vietnamese Catholics had many years previously made a pilgrimage to Rome, and the Pope had given them a five-foot statue of Our Lady of Fatima, which stood on the altar of the church in Haiphong. Tom had often prayed in this church and usually went there for daily Mass. He loved the statue and could not bear the thought of leaving it behind to be desecrated. "When I received orders at 1000 to leave at 1300," he wrote, "I went to the church and talked to the two Vietnamese priests, old barefoot gentlemen. They were reluctant to see the statue go, but they finally agreed it would be for the best. So I took an American Aid blanket, we lowered the statue from the main altar, I stole it out to the airport, put it on the plane and brought it to Saigon. I turned it over to the Saigon mission, and they were absolutely jubilant."

The next day in Saigon was one that Tom called "the proudest day I have had." Tom was preparing to go aboard the U.S.S. *Cook,* leaving at 1500. The ship would take him first to the Philippines, then Hong Kong, and finally his home base at Yokosuka Naval Hospital in Japan. Stopping by General O'Daniel's office to thank him before he left, Tom was startled to learn that they were looking all over Saigon for him. President Ngo Dinh Diem had requested Tom's presence at the Presidential palace at noon. "So without even a chance to change my shirt," wrote Tom, "I cleaned up as best I could and went over." With him were General O'Daniel, Commodore Winn, and the military attaché. They were ushered into the Cabinet Room where several Viet Nam dignitaries, including the Bishop of Saigon and members of the Cabinet, were waiting. President Diem read the following citation:

It gives me great pleasure to speak on behalf of my people. They have asked me to award you recognition for the outstanding work you have done for the past ten months in the refugee camps in Northern Viet Nam. You are well known and beloved by my people. In the resettlement areas here in Saigon the name of the "Bac Sy My" Dooley is well known. I have heard it mentioned often by the refugees and by the members of the various committees concerned with the evacuation. In the greatest majority of cases you were the first American that the people of the Tonkin rice fields came in contact with, and by knowing you and loving you they grew to understand the American people.

Your medicine and your knowledge have saved many of their lives and brought comfort to their suffering. More than this, it has shown them the true goodness and the spirit of help and cooperation that America has displayed in Viet Nam, and in all the countries of the world who seek and strive to achieve and maintain their freedom. Again, Doctor,

I want to thank you personally and in the name of my people, who will long remember their Bac Sy, his work, and his love.

President Diem then awarded my son the highest honor that his country can give to a foreigner, pinning on him the medal of an Officier de l'Ordre National de Viet Nam. "The medal is beautiful," Tom wrote, "and after approval by the Navy I shall be allowed to wear its ribbon. Commodore Winn was just as pleased and proud as I. He said it was extremely unusual for a junior officer to receive a decoration of a foreign country. He told me that to have it personally awarded by the country's President in the midst of strife was also extraordinary. So Mother dear," Tom could not resist adding, "it's a long time since I flunked those exams. Several of my teachers did not think I was adequate, but the President of Indo-China thinks I am."

In closing this letter, written at sea aboard the U.S.S. *Cook,* he said:

"That is it for now. I am really tired. Sort of tired for the whole year. A four-day sea trip with nothing to do but sleep. Then Hong Kong. I wired you yesterday from Saigon, and I will try to phone from Hong Kong. It is all over. I am in good health, and very pleased, and tired. If you looked at me now and said your usual, 'You look tired,' this time I would agree. Good night, Mother. I wish you could have been with me today and Dad too. Thought of you both so much. I think Dad would have been proud too."

It was not until long after his arrival in Japan when he began to work on his book, *Deliver Us from Evil,* that he told me the full story of the last days in Haiphong. It has never been revealed that he was held incommunicado by the communists for a day and a night. The story came out almost inadvertently, when a Navy friend of Tom's visited me in St. Louis enroute home on leave. Speaking of the job Tom had done in Viet Nam, he said, "Well, what do you think of our POW? Quite a guy, isn't he?" I knew that POW stood for Prisoner of War, and the explanation of Tom's friend that this was merely a figure of speech did not convince me, since he had also used the word "detention." So I wrote Tom at Yokosuka that I had a right to know the truth. Finally on August 26th he replied:

"Many around here know that there was a period of some silence between the Communists coming in on the 4th (the Committee of Experts) and my sudden departure to Saigon on the 12th. The full particulars of what happened during this time are not going to be told to anyone for some time. The Commodore, not having my walkie-talkie radio check for five days, came ashore himself and went to the Control Commission. My friends, the Poles, did some intervening and my brief 'detention' came to an end. This is all there was to it. I was whisked off to Saigon before anything else came about.

"I was in a communist-held city, though under the 'theoretical' control of the International Control Commission. As an American I had no diplomatic immunity whatsoever. I was held in a building right in the town. No one missed me, as I had no corpsmen, and my Vietnamese corpsmen and nurses were never sure if I had left, or what. I was not permitted to contact anyone.

"The only harm that came to me is that I was just scared to death. All the time. I was given food and water, of sorts. No head facilities, and no place to go. My clothes were taken away. This humiliation plus the mess (my own) that I was forced to stand, sit and sleep in was all I had to take. Questioning, yes, a good deal of it, in a fashion that has been well publicized. But I was never touched. 'Sir, do you own an automobile? And is it not true that this car cost the equivalent of many people's yearly salary?' This was the type of questioning.

"I have in no way been brainwashed or tortured or anything, Mother. I don't like to even use these words. I have an enormous amount of sympathy, in a noble sense, for those Americans held in China—and other areas. Remember my patient, Bob Coffee, back at Pendleton, who had those three years in POW camp in Korea? I understand so much more about it now. It is an experience that I would do everything in my power to escape from; yet I am glad that I had it.

"You knew a great deal, Mother, and thank God for it. You never wrote of political things in your letters. Your last eight or ten that I had on hand on the 4th were taken from me and reread back to me line by line, with a great deal of intimation between the lines. Had you mentioned anything political, things might not have been so soft for me.

"I had burned all issues of *Time* and many other things before the 4th on the advice of John McGowan, who went through hell in Hanoi a year before and who taught me what to say and how, just in case. (Only the "case" happened to come about.) All my possessions were taken away from me, and later returned with the seams opened, pockets slashed, etc.

"I do not want you thinking that I am ill. Your worrying about this worries me a great deal. I am in excellent health now, my weight is going up every minute. You have seen that picture of me at the Palace in Saigon. That was just after leaving Haiphong, when I was in my poorest health. I look a lot better now. I am not in the least changed mentally, just matured and cognizant of so many more things, as I am trying to bring out in my book. Most of all, I have learned how frightened you can become, and how many millions of people are living in this state by day and by night.

"I could never have kept my head if I didn't have the background, the stability, and the God that you and Dad gave to me. Stop being distressed about anything. Thank God, as I do every morning at Mass, that I am all right and sane in mind and body. Stop being distressed about little things, and see the great and good things God has done for me, and the horrors that He managed to keep me from.

"I don't want to write any more now, Mother, because it is so hard to write things that bring up such emotions. You can't hear the passion that I want to speak with. There is no need to think of those words of Earle's, *chin up,* because they imply difficulties and hardships. The Dooleys don't have problems of any magnitude now. We have our little problems and irritations, but no real big problems, as we might have, so very easily.

"If my letters have been different lately, I don't know why, other than that I have been working a good deal. This book, while a good idea, was bad in this sense: it has made me remember too much."

four

towards the edge of tomorrow

I knew the promises I had to keep.

In one sense the "temporary additional duty" that started for Tom in 1954 never ended. It really went on for the rest of his life.

Two decisions which he made while still in Japan misled me about his future plans. The first was his desire to write a book about the evacuation of Viet Nam, and the second was his decision to apply for a one-year residency in orthopedics at the National Naval Medical Center in Bethesda, Maryland. The book, as he said, was bound to reawaken all the misery and horror he had been through, but I felt that until he put the story on paper he would never be finished with it. As for the residency, it was Dr. Casberg who advised it. "My old medical mentor," Tom wrote, "told me I'd better get on with my postgraduate training if I hoped to be a good orthopedic surgeon."

I thought these two decisions made great sense and told Tom so. He later wrote: "Mother reminded me of all the things I had always wanted and now might have. A home, a wife, kids, a nice medical practice, maybe a few fine hunting horses." It seemed to me that Tom was now moving in this direction. Perhaps he even thought so himself.

114

If so, we were both wrong. Other forces were working within him throughout this period. Tom had a mission, one might even call it a vocation, which could not be denied. Everything that happened during this period underlined it and pointed to it. At least it seems so now, looking back at it. But at the time, when he made his choice, I was wholly unprepared. I was stunned at first, then terribly worried. Yet it was meant to be, and it finally prevailed.

At sea, aboard the *Diachenko* returning to Japan, Tom wrote: "I spent all last night and all today working on the book. Doesn't that sound formidable? But that is just what it is, a book. Before we got to Hong Kong, I slept until ten every morning, did some typing, then got out on deck for a sun bath. I slept every time I put my head to a pillow. Guess I was more whipped than I thought I was. My weight is down, that is true, from 180 to 130, but I am already gaining and I will get the rest back in no time whatsoever." After Hong Kong he wrote: "I was the tailor's delight in Hong Kong with a 28 waist, but I had the pants made for 32."

Tom had sent me flowers by wire from Hong Kong. "I am very pleased that you took the flowers to the cemetery. That way they were enjoyed by all I love, living and dead. I read Earle's letter frequently and I quote it in my book. It is applicable, even more so, ten years since the day he wrote it. Wonder if he ever dreamed that we would be reading it under such circumstances, so many years later, without him. *'I charge each of you...'*"

Back at Yokosuka Naval Hospital he found that writing the book was not easy: "I know I have been remiss in my letters, but blame THE BOOK. It is consuming every free moment of my day. When I finish my work in the evening, I start typing and find that I cannot tolerate the least disturbance. It breaks my train of thought and I can't seem to pick it up adequately again. Now I know why authors go to cabins in the north-woods to write a book. The title is still unsettled. What do you think of *Treatment for Terror*? I have definitely rejected *Exodus from Agony*. Commander Bill Lederer was certainly right when he said, 'Giving birth to a baby is a cinch compared to fathering a book.' I haven't a finished manuscript to show him yet. Do you like *Trial in Tonkin*? Another possibility is *Bamboo and Blood*. I guess not."

Late in the summer he wrote: "Yesterday I had a telecon

conversation with Commander Lederer in Hawaii. He is stationed there at CincPac headquarters. Told him of the book, and he said he would like to go over it with me, would I come to Hawaii for a few days? Taking a deep breath, I said I could not arrange such a trip, would have to come on orders. So he said he would talk to Admiral Stump. A chance to go over the manuscript with an expert would be great!"

Two weeks later Tom announced: "I finished the book, or at least so I thought. I gave it to several of my friends (therefore my severest critics) here. The reactions were different, but the consensus is that it has a tendency to fall apart. No unity. Everyone was surprised that I did not use TAD (me) as the unifying theme—the evacuation as TAD lived it, the orphanage of Mme. Ngai as TAD saw it, etc. I thought egocentricity was bad. For this book, they tell me, it's good. It is going to take forever to be written. What long hours this typewriter demands. I'm glad there's no word on Hawaii yet, because the ms. is far from ready to show Lederer."

Finally in September Tom's orders came, detaching him from the U.S. Naval Hospital at Yokosuka: "When directed by the Commanding Officer about 1 November 1955, proceed to the United States and upon arrival further proceed and report to the U.S. Naval Hospital, National Naval Medical Center, Bethesda, Maryland for duty under instruction in residency training." He was to have thirty days leave in the U.S. before reporting for his new duty.

About the same time he was informed that he had been awarded the Legion of Merit. "I was notified yesterday," he wrote, "that the Commanding Officer here has received the medal, and that it will be presented Friday evening at dress parade. The Marines, 2,000 strong, will pass in review with the band. All the officers and enlisted men will be given two hours off to attend, and all my patients should be there. My phone has been ringing with congratulations. My health is excellent," he added, "except for those damned intestinal worms which I am still battling. In spite of their eating most of my meals for me, my weight is rising daily."

A few days after this ceremony Tom took off from Tokyo International Airport at 11:30 P.M. on November 10, 1955. He stayed in Hawaii two weeks, not only conferring with Commander Lederer about revisions on his book, but briefing Admiral Stump's staff on his experiences in Viet Nam. As he described it in the opening chapter of his book, it was "the

Walter Mitty moment that every junior officer has dreamed of since the Navy began. How often I had sat in the ship's wardroom saying, 'Well, if I were running this outfit...' Or 'Why the devil didn't the Admiral do it this way?' And now the Admiral was saying, 'Well, Dooley, what would *you* do if *you* were wearing the stars?' " Needless to say, Tom told them exactly what he would do.

In Hawaii Commander Lederer not only made suggestions for revising the book, but arranged an appointment which was to end Tom's writing problems. He had a date to meet with the editors of the *Reader's Digest* back east. Tom took a plane to San Francisco, joining a group of cadets in the Vietnamese Air Force on their way to Texas.

I joined my son in California. My happiness and relief at seeing him safe in this country at last cannot be described. We then took a train home to St. Louis. In his book he explained why he preferred a slow return: "I wanted to see America's fields and mountains, her canyons and plains. I even sat up most of the night looking out the window. I was home. I was back in America—though truly I had never left her at all. She was in my heart."

It was in December that Tom met Mr. and Mrs. DeWitt Wallace of the *Reader's Digest,* who took a great interest in him. Through them he met James Monahan, a valued friend and a crucial influence in his life. Mr. Monahan, Senior Editor of the magazine, has described their first meeting:

"On December 14, 1955, a half-dozen *Reader's Digest* editors were hosts at luncheon to a tall, lean, handsome young (28) Navy doctor, Thomas A. Dooley, Lieutenant (jg), who recently had been awarded the Legion of Merit for the singular part he played in the U. S. Navy's heroic peacetime operation 'Passage to Freedom' in Indo-China. Tom Dooley began his rapid-fire recital that day even before he sat down at the luncheon table. Two hours later his listeners were still spellbound by the story of his adventures in the wretched refugee camps of Haiphong... The *Digest* editors recognized at once that Tom Dooley was a singularly colorful personality with a great story. An agreement was made for its publication."

Before inviting Tom to join him in Florida to finish the revision of the book, Mr. Monahan introduced him to Roger W. Straus, Jr., head of the publishing firm of Farrar, Straus & Cudahy, who presented Tom with a book contract. It was a good augury for the New Year, being dated January 3, 1956. It never remotely occurred to me that before the year was much older, Tom would have resigned from the Navy and completed plans for returning to Asia.

Tom had reported to Bethesda for residency early in December, but soon word about his book began circulating through the Navy Department in Washington, where the manuscript had been submitted for clearance. The top line-officer himself, Admiral Arleigh Burke, Chief of Naval Operations, not only read it, but contributed a foreword in which he said:

"Today's naval traditions have been built by generations of men like young Doctor Dooley who have served their country well under arduous and challenging circumstances. The American sailor is ofttimes, as was Doctor Dooley, confronted with situations in which proper courses of action could not have been pre-planned or pre-determined. . . . Lieutenant Dooley contributed greatly to the welfare of mankind and to an understanding of the fundamental principles of the United States, as he participated in this epoch-making period of world history. In *Deliver Us from Evil* he has written that story with freshness, clarity and force. It is a story that will be told and re-told. It is a story of which the United States Navy is proud."

Since book publication was planned for April, the Navy Department decided to modify Tom's orders and attach him to the office of the Surgeon General for three months. It was in Washington at this time that he and I met Clare Murphy, longtime secretary to the Surgeon General, who became one of our dearest friends. Clare has described Tom at this juncture:

"He was the snappiest, best-looking young naval officer I had seen in a long time, and he was blessed with a keen sense of humor and all the charm of his Irish ancestry. He always knew exactly what he was doing and where he was going, which made it a pleasure to work with him. Even at 28 he was master of the spoken and written word, and his dictation was perfect and so fascinating you were sorry when he stopped. When it was transcribed, never a word needed to be changed. He was a secretary's dream from that angle alone.

"He was always in a hurry, and the consensus in the Navy Department was that if Dooley kept up this pace he was headed for a breakdown, either mental or physical. . . . He was attached to the Office of the Surgeon General for the first three months of 1956, and he worked out of my office. During that time he made hundreds of talks at various naval activities, and at many colleges and universities. The public relations officers were wild about him, because he was in great demand and always made good copy. They could not get enough of him, and they regretted his decision to resign from the Navy in order to work in Laos, which he had to do as a civilian."

I have in front of me the schedule of lectures which Tom made during this period, and as I look back it seems almost super-human. The frequency of his appearances, sometimes three in one city a day, was not only very demanding, but he would agree to dates without regard for the wear and tear of space and geography. On January 31st he talked at the Pentagon Auditorium in Washington, on February 1st in Miami, next day again in Washington at the Press Club. The sequence of places is almost bewildering; he talked only single days apart in these cities during February and March: Philadelphia, New York, Columbus, Charleston (West Virginia), Dayton, Louisville, Chicago, St. Louis, Westchester, New Orleans, Kansas City, Denver, Phoenix, Oakland, Seattle, Richmond, Atlanta, Baltimore, Nashville, and New York. He talked to medical societies, sororities, high schools, colleges, grade schools, Rotarians, press clubs, Chambers of Commerce, U.S. Navy stations (including a submarine base), and religious groups of all faiths. He gave TV interviews, radio interviews, and press interviews; he addressed hospital staffs and luncheon clubs. He even spoke at the Willys automobile plant at Toledo. Everywhere he went he told the story of the "Passage to Freedom."

I heard some of the lectures, spaced widely apart. Each time he seemed more eloquent and effective than the time before, and seldom repeated himself. The talks he had prepared so long ago in the Baie d'Along and Haiphong, to "brief" the sailors and officers aboard the Navy ships, now stood him in good stead. He reviewed the history of Indo-China and the French colonial occupation from the eighteenth century to the fall of Dien Bien Phu. He explained the Asian point of view, the centuries of neglect of a fine people which had created hostility and hatred of western nations. He showed the reasons for the identification of the United States, in the eyes of Asians, with the imperialistic colonial powers. He described the Geneva Convention and the partition of

Viet Nam. And when he came to the story of the evacuation itself, the misery and terror of the people, their suspicions and fears of Americans, and the daily life in Camp de la Pagode, he began to relive it all over again. His accounts would become so real and vivid that not a sound could be heard in the audience. He spoke so simply and clearly that children in the audience would be just as rapt as grown-ups. He held attention not by tricks and rhetoric, but by simple sincerity. When people hear the truth, they recognize it.

"How many times have I told that story?" Tom has asked. "I told it whenever and wherever I could find Americans who were willing to listen. But at least it was never told in vainglory. For what we did in dying Haiphong was far less important than what we learned there. We had seen simple, tender, loving care—the crudest kind of medicine inexpertly practiced by mere boys—change a people's fear and hatred into friendship and understanding. We had witnessed the power of medical aid to reach the hearts and souls of a nation. We had seen it transform the brotherhood of man from an ideal into a reality that plain people could understand. To me that experience was like the white light of revelation. It made me proud to be a doctor. Proud to be an American doctor who had been privileged to witness the enormous possibilities of *medical aid* in all its Christlike power and simplicity. Why was it that foreign-aid planners, with their billion-dollar projects, found it difficult to understand? I preached so ardently that my folks began to worry . . . How could I make them see that things would never be the same? I knew the promises I had to keep. I knew the keeping of them would take me many miles, back to Southeast Asia, to the very edge of tomorrow, where the future might be made —or lost."

To me that experience was like the white light of revelation . . . How could I make them see that things would never be the same? . . . I knew the promises I had to keep.

These words should have warned me that an ordinary, routine life was not for Tom. We were living then at 4301 Massachusetts Avenue in Washington. I was waiting for his book to come out, for his change of orders from the Office of the Surgeon General to his residency in orthopedics at Bethesda. Then one evening in February he told me: "I'm resigning from the Navy, and I'm going to Laos." It was as simple as that.

Before I could recover from the shock, he related how, a

few evenings before, he had gone to a dinner in the Viet Nam Embassy. "I had a premonition that any chance I had of returning to Indo-China with a medical team of my own would hinge on whatever happened at that dinner." The Ambassador had invited some Cambodian and Laotian diplomats to meet Tom. After dinner Tom talked about the kind of medical mission he had in mind—small, privately financed by funds which he would raise by his own efforts, by writing, lecturing, begging. There would be no political or religious sponsorship. Neither the government nor the church would be involved. The team would consist of himself and a few young Americans who had served with him in Viet Nam. He said that perhaps, if they did a good job, they would inspire other Americans, doctors and laymen, to follow their example of international cooperation on a people-to-people basis.

Tom said that the Cambodians listened politely, but he noticed that the Laotian Ambassador, Hon. Ourot Souvannavong, was following him with keen interest.

"Dr. Dooley," he asked, "why should you, a young man with a career before you, choose to make this sacrifice? Obviously you have much to offer. But what do you stand to gain?"

Suddenly Tom remembered a remark of Boatswain's Mate Norman Baker, who had served with him as corpsman in Haiphong. Pressed to explain their motives, Baker had simply said, "We just want to do what we can for people who ain't got it so good!"

Ambassador Souvannavong beamed when he heard this. "Dr. Dooley," he said, "my country will be honored to receive your mission." When they met again next day, he said: "Many times before white men have come to help us. But always they had other motives—colonization, trade, even our religious conversion. I really believe your motive is purely humanitarian. That will make your mission unique in my country." Then, with a smile, "And also, for some of my people, a trifle hard to believe."

Operation Laos, as Tom decided to call his mission, was to start in July. He persuaded his three Navy helpers, Norman Baker, Peter Kessey and Dennis Shepard, to leave their families and commitments and accompany him to Laos. Angier Biddle Duke and Leo Cherne of the International Rescue Committee arranged to take Operation Laos under the aegis of I.R.C. Then Tom, with hat in hand, made the rounds of the pharmaceutical companies and surgical supply houses and met with generous responses. Walt Disney presented him with a projector and a collection of Disney movies for the children of Laos. The Willys Company donated a jeep, which he named "Agnes." CARE donated fifty midwife kits, and Meals for Millions gave five thousand pounds of their multi-purpose food.

In the midst of his planning and begging, his book *Deliver Us from Evil* was published. Its reception was enthusiastic, both as to sales and criticism. It was reviewed in the New York *Herald Tribune* by former Ambassador Edwin F. Stanton, who wrote: "If other true stories were told as effectively as Dr. Dooley's, we might glean from the minds of many the poisonous, Communist-inspired picture of an America intent only on The Bomb, and implant in its place the truth." The *New Yorker* review especially delighted Tom: "His story of how he and his assistants conquered the refugees' fears and restored them to something like well-being is a moving poem of the human spirit victorious." The *Library Journal* called it "a story filled with courage, human love and kindness for fellow men. Inspiring, it will fill any reader with pride in our American heritage . . . Highly recommended." The *Episcopal Church News* said: "As a human document it is extraordinary . . . Dr. Dooley had limited equipment, a tiny band of assistants, and vast reserves of innate human faith, dignity and patience in suffering on the part of his charges. It is a stirring document." Monsignor John S. Kennedy, in his syndicated book column in the Catholic press, wrote: "One suspects that Dr. Dooley might be a figure of fun to the Graham Greene of *The Quiet American*. He is young, earnest, ebullient, intent on publicizing the fact and the extent of American assistance to the refugees. And yet, as to essentials, he is indubitably right. The overwhelming evil of communism is clear to him. Patriotism burns strongly in him, but the dominant motive in all that we see him doing is charity—love, and supernatural love at that."

Hundreds of reviews continued to appear throughout every section of the country, and finally the book made the bestseller lists. The *Reader's Digest* ran a condensation in their April, 1956 issue, as a result of which Tom received thousands of enthusiastic letters. The book sales passed the 90,000 copy mark in the original edition. In the paperback editions later on, *Deliever Us from Evil* sold over half a million copies. It received the Christopher Award for 1956.

Tom was very happy about the success of his book, of course, but I believe the thing that pleased him most was the fact that *Deliver Us from Evil* appeared in translation in these languages: Arabic, Assamese, Bengali, Burmese, Bicol, Cambodian, Cebuano, Chinese, Farsi, French, German, Greek, Gujerati, Hebrew, Hiligaynon, Hindi, Icelandic, Ilcaro, Indonesian, Japanese, Kachin, Kannada, Korean, Laotian, Latvian, Macedonian, Malay, Malayalam, Marathi, Oriya, Portuguese, Punjabi, Serbo-Croatian, Sinhalese, Slovenian, Taglog, Tamil, Telugu, Thai, Turkish, Urdu and Vietnamese.

Tom now drew up, in the name of the team, a summary of the concepts behind Operation Laos. This document represents the embryonic stage of Medico. He entitled it *Plans for the Medical Mission to Laos:*

AIM. (1) To give medical care both to the people of the mountains and of the cities, through the Minister of Health of Laos. (2) To illustrate to these people some of the principles and achievements of America, and especially to show them that we are anxious to help them on a person-to-person basis.

EQUIPMENT. Two small vehicles, pharmaceuticals, vaccines, portable tape-recorder, sound-track movie projector, lots of baseballs, several consumer-goods catalogues, an accordion, and a bucketful of good-will. The former will be gifts from individual companies. The last is characteristic of my volunteer ex-Navy corpsmen.

APPROVAL. This mission has the complete approval of the State Department, the International Cooperation Administration, and the Laotian government.

BACKING. We shall work under the auspices of the International Rescue Committee. However, the major part of the financial support will be from private pharmaceutical concerns and CARE. Also there will be personal contributions of fellow Americans.

THE REASON. If America as a nation (composed of individuals such as we) ignores the Asian's physical needs while handing him pious platitudes, we justify the Communists' characterization of our religion as an "opiate of the people," and "pie in the sky by and by." While we are preaching God's precepts and the Voice of America proclaims our good intentions, the Communists are moving in among the masses of humanity who never saw a missionary, nor heard a radio, and they appear to practice exactly what WE preach. This was seen by the members of our unit and it illustrated to us the need for a mission such as this, over and above the already functioning government organizations. We shall be a small mobile unit composed of men who have had experience in this line (Haiphong, Viet Nam) and who now fully realize the significance of our actions. We want to take positive steps for America, not just denying what the Communists say about us, but getting there and doing something about it. We shall try to translate the democratic ideals we DO possess into Asian realities that they CAN possess. Our instrument for this shall be medicine. The future of Laos is shrouded in a mantle of uncertainty. Rather than curse the darkness, perhaps we can light a few candles.

CHANNELS. We shall work through the Ministry of Health of Laos, with the already established (though inadequately trained) village dispensaries. In this way we shall avoid the impression of meddlesomeness and/or neo-colonialism.

TIME. This is a pilot project. Because of this and because of the monsoon season, there is only a six month period when the roads of the mountains are usable. Our present intention is to remain but six months. Estimated time of departure is August, 1956.

METHOD OF ACTION. Vientiane, the capital, shall be our headquarters. Upon arrival we shall pay our respects to the Minister of Health, Doctor Souvanna Vong. Then with one of his "nurses" or "corpsmen" we shall leave the city and drive to a mountain tribe with our jeeps loaded with medicines, etc. We shall go to the tribes of the Meo, the Yao, the Muongs, etc. We will present ourselves to the village "ban" or chief. He will show us a place to build our tents and park the vehicles. Then we shall throw a baseball around, play with the kids, and that evening eat with the villagers. Our small cans of food will be of interest to them. We shall show them our catalogues which will amuse and amaze them.

That night we will show them a movie, *Bambi, Fantasia, Snow White,* or another Walt Disney film. The Laotian Ambassador in Washington is making a sound-track for this in the Lao tongue. Most of them have never seen a white man, nor a doctor (there is one physician for the two million people of Laos). After the movie the kids will say, "Not only do Americans have colorful animals who dance and sing, but the animals can speak Lao."

The following morning we shall say, "Look, we possess medicines that can cure your yaws, your congenital syphilis, your malaria, your trachoma. Let us help you." We will treat the people, learning the characteristics of their honest and gentle Buddhist life. We have no intention of trying to foist our way of life on them, nor convert them. The only aim is 50% medicine and 50% contact with Americans who want simply to help.

The corpsmen who will do this have had equivalent experience in Haiphong, North Viet Nam. They did a superb job when they did not realize the full significance of their task. Now they shall do a better job. The Laotian Ambassador says that the legend of the "Bac Sy My" and his American corpsmen has reached the foothills of Lasha in Tibet. The "American Doctor" and his corpsmen are returning.

Under the Geneva treaty no military personnel are allowed into this area. Therefore we are going as civilians, on a purely personal basis. We will not be members of the State Department or of any affiliated government organization. Rather, we shall be under the auspices of the International Rescue Committee, a private institution.

After working in one area a while, we shall return to the capital to restock, and then go to another tribe. We want them to want us to return.

When the Communists say that we are monster Americans, these tribes shall say "Why, that is not true, we met some Americans, and they were very nice, they were *tot lam.*" These are our plans.

> THOMAS A. DOOLEY, M.D.
> NORMAN M. BAKER
> PETER KESSEY
> DENNIS D. SHEPARD

Tom and his three co-workers left San Francisco on August 7th. After stop-overs in Hawaii, Hong Kong and Tokyo, they arrived in the Philippines, and in Manila were the guests of President Magsaysay, who wished their mission Godspeed. On September 6th they reached Saigon. President Ngo Dinh Diem of the Republic of South Viet Nam not only received them as his guests, but put his personal plane at their disposal for a seven-day tour of the refugee resettlement areas of free Viet Nam. "In each village," Tom wrote, "we found people who knew us in Haiphong during that city's death. There were people who said, 'Look, Doctor, my arm is all healed now' and 'Look, Baker, my eyes are better.' It is a tremendous thing to be remembered. President Diem is having some 3,000 pounds of our equipment flown for us (and with us) to Vientiane, the capital of Laos."

In Vientiane Tom had his first meeting with Dr. Oudom Souvanna Vong, Minister of Health, and the only doctor of medicine in Laos. He was the nephew of Ambassador Souvannavong, with whom Tom had discussed the country's medical needs in Washington. It seemed clear that the northern province of Nam Tha was the section most in need, and that is where Tom asked to go.

"I have heard of your wishes to go to the north," Dr. Oudom told him, "but there are many hazards there. Isolation, the precariousness of border life, communist banditry, the monsoons, lack of transportation." He said that the white man was almost unknown in the region, and there might be difficulty among the primitive and superstitious people of this Himalayan foothill world. Dr. Oudom said he was pleased that Tom and his co-workers were willing to take their medicine to these needy people, and they had his approval, but it would also be necessary to get the approval of the American embassy.

This was refused by Ambassador J. Graham Parsons. He explained that the political situation in Laos was explosive, and they would be accused of being American espionage agents, no matter how absurd the charge. However, as the Ambassador pointed out, there was scarcely any part of Laos *not* in need of medical aid, and he suggested instead that they go to the area around Vang Vieng. Dr. Oudom agreed that they could perform a real service in Vang Vieng, and that is where their first clinic was set up, in this village about 120 miles north of the capital.

Tom sent home this account of their first days in Vang Vieng: "We finally arrived in this village covered with mud and red dust. After having spent the night on the road, we were unshaven. Our truck and jeep were full of dents and scratches, and our crates covered with dirt and hardened mud. Instead of giving the impression that we were arriving to help the village, we looked as though we were arriving in the village to be helped. For the many who had never seen an American, I'm afraid we were something of a disenchantment.

"There are about 2,000 people living in Vang Vieng, and a few kilometers up the road there is another village of 2,000. In the surrounding mountains there are tribes of Meo, Yao, and Kha, numbering about 20,000. Our hospital will, therefore, serve quite a large community.

"Although the Chao Muong, or village chief, met us and offered us a fine little hut to live in, we had something else on our minds. As soon as we could, we found the nearest river, only a few hundred yards away, and took a swim with a bar of soap. I'm sure the Nam Song River will never be the same.

"The next thing on the agenda was to set our house in order. This involved gallons of water, much scrubbing, much scouring, and plenty of paint. A lot of the village kids helped us. The man next door (that sounds stateside) pitched in and sawed down enough bamboo to help build an extension for our bedroom.

"We now have a living-room about twenty feet square, with out most prized possessions—our kerosene-run ice box, several wooden crates constructed into couches, another on the deck for the dining-room table, and four-inch high Laotian stools for chairs. The bedroom is just large enough to put our four cots down and squeeze Chai, our interpreter, in also. Hanging off the side of the house is a 55-gallon gasoline drum with water in it for washing.

"This hut-of-a-house stands on stilts about 5 feet high. Underneath, the neighborhood pigs, cows, chickens and ducks meander in constant search for nourishment. Above we have a large American flag flying. This is a warming sensation. I am sure, save for the USIS flag at Luang Prabang, that ours is the only American flag north of Vientiane. Over the door of our house Dennis Shepard painted a sign reading UNCLE TOM'S CABIN in English and in Laotian.

"As for our own nourishment, we have plenty of C-rations which we alternate with rice and fish. The next day we alternate with fish and rice. I'm not sure how we shall feel a year from now. There are some cucumber-like "melons" here, and plenty of oranges and bananas, so we really can't complain.

"Pete Kessey from Texas, Norman Baker from New Hampshire, and Dennis Shepard from Oregon are all working very hard, but I believe they are thoroughly enjoying it. I'm fortunate to have three such as these. Every day I realize this a little more. At the present moment Baker is sitting across from me looking at a Pan American Airways time-wheel trying to figure out what time it is back in New Hampshire. His wife is due to have her baby soon.

"After fixing up the house, we next set our sights on the dispensary belonging to the Laotian government, and converted it into our hospital. As we are working with and through the Laotian Public Health Department, we are ultilizing their building and their nurses, a man and his wife. With all pitching in for the next two days, we cleaned the dispensary up, painted it, and stocked it with our supplies. We have three rooms, one for the nurse and his wife, one for daily sick-call, and the third for our hospital ward, only we don't have any beds, just mats on the deck. It is a fine little building made of sun-baked mud, white-washed, with neither electricity nor plumbing. We are very pleased with it, and think we can do a lot of good. We'll try, anyway.

"So far our sick-calls consist of several hundred per day, with a tremendous lot of malaria, and pneumonia in children. In some other letter we will go into the medical situation.

"We have a teaching program outlined with the Chao Muong. We are going to try to have three distinct classes, one for those who want to learn English, one for pregnant women in general prenatal care, and a third for some 25 young people the Chao Muong will choose as outstanding so that we may teach them hygiene and sanitation.

"It is getting late in the evening now—Baker hasn't figured out what time it is yet, and we are all quite tired and think we had best hit the proverbial sack, which here consists of a bedding roll on the floor. We shall send the jeep down to Vientiane about twice a month to pick up mail, supplies, and for a "break" in the routine of the weeks.

"We are really glad to be here, as the people need help. They are gentle, hospitable and good. It is a real joy to work with them. From February to now, when all the planning, programming and blueprinting for our Operation Laos was being done, there was a great deal of talk. Now we are *doing* rather than talking. As St. Augustine said long ago, 'Words sound, but it is actions that really attract.' "

Tom explained that he had met Chai, their interpreter in Vientiane, where he had graduated from the lycée. A husky fellow with clear bronze skin and jet-black hair, he spoke French as well as the native dialects, and Tom offered him a job. Chai had short, stubby fingers ("I didn't realize they would one day serve me expertly across the surgical table") and as a Buddhist he would not kill anything, though he liked fishing (*"Non, mon docteur,* I merely take the fish out of water. If it dies, I have not killed it").

The medical picture promised in Tom's first letter soon followed: "In most countries hospitals are classified by their capacity. We don't use beds but mats. Our hospital, which has but one ward, has 25 mats. The second room of our hospital is being used as quarters for our Laotian nurses. The other room triples as a delivery-room, operating-room, and sick-call room.

"A typical day might go like this: we get up with the dawn (we don't know exactly what time that is, no one here is strapped to the watches on their wrists) and after breakfast of eggs received as yesterday's fees, we walk several hundred yards to our hospital.

"There is already a line of people from this and surrounding villages, as well as a sprinkling of brightly clothed tribal people, such as the Meo and Kha. I first hold rounds in the ward, and the boys start sick-calls with our Lao nurses. We do all our work through the Lao nurses, as we want to be working with and through them, not around or above them.

"Sick-call manifests the usual run of tropical ills. The mosquitos here are malignant with malaria. This is our greatest problem. Then there are all sorts of upper respiratory infections, yaws, tropical ulcers, dysentery, and a goodly amount of the traumatic injuries sustained by a people who must wrest their meager existence from a savage jungle. We have one young patient who has been horribly mauled by a wild boar.

"Many of the children here suffer from some degree of malnutrition, beri-beri, and other deficiency diseases. There are the tuberculous oldsters, and scabby-headed infants. What a need there is here for medicine! These people, shoulder-deep in omens, portents, witch-doctors, herbs, symbols, beneficent and malicious spirits, have never seen a doctor, never seen an American, indeed few have even seen a Frenchman.

"After a lunch of C-rations (a gift of the Navy) mixed with some local greens, well permanganated, we load up the jeep 'Agnes' and head for a village an hour or two away, tucked high in the mountains. Here two of the team hold village sick-call to take care of those who couldn't get down to our clinic in Vang Vieng. These sick-calls are held on the tailgate of the jeep, where our boxes of magic and miracles lay.

"The two men who remain in Vang Vieng during the afternoon hold classes there. One lectures at the local school on hygiene and sanitation. The other speaks at our hospital to a dozen bright-eyed girls who are in training to be midwives. The children think Americans most strange. ('Do you know they claim fever comes from mosquitos?')

"When the midwives complete two months of training and have assisted at 25 deliveries, we bag them. At home a nurse gets her cap as a sign of graduation; here she gets her bag. That is, we give them a CARE Midwife Bag, in which there are the proper accoutrements for delivery.

"In the evenings we bathe in the river with the rest of the

village, but we use soap. However, Pete Kessey's 'hot shower' will be done soon. It is an 18-foot bamboo-enclosed,
double-barrelled shower which looks like an illegitimate union between the Leaning Tower of Pisa and a Texas oil
derrick.

"The Laotians are not as gastronomically ingenious as the
Chinese (who have made even the snake edible) so our din-
ner is again C-rations with a few herbs and greens thrown in.
For vitamins and mineral content, we take pills.

"We show a Disney movie every night, either here or in
the surrounding villages. I am not sure just which is more
powerful—our medicines or *Bambi*. However, both seem to
be working.

"Late last night a group arrived from a village over 100
miles away. They had come to see, and brought with them
a sickly-looking young mother who thrust under our sleepy
noses a bundle of clothing. Wrapped in layers of cloth was
a child. We undid layer upon layer and found a huge dis-
tended abdomen. There was practically nothing but a glistening abdomen, enormously enlarged, semi-transparent, netted
in a lace pattern of veins, looking as if at any moment it
might burst like over-blown fruit. Around the edges of the
navel were a dozen of those round brown marks where the
local witch-doctor had burned the skin with pieces of hot
ginger-root, to draw the sickness out. Above this monstrous
sphere sat the tiny bird cage of a thorax, and above it the
miniature face of a querulous baby, wth sickly eyes and a
deathly pallor. This is another case of malnutrition, a bit
more hideous than the others. The mother fell sick and was
unable to nurse the baby. They fed it rice, at the age of five
months, rice and water. It doesn't take long for beri-beri to
conquer.

"One has heard of these things, but what a terrible sight
to encounter it personally. What a lot of misery and pain
there is in the world! Politics may come and may scud past
like clouds, but pain and hunger and poverty are the real
internationalists. They seem to go on forever.

"Pete Kessey, Denny Shepard and Norm Baker are working long hard hours, and they say I am a son-of-a-gun to
work for (hyperthyroid is the word, I think). All of us are
out of contact with what is usually termed civilization: plumbing, hot water, television, and so on. But we are learning
that there is nothing stronger in the world than gentleness,
and that there is an intense and vivid joy that comes from

serving others. We have found a challenge and are giving our response. This is satisfying in itself, and any complaint fades into a very slight grumble. The brotherhood of man transcends the sovereignty of nations, and service to humanity is the best work of life."

Another American, Jefferson Davis Cheek of Comanche, Texas, arrived in Laos about this time (October, 1956) to work at the U. S. Information Agency in Vientiane. He had never heard of Dooley or his work, "but I heard plenty about Tom Dooley in the first few days after my arrival. Dooley was very unpopular among the Americans of Vientiane. They were critical of his ego, his fanatical zeal, his flair for personal publicity. The more I heard, the more I wanted to meet the guy." Jeff decided to visit the clinic. "On Thanksgiving Day, 1956, I had my cook get up very early and start roasting a turkey. I figured that any American would appreciate a turkey on Thanksgiving, and I was pretty sure Dooley and his team-mates didn't have one in Vang Vieng. By 7 a.m. the turkey was ready. I loaded my jeep with extra gasoline, extra food and Dooley's mail, which I had picked up. I arrived there about eight hours later and just introduced myself as Jeff Cheek of Comanche, Texas, and the name stuck. The boys were bowled over by my American-style turkey dinner . . ."

Jeff describes the clinic and house in Vang Vieng as he saw it in those first months in Laos: "The house which Dooley and his team had chosen for themselves was no worse than that of the other villagers. It was a three-room hut, made of bamboo, with the joints of the house secured by a vine called *wy* in the Lao language. But it had one item which differentiated it from all the others—a large American flag hung from a bamboo flagstaff on the front porch. The single concrete building which the villagers had offered Dooley had been rejected. It would serve to set the Dooley crew apart from the villagers they had come to serve. Instead, he converted that house into a hospital.

"I got a fire going, and when Dooley and his boys came back from work, we all sat down to Thanksgiving dinner. To say that they came back from work is inaccurate, however. Actually they were always working. They got up in the morning to find patients waiting for them on the doorstep. While they ate breakfast or lunch or dinner, other patients materialized out of the jungle, and squatted patiently in the dust, waiting.

"My first impressions of Dooley were these: He was a young man with tremendous driving energy, with a desire to get things done. He had an ego that was mountainous. He had absolutely no patience with mediocrity. He was brilliant in the intellectual sense, and full of charm which he could turn off and on as with a spigot. I could see that these were the characteristics that people disliked in Dooley. But I soon learned that most people did not make the effort, as I and a few others did, to look behind the Dooley façade. There they would have seen a remarkable human being—a man full of deep love and pity for the suffering people of the world....

"In those early days he could not speak a word of Lao. So, when I visited him, I would go with him on sick-call to distant villages, serving as both driver and interpreter. We would stop in some little village. Dooley would drop the tailgate of the jeep, set up his medicines, and treat anyone who came. I watched him closely at these occasions. His manner became completely different. The inner tension disappeared, his voice would soften, he would almost croon to the sick children, as he gave them shots of penicillin, and quieted them with a stick of candy or a toy balloon... That's when I saw the real Dooley emerge—a shy, lonely man, ridden by doubts and fears, possessed with a burning desire to help, but fearful that he would be (and he was) misunderstood... Dooley said many times that he was happy only when working in Laos. Some Americans have ridiculed this as a publicity gimmick, much as they used to hoot at the late Carole Lombard for saying that she liked to pay taxes. They were wrong—Dooley *was* happy in Laos....

"Dooley was a very practical person. On my first visit to his hospital at Vang Vieng, I did most of the cooking, simply because this freed him and his three medics for more important work. This task I volunteered for. But, later, Dooley said to me: 'I have to make several night calls. I will wake you up and you can drive me.' It never occurred to Dooley to *ask!* To him, this was the practical way to arrange things: The medics were busy all day, and *they* needed sleep. I could drive him, and interpret for him, as well as cook for him. I didn't resent this, but I remember that it did seem tactless, almost rude, at the time.

"I remember one patient we handled on such a night call. He was a Lao male, about 40 or 45 years of age. He had come down with pneumonia. After the witch-doctors tried to cure him and failed, the family sent for the *Khun Ma Farang* (Friend Foreign Doctor). The messenger woke us at 3 a.m. A few minutes later we left for the village. Luckily the sick man lived in a village that could be reached easily by jeep.

"The patient was near death when we arrived. Doc decided that he was too sick to move. He put the patient on an improvised stretcher, and elevated the lower portion of the body at a 30 or 35 degree angle. He constructed a crude vaporizer by using a *tao* (fire pot), an old blanket, and a length of bamboo attached to a tea kettle. This was nineteenth century medicine all right, but it saved that man's life. We returned at about 6:30 a.m. I stayed up to fix breakfast. Doc took a half hour rest, then went right ahead with the day's work.

"I needn't repeat here the well-known story of Savong, the little Lao girl that I brought to Dooley, and whose life he saved. But after Savong recovered, Dooley took a picture of her which he gave me on his next trip to Vientiane. Ever since, I have carried that picture in my wallet. Whenever I heard some loudmouth in Vientiane or Hong Kong sounding off about Dooley's ego and his phoniness, I would whip out that picture and say: 'Dooley saved the life of this little girl. Tell me, how many lives have *you* saved?'

"I left Laos in September 1958, and my wife and I settled in Hawaii. In August 1959, when I heard that Doc had cancer, I was stunned. I remember saying to my wife, Denise: 'There are thousands of jerks in the world whom we could live without. Why does someone like Tom Dooley have to get cancer?'

"When I saw Tom Dooley, an obviously sick man, in Hawaii in July 1960, I kept thinking: 'There are lots of Savongs in northern Laos who owe their lives to you—babies, small children, pregnant women, old folks, people who would have died long ago in that land of filth, misery, poverty, and without doctors. There are lots of loudmouth Americans who also know this in their hearts. But there's something else that's more important. And that is that there are *people* in Vang Vieng and Nam Tha and Muong Sing who know that they are a little better off because you, Tom Dooley, the *Thanh Mo America*, happened to pass this way.'"

In Jeff Cheek of Comanche, Texas (he was always given his full credentials) Tom found a friend he cherished. It was Jeff and Denise with whom Tom stayed in his passage through Hawaii in the last summer of his life.

In Vang Vieng at the end of January, 1957 Tom called a meeting of his three co-workers to review their situation. The mission had been set up as a six-months' venture, and already five months were gone. They found that they still had medicine, that *Deliver Us from Evil* was still bringing in royalties to keep them going, that they still wanted to continue their work. They voted to stay on until the summertime.

However, a change in their plans was brought about from the outside. Tom was called to Vientiane by the Prime Minister, Prince Souvanna Phouma. "He spoke from his heart," Tom said, "gave us many fine compliments for our work, and asked us if we would move our unit to the northernmost tip of his country, to the village of Nam Tha." Tom was delighted, for this had of course been his original wish.

The town of Vang Vieng gave the boys an elaborate *baci* or ritualistic feast as a farewell. At the banquet they tied the cotton strings of friendship on the wrists of the four Americans, and chanted their lovely wishes: *"May you possess all wisdom and health, may you have many wives, may your airplane not fall from the sky, may you always carry our love with you, may you return to us, your friends."* Next day hundreds of people gathered in the village square and waved farewell as government trucks carrying the boys and their equipment pulled out.

With the move from Vang Vieng, Norman Baker left for the United States and two new corpsmen, John deVitry and Robert E. Waters, arrived. The new men, both undergraduates at Notre Dame, had been recommended by Erma Konya, and they proved to be excellent team-mates.

Tom described the move to Nam Tha: "In Vientiane we transferred to two antique planes and flew the four-hour trip straight north to Nam Tha. We bumped and skidded to a stop on a dried rice field, and found ourselves surrounded by the tribal mountain people of this region. After they recovered from the shock of such a large plane on the ground, they all pitched in and helped unload.

"As in Vang Vieng, we took over the already existing Lao dispensary. In three days we converted it into a fine little hospital, complete with small operating room, and a large clinic. Across a buffalo wallow that we call 'The Front

Lawn' we have another building. This is on high solid bamboo stilts and is our ward. It has 17 beds, and 30-odd mats. Down the patch is our house, given to us by the head of the village. We went to work immediately and built a hot shower of bamboo, a 55-gallon gasoline drum, and bamboo posts."

Three days after their arrival, Tom, Pete and Denny saved the life of little Ion, the boy almost fatally burned, whose story is told in *The Edge of Tomorrow*. As the exhausting and unrelenting daily routine continued at the Nam Tha clinic just as it had at Vang Vieng, it was not surprising that there were moments when Tom felt overwhelmed by the immensity of the task. At those times he would ask himself whether a small medical mission could really combat the onslaught of disease in a primitive country, and in a village where the dynamic appeal of Communism was ever present.

"On the porch of the hospital there are men with yaws morning when I go to the hospital the sight of the waiting crowd is a vista of awe, rather horrible to a 20th-century eye. There are nearly a hundred people, many of whom have traveled on foot and by Tibetan pony for three or four days. Many come to us from deep within Red China. The tribal people are varied in physical characteristics, ethnic languages and costume. But all are sick. There are the mongoloid Lutan in blue, with a red-splashed sash. The gaunt-looking Chinese with his historic pigtail is next to the full-faced Yao woman, whose neck is looped round with hoops of solid silver. There are the Kha Kho, whose tribal women wear heavy rings in their ears. You can see and smell their diseases a dozen feet before you get to the hospital. It is at this time that I realize so vividly that I'm half a world away from home—and five centuries behind the times.

On May 18, Tom sent this letter from Nam Tha: "Each sitting beside infants with whooping cough. Under the trees, in clusters apart, are the wretched lepers, who have just a fleck of hope left and who come daily to the American doctor. There are children with foul smallpox in the arms of young pregnant girls. Old men, their faces gnarled with pain, skin parchment-yellow, are hacking out their tubercular lungs and the remainder of their lives. There are sweet-tempered smiling kids with flies over their sores; women with excoriated lips and huge goiters hanging pendulously from their necks. All those diseases which are ancient in the sense of the 20th

century are our daily problems in Nam Tha, on the China
border, in Northern Laos.

"The child here is different from the American child only
in geography, chronology, dress and opportunity. The American child has the advantages of civilization and the security
of being in a free land. The Lao child (identical in body and
soul) has no advantages and little security. His nation is a
pawn in a game of power between Slavery and Freedom.
There is a simple, clean-cut vivid challenge to those who live
in freedom. This challenge demands that to those in need
we give some of our time, some of our humanity, some of
our life, and some of whatever light we may have to give.

"I wish I could bring every medical student to our out-
patient clinic. Then, in the loneliness of the mob at sick-
call, these memories would race through their minds as they
do mine:

'Gentlemen, in this your fourth year of medical school, we
shall study the bacteriology of leprosy. This Biblical disease,
of course, you will never see.' (There are four in the line
this morning.)
'Gentlemen, don't worry, you will probably never have to
treat smallpox, but back in the 1800's . . .' (We had six
cases yesterday.)
'Men, modern vaccine therapy has eradicated the triple ter-
rors of infancy—diphtheria, whooping cough, and typhoid.'
(All three are regular visitors to my clinic.)
'Remember your surgical technique. Never prostitute technique, no matter how humble your operating rooms may be.'
(Last week we tried to put together a lad's face from the
ribbons of flesh that were left after he was mauled by a wild
bear, his left eye and bridge of the nose torn off.)

"The four horsemen of the Apocalypse have roamed the
land of Laos for a long time. The white horse of war has
only recently left. The red horse of strife still stomps on
the political scene. The black horse of famine is quiet now.
The pale green horse of pestilence is always with Laos. We
fight against him and frequently feel that we're losing the
battle. Sometimes, feeling overwhelmed, we ask ourselves,
'How can such a small mission be a firm buttress against
the onslaughts of disease and Communism?'

"Reassuring words came last week in a letter from Dr.
Melvin Casberg. He wrote, with uncanny timing: 'Tom, you
will face periods of abject discouragement when your efforts

will appear negligible in the face of such a tremendous task. But remember, nothing of any great consequence was accomplished by the majority. Rather, one can trace all major steps in the progress of humanity to the individual and to the minority. So keep up your courage and, as St. Paul said, *Be steadfast in faith.*' "

Tom's last letter of this first year in Laos was written on August 1, 1957. He felt that the combination of "empty cash-box and exhausted energy" demanded that he leave Laos in September. Denny Shepard had left in March, Pete Kessey in May, and Bob Waters and John deVitry returned home in August. Of the five men who worked with him up to this time, Tom said: "They served Laos and the mission well. Their many months of hard work were productive of much good, and life was not always easy for them with the not-too-patient Dooley in charge."

Tom stayed in Nam Tha long enough to effect a transfer to native hands. His relief was a young medical student who had two years of training in Cambodia. The men were replaced by two Bangkok-trained Lao nurses. Chai, the interpreter, and Si, the other Lao helper, both of whom had learned a great deal in their work, also remained. The hospital was given a charter by the Lao government, henceforth to be administered and financed by their Public Health Service. Tom donated all the medical stocks, surgical gear, generator, lights, furniture, equipment and, as he said, everything else he had "brought, built, borrowed, bought and begged." Unfortunately, the young man in charge was a source of future disappointment for Tom.

In September, on the day of his departure, hundreds of villagers gathered on the airstrip to see him off, as he walked out with Si and Chai. "I felt some guilt in leaving," he wrote, "and some pride in knowing there was now a hospital in Nam Tha. These people had become important to me. I had learned to love them." As the plane took off, the blasé French pilot from Vientiane said to Tom: *"Ils vous aiment bien."*

On his way home, Tom stopped over in Lambarene, French Equatorial Africa, to visit there at the invitation of Dr. Albert Schweitzer. "Since my earliest days in medical school," Tom wrote, "the work of Dr. Schweitzer has been one of the great inspirations of my life. To enter into correspondence with him was a great satisfaction, but the biggest thrill of all occurred when I visited the great old gentleman himself. He has sensitiveness and forcefulness at one and the same time."

In the back of Tom's head was a plan for putting his concept of a medical mission on an organized working basis, with medical teams operating throughout the world. They would be independent of government control, and financed with the help of public donations. "International medical cooperation" was the phrase he used to describe his ideas. This is precisely what the name Medico, which he founded in November of that year, means. Dr. Schweitzer was most interested in Tom's plans and promised to help him in any way he could. As he put it in a letter to Tom: "I do not know what your destiny will be, but this I know. You will always have happiness if you seek and find: *how to serve.*"

Tom returned by ship and arrived in New York on October 17. He was already in search of an administrative head for the body he envisaged, and at once arranged a meeting in Washington with Dr. Peter Comanduras. Having been in correspondence with Dr. Comanduras, who was associate professor of clinical medicine at the George Washington University Medical School, Tom felt that his thoughts on American medical aid to the rest of the world, not dependent on government control and performed by individual doctors, were very much in sympathy with his own concepts. Dr. Comanduras, Tom hoped, "had what I lacked—the experience, temperament and ability to plan and direct operations." Their meeting in Washington was a success.

The support of the International Rescue Committee, which had sponsored Operation Laos, was also of great importance to Tom. Since the I.R.C. charter did not encompass medical programs, Angier Biddle Duke called a board meeting to consider the matter. Tom's talk and the persuasiveness of Mr. Duke and Leo Cherne, chairman of the board, effected an amendment to their charter. Thus Medico was born.

The first six months of 1958 became one of the busiest and most productive periods of Tom's life. He had three big jobs going at one time—work on his second book, *The Edge of Tomorrow;* the setting up of Medico; and the planning of a whirlwind lecture tour and money-raising campaign. He also decided to return to Laos with a new team of coworkers in June and open a hospital at Muong Sing.

Medico set up its first office at 255 Fourth Avenue, near 19th Street, New York. (Their cable address appropriately was INTERESCUE.) Dr. Comanduras set out on a round-the-world tour. At Lambarene Leo Cherne saw Dr. Albert Schweitzer, who readily agreed to serve as Honorary Patron of Medico. Despite his long-standing policy of not endorsing or sponsoring projects regardless of their merit, Dr. Schweitzer said: "I endorse Medico with all my heart."

A Medical Advisory Council was formed and included such distinguished physicians as Dr. Melvin Casberg, Dr. Howard A. Rusk, Dr. Paul Dudley White, Dr. Henry L. Bockus, and Dr. Alphonse McMahon. Dr. Gordon Seagrave, the famous "Burma Surgeon" who for 35 years had worked at Namhkam, announced that he would affiliate with Medico. His mission in Burma and Tom's in Laos were Medico's first two programs-in-being.

At the press conference announcing the founding of Medico, Tom said: "Today, on the fourth of February, 1958, I feel as though I were on the verge of the longest journey I have ever taken. On this day a new organization is being founded. It will be entitled Medico, which stands for Medical International Cooperation Organization. Medico's reason for existence is simple. We wish to take care of people who are sick, in areas where they have little or no chance of receiving medical aid. We are in no way a religious or political organization. We are not trying to replace any already existing programs in the field of health. What we wish to do is a job in simple therapeutic medicine. The simplicity of Medico's program is this: we actually believe that we can win the friendship of people only by working beside them, on equal terms, humans-to-humans, towards goals that they understand and seek themselves. Medico is a person-to-person, heart-to-heart program. It will aid those who are sick and by that simple act it will win friendship for America."

It was a source of disappointment to me that after my son's death the work of Medico deviated from these original concepts. That is why the Thomas A. Dooley Foundation was established late in 1961. I consider it the *only* organization which is truly dedicated to carrying out my son's ideas according to the principles he defined over and over again. In any event, as the founder of Medico, Tom could not have stated the true aims and goals of the new organization more clearly or more simply than he did at that first press conference.

"I left the very next day to begin a lecture tour of America," he wrote, "covering all parts of the country. I spoke in high schools, in women's clubs, in medical societies. I spoke to people on trains and planes. I stayed in cheap hotels in small towns, in magnificent suites in large cities. The lecture tour consisted of 188 speeches in 79 different cities over five months."

Through the good offices of the International Rescue Committee, Medico acquired a warehouse, and soon the medicines and supplies began to pour in. Tom went to the leading pharmaceutical houses and again they demonstrated their great generosity—Chas. Pfizer & Co., Mead Johnson & Co. and Eli Lilly & Co. were especially generous, Tom reported. The A. S. Aloe Company of St. Louis supplied all the surgical equipment they needed. "Everywhere I went in America people showed their warm admiration towards our program, and backed it up with cold cash. Over six hundred doctors, corpsmen and nurses applied for our teams. I started out to raise money, men and medicine. And with the luck of the Irish and the grace of God, Medico had these three. After the tour ended, Dooley was nearly voiceless." By June, when he completed this tour, Medico had about $300,000 in cash donations and well over $1,000,000 in medicines, Tom reported.

Life magazine in March ran the first of the three articles they were to do on Tom over the next two years. Their first piece was entitled "Do-It-Yourself Samaritan" and featured a large photograph of Tom teaching the Laotian gesture of thanks to a gymnasium full of Illinois schoolchildren who had donated clothing. The caption quoted Tom as saying to them: "I'm going back to the jungle where my children don't have any clothes, nor any of the nice things you have. And you must never feel that what I do or anyone like me does was possible because I am an extraordinary person. I am not. I'm an ordinary man. This country was founded on the idea that the ordinary man can accomplish extraordinary things."

They showed a picture of Tom and me saying goodby at the door of our St. Louis apartment. They also correctly quoted me as saying: "At my age I've learned to type and become a secretary to my son. The most personal talk we have is when he comes in the door."

Tom's second book, *The Edge of Tomorrow,* was written with much less difficulty than the first, due to the expert advice of James Monhan of *Reader's Digest* and Robert Giroux, editor-in-chief of Farrar, Straus and Cudahy. Tom did most of the work on his book at the Waldorf-Astoria.

He had learned a great deal about the importance of keeping notes, and had brought back many parts of the narrative, drafted in the small hours of the night in far-off Vang Vieng and Nam Tha.

When it appeared in April, *The Edge of Tomorrow* was warmly received. Peggy Durdin reviewed it in the New York *Times* as follows: "Through anecdote and an Irish gift for the felicitous phrase he brings the reader an understanding of Laotian individuals, their ways of living, their attitudes, beliefs and superstitions—and their tragic needs, among them the need of simple, elementary medicine." William Hogan wrote in the San Francisco *Chronicle:* "The tall, good-looking, idealistic Tom Dooley emerges a kind of 'Mister Roberts' of classic tradition. He is a good guy with a good cause—and the privately financed cause is working. I think more people should know about the Dr. Dooley story. This book (proceeds of which will be plowed back into the bamboo hospital) is the place to hear about it." Harry Hansen detected a special quality in Tom's character and wrote in the Chicago *Tribune:* "His book reflects a radiant personality that must have influenced the villagers to accept him as their big brother. A man who can win over the witch doctor by convincing him both are working for the same ends is more than a practitioner."

The Edge of Tomorrow made the bestseller lists almost immediately. The condensation in the April issue of *Reader's Digest* helped to make it a bestseller, and Tom's mail at once began to swell. Before he left for Laos in June, the trade sales of the book had passed the 80,000-copy mark. Eventually, of course, the total sales were much greater than this. Again publication around the world in many foreign tongues was arranged by his publisher.

I had an unwitting part in Tom's choice of team-mates for the new mission to Laos. When the *Life* article appeared, two young men in Austin, Texas named Earl Rhine and Dwight Davis read it and thought, "This is the kind of work we want to do." Their joint letter of application reached Tom like hundreds of others but, in addition to writing, they phoned me in St. Louis and told me their story. Tom was very much impressed by their initiative in doing this. "My mother," he wrote, "has a very good sense of business about her and endorsed the boys by the sound of their voices and their go-to-itiveness." Because of their Texas address, he also asked Pete Kessey to look them up and Pete reported "they were both tops."

A week later Tom met Earl and Dwight in Houston. They were both married, both pre-med students at the University of Texas, both Air Force veterans, both working as surgical technicians at Breckenridge Hospital. In fact they had met at the hospital and become fast friends. "What Pete told me," said Tom, "plus my mother's intuitive knowledge and my own interview convinced me that these were my new crew." Tom considered their friendship one of the chief things in their favor; he would not have to find out in Laos whether they could work successfully together. They joined Tom in Hawaii in June. After a stop-over in Tokyo, the team reached Hong Kong.

In that colorful city, Tom went on a piano-hunt. The Wilson Club of Bridgeport, Connecticut, had asked him if there was anything he would like to have for his personal use and he had blithely answered, "A piano so I can have Chopin in North Laos." Their thoughtfulness resulted in the zinc-lined upright he found in a Chinese shop.

There were two more stop-overs. In Saigon they visited the An-Lac Orphanage of Mme. Ngai, and in Cambodia they stopped at the Courtyard of the Leper King in ancient Ankor Wat. After this Tom was home again in Laos.

five

the burning mountain

*I had pain in my right shoulder
and chest . . . On that particular night
I had a feeling of apprehension difficulty to describe to myself, more
difficult to explain. . . .*
—MUONG SING, MAY 1959

Soon after he reached Laos, Tom wrote me this note from
Vientiane: "Midnight, 15 September 1958—Wonderful news!
Just left the dinner given by the new Prime Minister and
other officials. They have all okayed, completely and totally,
my going to Muong Sing. Not only that, but they have
granted each and every one of my requests, even to paying
the salaries of indigenous personnel. I've located Chai (he's
now married) and Si, and found an English-speaking Lao
(really a Thai Dam) through the Bahi center here. The team
is complete, the location approved, the government behind
us. Hurrah!"

As he flew to the northern village of Muong Sing, only six
miles from the China border, Tom noted the beauty of the
landscape. There were craggy mountain peaks alternating with
the checkerboard valleys of rice paddies. Through each valley flowed a river which from the plane looked like an artery

143

of clear, cool water. From above, the view suggested a lovely Shangri-La. "It is not that at all," said Tom. "It is another unsanitary, underdeveloped Asian village, alive with sickness and disease."

He described Muong Sing as an "almost enchanted village which sleeps on the floor of the valley." Encircled on three sides by mountain peaks, the highest being 10,000 feet, with the south end of the valley open, Muong Sing lay north and west of Nam Tha, with an 8,000-foot mountain separating the two villages.

Since this was the northwestern outpost of Laos and war rumbles were already being heard, Tom was not surprised to find that their hospital site was across the road from a fortress. Tom called it a *Beau Geste* affair, built of mud and encircled by a moat. The Chao Muong or village mayor, who lived in a house next to this military encampment, showed them two dilapidated straw-mud huts nearby. "Our dispensary," he announced. Earl and Dwight, who had not seen the Nam Tha transformation, were aghast.

Hard work, perspiration, and aching backs accomplished wonders. "Perhaps our hospital at Muong Sing was unattractive, white-washed, utilitarian and ugly," wrote Tom, "but it was also a compassionate candle in the darkness. It took only a few weeks to put the clinic building in usable shape. It had three major rooms and two smaller ones. The largest central room, a long rectangle with the door at one end, was the clinic."

Across the center of the clinic stood a wooden railing, one foot high, through which the patient entered. He would sit in a chair in front of Tom, with interpreters and students on either side of him. The other patients remained behind the railing, awaiting their turns, and Tom said they always listened in on the patient's recital and even made comments like, "Oh, explain yourself better than that, Houmpenh."

Neither Tom nor the American corpsmen handed out medicine. The Lao helper would be told what was needed, locate the bottle on the supply shelf, put the correct number of capsules in a little envelope, and explain the dosage schedule to the patient. He would usually add a word of advice: "Why don't you wash your hands?" or "Why didn't you bring your child back last week as you promised?" Tom expressed the philosophy behind this method: "Asians helping Asians is better than Americans helping Asians. The Asian students will be here all their lives, I will not."

Perhaps this is what Norman Cousins meant when he wrote, after Tom's death: "Dooley was not just a doctor. He was an educator. And he knew the success of an educator was to be measured by his ability to teach others how to pass their knowledge along. According to such a yardstick, Dooley may well have been one of the most useful teachers of his time."

Dr. Carl Wiedermann, who worked with Tom in the field, spoke from experience and observation when he said: "Tom Dooley was a *good doctor*. He didn't have much time for pre-operative or post-operative care, but he was a good diagnostician and he did good therapy. He was an all-round doctor. He knew the latest treatment for malaria, for example, or the amoebic diseases. He had brushed up on his tropical medicine and other specialties. He read not only journals of general medicine but also the specialized journals. He had his books on ophthalmology, for example, and he would read them. He was always interested in acquiring new instruments . . . or the latest system for giving anesthesia. He was a good doctor, and obviously interested in his job . . . He would say: 'I am a jungle doctor and I am practicing 19th century medicine.' *But he left it up to his colleagues and associates to find out that he really was doing an excellent job under difficult conditions.* I was very much impressed." (Those italics are mine.)

Tom himself had this to say about his medical philosophy: "The powerful and sometimes immaculate dispensers of American aid believe that my philosophy is short-sighted. They claim that the villages cannot maintain what I build. I admit they perhaps cannot maintain it at my level, but I am confident they can at a lesser level, which is still superbly higher than the medical level of the area. I have had many, many visitors to my hospital from Washington. Most of them arrive with that chip on their shoulder, looking around to find the weak spots. *Among 'jungle doctors' the world over, adaptation to the environment in an effort to maintain simplicity is the keynote of survival.*" The precept which I have italicized is one that he took directly from his beloved mentor, Dr. Albert Schweitzer. Another well-known Dooleyism on this subject goes as follows:

In America doctors run 20th century hospitals. In Asia I run a 19th century hospital. Upon my departure the hospital may drop to the 18th century. This is fine, because previously the tribes in the high valleys lived, medically speaking, in the 15th century.

Meanwhile Tom's work in Muong Sing was proceeding on schedule. "All here is going excellently," he wrote, "now that we are finally at full speed. The sick-call now hits 100, and we have had a sprinkling of gunshot wounds from the border. There is raiding going on to our northwest. The boys are working out splendidly, fine surgical technicians who also know the honor and drudgery of manual work. Your judgment was superb. Chai's hepatitis is clearing up, and Si is wearing the same hat you sent him years ago, still without starch."

I found it rather interesting to receive news, by way of Laos, of Medico's money-raising campaigns in America, such as this: "A fashion show in New York City last week, under the leadership of Anna Matson, brought in $4,000. The former Dooley fan clubs, now called the Medi-Corps, also brought in over $4,000 during the past few months. We approached Adlai Stevenson, for whom I have much admiration, and he signed a fund-raising letter which has brought in almost $50,000 to date. In the fall we shall have another series of letters going out. Senator Kennedy has agreed to speak at a dinner in my honor in Boston this fall, if we can work it out. I'm sorry I can't be there."

The Edge of Tomorrow continued to receive notices in all parts of America and it was selling very well. "The overall press has been superb," Tom wrote in September, "and the constancy of book sales is creating much interest in Medico. The success of my work and my book is remarkable to me. I am surrounded by dear friends, well-wishers, and admirers. I have security, sanity, and faith. My health has been good. I think I owe gratitude to God."

In early December his hospital had a medical visitor: "We have a delightfully quiet, easy-going young American Baptist missionary doctor, who works at a fine modern hospital in Thailand. He wrote months ago and asked if he could spend some time with us and do surgery while here. He is an ideal guest. He is neat and keeps things in place (essential when a dozen people live in three little rooms) and his services are first-rate. His only flattering comment so far, to one of the crew: 'When I go back to Thailand I shall have to tell people that this young Dooley is not what he is reputed to be, he's better.' "

Around this time Tom received a copy of the New York Times *Book Review* of November 30, 1958. It contained a Christmas list of the 250 outstanding books published during the past year. "Under the heading 'World Affairs' there are only 26 books," he wrote, "including Thomas Finletter, Dean Acheson, George F. Kennan, and believe it or not, Dooley. To my mind this is quite an honor."

On December 24, 1958 he was writing this letter at dawn: "The sun has just come up on the day before the night before Christmas. It is really the day *of* the night. I dreamt last night of the wonderful Christmases of old, with the huge trees, the big cardboard Santa Claus, and the wonderful family life I have always had. We are planning a little *baci* or banquet for the Lao nurses and have three bottles of champagne to drink out of coffee cups. So we shall have at least half a day's vacation. (People get sick on Christmas too.) I have already recorded my Christmas message which KMOX will broadcast from St. Louis."

In his broadcast message he said: "From Africa, England, Sweden, India, Taipai, Viet Nam, Indonesia, and from all over America we have received Christmas cards this year. These cards have all come to the mountain valley of Muong Sing and they all bespeak a great unity—a unity of all races and all faiths. There is a unity of Protestant, Jew, Catholic, Mohammedan, and Buddhist. They all unite in this spirit of the brotherhood of man which exists as certainly as the Fatherhood of God. Christmas of 1958 reminds us that the challenge of our era is the godlessness of Communism. The keynote of 1959 must be to seek more ways on a worldwide basis to serve with courage and love the humanity of man."

In February he and his crew decided to make a river trip to some of the outlying villages where misery and sickness were rampant. They had heard radio reports of border infiltrations and skirmishes, but they felt they should make the trip despite them. Tom described one little hamlet, Ban Saly. Located on the Nam Tha River, it consisted of 100 people "of whom 80 per cent were at sick-call in the morning. Real illnesses—malaria, tuberculosis, pneumonia, hookworm, anemia, and always malnutrition. The people of Laos are not a carefree, happy people. They laugh and smile, but they suffer. Their existence is eked out with great effort."

On the eleventh day of "this journey into wretchedness, misery, stink, and poverty," they reached the confluence of

the Nam Tha and Mekong Rivers. Here they had to pole
upriver, as they wished to reach the village of Ban Houei Sai.
At the end of the first day of poling, they were exhausted
and stopped at the riverside overnight. As Tom and Chai began to climb up the slope, Tom tripped and lost his balance.
Head over heels he fell, gashing his head and badly hurting
his chest. He described it as follows:

When I hit bottom, I had to lie doubled up to get my
breath. Chai came down to my side and asked if I were all
right. I told him I had badly skinned and bruised the right
side of my chest wall, just below the shoulder. I had tripped
on the lace of my boot, plunging headlong down this 25-foot
drop, bouncing my rib-cage off a few of the rocks. I was
really sore.
I did not of course realize it, but that fall was to become
a pivotal point in my life.

Soon after their return to Muong Sing, a little boy of
seven named Tao Koo was brought to the hospital by his
father. The terrified man explained that a month earlier his
son had had a scorching fever, the village witch-doctor had
treated him with baboon's blood, and the child had developed
a sore. Soon this spread until all the flesh of his lower back
and buttocks was ulcerated. In addition the boy had diarrhea
and the constant soilage worsened his condition. By the time
he arrived at Muong Sing, he was shrunken and withered,
a mere shadow of a child.
Earl Rhine and Dwight Davis took him to their hearts,
washed him with tenderness and care, and dressed his sores,
but the child was too sick to respond. In the few days of
sunlight left before the monsoons, they took his bed outside, draped it in a mosquito net and let him lie in the sun.
The dressings were removed and the sores aired. After a week,
Tao Koo's eyes began to brighten a little. The boys tied bal-
loons on the crossbars of his bed, gave him a color book
and a toy rabbit that squeaked. They taught his father how
to bathe him and tend him without injuring what good tissue
was left on his bones. Earl and Dwight even devised a rig so
that his incontinence would not soil everything. The little
boy once again began to live; he no longer whimpered and
even smiled. His skeleton began to pick up weight, his sores
began to close, and soon he was one of the happiest and
cleanest boys in Asia.
Tom watched all this. He had done nothing, Earl and

Dwight everything, but he was as happy as they for he knew he had created the conditions which made it possible for them to do something. "At such moments," he wrote, "I remembered just why we were here. Maybe the dream of Anne Frank is closer than we know: 'Things will change and men become good again and these pitiless days will come to an end and the world will once more know order, rest and peace.' "

Not long afterwards Tom had a strange experience. It occurred on the night they burned the mountain. Tom was not aware of the Lao custom of preparing for the great rice planting season, when the dry spell had reached its peak before the rains came, by burning the arid mountain slopes. At that time he and his team were under attack by Radio Hanoi, which denounced them as foreign spies and accused them of shipping guns to the renegade KMT soldiers. In May the war scare was worse than ever, and on some nights they could hear gun-fire in distant hills.

Tom felt that the approaching rainy season would make it difficult to fight. "I had a vague, uncomfortable feeling," he wrote. "I was not especially worried about the war, yet on the other hand I feared the poison of China flowing into our valley. I had a pain in my right shoulder and chest, dating from my fall of several months before. The pain had never eased; in fact, several times I sneaked over to the hospital and took some codein."

On this night he was sitting at the table before the typewriter, stacks of mail around him. Earl and Dwight were asleep in the bedroom. "I was writing to my family and friends in America, but more than ever they seemed distant to me now. On that particular night I had a feeling of apprehension difficult to describe to myself, more difficult to explain.

"The night seemed noisier. I had a sensation of activity outside the house, so I took a flashlight and walked out on our front porch. The mountains all around us seemed covered by swarms of lightning bugs. As I looked at these blinking, flickering lights moving in all directions, I thought to myself. 'Almost like Japanese lanterns in a parade.'

"Suddenly as I watched I saw one whole section of the mountain catch on fire. Then more fire. And more fire. Almost in a flash the whole mountain slope burst into a blinding glare of yellow flames. I walked out to the field across from our house and a whole panorama opened up

—the slopes to my south, north, and east were also aflame. Huge billows of clouds were spreading up towards the sky.

"Oppressive rolls of heat poured down into our valley. I had an almost terrifying feeling. Were the Communists burning the jungle down, aiming at the complete annihilation of Muong Sing? Just weeks ago they had destroyed a village only a few miles away, in retaliation for the villagers taking refugees from China into their huts. Was this another atrocity?

"In a few minutes Earl and Dwight, awakened by the heat, ran to the porch and looked with amazement at the sky and the night on fire. The whole forest covering the mountains around us was alive with flames. In the bottom of the bowl of the Muong Sing valley it seemed as though all three sides of us were blazing, the yellow flames licking at the clear sky, the smoke rolling higher and higher.

"Ngoan came out, looked at the mountain slope, then looked at us, and said, 'Do not fear, this is the night they burn the mountain.' For the mountain tribes the last week of the Duong Pet is a time of great work. The village sorcerers and astrologists choose the most felicitous night, and the people light their bamboo torches and go up into the mountains. These slopes burn for several days, and then the rains come and make rich, fertilized soil. In this they plant their rice roots, and from the seedlings they get mountain rice, inferior to paddy rice, but rice.

"We watched the mountain burn for many hours. The strange vague foreboding feeling that I had had in the house seemed all the stronger now, though perhaps it should not have been. What would become of these mountains and these tribes? What would happen to Laos—would the flames of communism conquer it and the flames of disease destroy its people? Would there ever be another free May?

"In spite of the heat and roaring flames, I went to bed. I slept until dawn came over the scorched mountains. It seemed as though the astrologers were right: only a few days later Nyam Fon (season of rains and monsoons) came."

Soon after the rains came, Tom flew to Vientiane as the first leg in a trip to Phnom Penh, the capital of Cambodia, where Dr. Emmanuel Voulgaropoulos headed the Medico mission. "Manny's hospital," said Tom, "comes closer to the realization of my dream of Medico than any other, with the small hospital in Kenya second." He was proud of Medico's surgical programs in Jordan and Viet Nam, eye programs in Hong Kong, dental programs in Africa, "but closest to my heart is a village team such as Manny's." He reported that Manny, who had recently married, "was doing a wonderful job, and the touch of a woman was very easy to see—curtains on the window, flowers in the vases, a little study fixed up over the main clinic. Maybe there is something in this connubial bliss."

On his return to Muong Sing, Tom came down with malaria. After twenty-four hours in bed, the fever and chills stopped. He felt tremendously exhausted, yet he was able and glad to go back to work. During the month of June, the pain in his chest increased. A lump on his upper chest had grown from the size of a pea to that of a golf ball. His arm ached so badly that he no longer played the piano at night. One day, driving the jeep "Teresa" with Chai, he had to ask him to massage his neck and back because it hurt so to keep his arm lifted. He had visited Hank Miller in Vientiane one day and Hank had noticed the lump and asked about it. Tom jokingly said, "Don't worry, Hank, it's just cancer of the lung."

In July an old friend of Tom's from California, Dr. William Van Valin, arrived in Muong Sing. Tom asked Dr. Van to look at his chest, which was now causing him quite a good deal of pain. Dr. Van examined it and suggested surgery, agreeing with Tom's preoperative diagnosis of a rapidly growing sebaceous cyst. When the operation was finished and the tumor removed, Tom saw that it was black. "There is only one tumor that is black," he wrote later, "but I was not in the least concerned that this was melanoma, believing the tumor had something to do with my fall and was perhaps a calcified blood clot. Dr. Van was very insistent that the tumor be taken to a hospital in Bangkok for analysis. I dismissed the thought of cancer from my mind, and plunged into work."

Following the operation, after a night of sleep with drugs, Tom was awakened a little after dawn. A villager had come to ask him to do "the work I was put on this earth to do." The caller took Tom to a neighboring village to see "one of the most wretched humans I had ever seen." This man had a severe infection of the lungs and was dehydrated; an opium gourd lay at his side. Tom did not expect him to survive the thirty-minute drive back to Muong Sing. He began to respond to treatment after four days, only to beg for his opium pipe. He was a hopeless addict. On the fifth day they found him dead in bed. This loss of a patient beyond help depressed Tom very much. He knew he had done everything humanly possible, but a death at this moment plunged him in gloom.

In July the Communists attacked Phong Saly, and the bright young Lao commander of the fortress across from the hospital informed Tom that there was a build-up of Chinese troops on the Yunan border to their north. Tom and his men discussed what they would do in an emergency. Abandoning the hospital would be difficult, destroying it they would not even consider. In early August, while Earl was in Vientiane for supplies and Dwight in Cambodia at the Medico hospital, Tom received a letter from Ambassador Horace Smith: "I urge you to consider carefully the desirability of evacuating immediately your assistants and yourself at least temporarily to a place of safety such as Vientiane, until the situation is clarified."

Tom thanked the Ambassador for his consideration and advice, but said he thought that his duty was with the hospital. If there were sick and wounded in Muong Sing, he felt as a doctor it was his obligation to be there to help them. Earl returned and concurred in this decision completely. Then Dwight arrived from Cambodia, accompanied by Tom's good friend, Bob Burns, and Dr. John Keshishian. The plane in which they arrived brought along a good deal of mail, much of it trivial, and all of it reflecting the fact that the writers were utterly unaware of the dangerous situation in Laos. Tom was in a grim and angry frame of mind, with so much outer and inner darkness around him. That night he sat down and wrote me a long letter which I quote in part: "I am a doctor. This is the root of me—I am a doctor. Everything else, everyone, is second to that. First, I am a doctor. All my duties are entwined with that and they are clear and lucid. Everything else is second. Home life, social life, writing life, living life, loving life, family, friends, romance, fame, fortune, all these are secondary, because I am a doctor. Perhaps I take this too much to heart. It was a hard and humiliating fight for me to become a doctor. I want Ambassadors to stop thinking of me as an international figure and a threat to the tranquility of their post. I want publishers to stop thinking of me as a hand that holds a conversation with a typewriter, while a piece of paper listens in. I want broadcasting systems to stop thinking of me as a correspondent and stop sending me telegrams asking for my opinions of the news. I want people who write me for my autograph to stop writing. I do not care whether the American Economic Mission considers me annoyingly autonomous or not. Perhaps I am ranting and raving, but this is how I feel.

"It is very late, close to three in the morning, and everyone is asleep in the house. Even the frogs and insects of the jungle seem quiet tonight. Through the screen doors I can see tonight's moon. It is a lurid moon looking down on grisly things. Hundreds of dead in the north, major villages fallen to the Reds, a build-up of troops only a few miles away from us. Young men and women beheaded with their heads stuck on posts along the runway. The whole of the north suffering, crying, full of sadness. No wonder everything is quiet tonight. They are sad, soundlessly.

"Later. The dawn came today wild and fiery. There was a turbulence of cloud and wind and rain. And then almost miraculously (and I expect miracles here all the time) the thunder stopped and the lightning no longer staggered across the sky and the whole valley fell into unearthly silence. We all noticed the noise of the silence. But then by noon the windless skies again grew disturbed and the sound of thunder was distant. Or was it the sound of guns? We are never sure. The noise rolled and crashed overhead, and the skies streaked with lightning and opened up and once again flooded our Valley. Dr. Keshishian is overwhelmed by the rains. Bob Burns is amazed at the downpour. I am scared. Scared."

At noon on Saturday, August 15, Tom was notified by a Lao soldier that there was a telegram for him at the radio-shack in the fortress. When he and the team finally made out the scrambled message, it read: "FROM PETER COMAN-DURAS—DOCTOR DOOLEY, URGENT RETURN TO UNITED STATES IMMEDIATELY." Tom was bewildered by this request, but he heeded it and at once headed for home. It was when he reached Bangkok and ran into Hank and Annie Miller that he learned the truth. The tumor that Dr. Valin had removed from him had been diagnosed as a secondary stage of malignant melanoma. Tom wrote:

"I tried to think with detachment. I tried to think objectively about illness and cancer. All I could think about was the statistic I had studied in med school, 'Only about 50% of people who have a malignant melanoma in the metastatic or second stage survive a year. Less than 30% live two years.' Yet I knew I was not going to abandon what I think is the correct thing to do in life because of shadows on a page. Nor was I going to quit this living, loving passion for life that I possess simply because of a statistic. I was not abandoning the beauty and tenderness that man can give to man, just for a statistic."

MALCOLM DOOLEY:

For the last ten days of August, 1959 my wife and I rented a cottage at Roules Beach on Lake Huron. On the Thursday before our weekend departure, the phone rang around seven in the evening. It was Tom. Immediately I said what a good connection we had; I thought he was calling from Bangkok. Tom interrupted to say he was at Idlewild. His voice was as usual clear, crisp and firm, but when he went on to tell me he had cancer, and then tried to tell me how it was discovered and what might happen to him now, his manner changed and he seemed overwhelmed by the seriousness of his fate. I was stunned by the news. As I remember, I merely said I would be there right away, adding that I supposed he would be at the Waldorf. He said, "Yes." Without excitement and with little conversation, Gay packed a bag while I got ready to drive to the airport.

That August night the air was chilly as I drove forty miles from Royal Oak, Michigan to Willow Run Airport. Thoughts, fears, memories, prayers raced through my mind as I drove. I didn't know much about cancer, but I did know Tom and I was alarmed because he had said, "I'm scared." His doctor's knowledge of disease should have removed fear, unless. . . .

I thought of the phone call. Had I said the right thing to Tom? Was my voice encouraging? I had had so many calls from Tom from far-off and unlikely places over the years. Sometimes he called about things he urgently needed in his work. Often he called to ask about Mother's health and happiness. At times he called merely because he knew how it thrilled Gay to hear the operator's "Hong Kong calling," or Bangkok or Tokyo or Honolulu. His calls usually came very late at night, when the Far East circuits were open. It got to be a family joke when the phone rang after midnight. And to outsiders our conversations would have sounded crazy: "Gay, Uncle Tom wants to know if you're pregnant, and if not, why not? Do you think little Maureen would like a beaded sweater? Why did we name our second boy Michael?"

Some time back this matter of names had almost developed

into a crisis. I had explained to Tom that he might some day get married, and who was I to steal his name and Dad's for a boy of mine? That's why my second son's name was Michael; we couldn't have two Thomas Anthony Dooley IV's running around. Tom accepted this and called a few months later to tell me I was forgiven, that he did not plan on getting married, and if we had another son ... Eleven and a half months later, Gay obliged by giving birth to our third son, who was christened Thomas Anthony Dooley IV.

When I reached Willow Run Airport and inquired about the next New York flight, there was a plane leaving in five minutes with space available. With the help of a good tail wind, I arrived at La Guardia one hour and fifty minutes later. Thirty-five minutes more, and I opened the door of Tom's room at the Waldorf. The lapsed time between Tom's call to me in Detroit and my arrival was less than five hours. To me it seemed five weeks.

We sat up and talked most of that night. I did the listening, Tom the talking. I felt very old, and Tom appeared very young. I knew that all his confidence would return if he could relieve himself vocally of his fears. And I marveled to see a man with a deep-rooted love of God and fellow-man come to grips with fears of the unknown. He called on the strength of his faith to lift himself back to his normal self-confidence and self-assurance. I knew he had found peace of soul when he said, "It's all in God's hands now. Let's get some sleep."

The next day Tom held a press conference at the Overseas Press Club in New York. He told the reporters that he had cancer, that there would be an operation, and that he would return to Laos. He spoke of his future with the assurance of a movie producer outlining a shooting schedule. The members of the press were spellbound by his confidence. One writer even criticized him for this confidence and asked: "How could a man about to undergo a cancer operation make announcements of his future plans?" If he had the faith of Dr. Tom Dooley, he could.

Tom and Malcolm phoned me in St. Louis from the Waldorf. I had no idea Tom was back in this country, and I was so happy and relieved to hear his voice. I had been following the war news in Laos with a heartsick feeling. It was terrible to read about the border incidents in the north, so near to Muong Sing. The thought that communist troops might take

the village and kill or imprison Tom terrified me; I could
not sleep at night. And now I heard his voice:

"Hello, Mother. This is Tom. I am in New York. Yes,
I'm all right but have come home because I have to have
some surgery."

I was so relieved to know that Tom was no longer in
northern Laos that his words about surgery made no impression on me. I was so happy that I almost broke down, and
Tom thought I was reacting to the news of his illness.

"Mother, are you all right?" he asked. "Do you understand
me? I am in New York."

"Yes, son. I know you are in New York and I'm so glad.
I was so afraid you would be taken by the communists and
tortured. The war news has been terrible. I have been so
worried about you and slept so little."

Tom then told me he would fly to St. Louis the next day,
and again my happiness was so great that his next remark
did not register. "Mother, I have just discovered that I have
a tumor which is believed to be malignant. Do you understand me, Mother?"

"Yes, I understand, dear. You have a tumor that may be
malignant. Well, take good care of yourself, dear. I'll be at
the airport to meet you."

It was not until I read the news in the papers next morning that I fully realized the seriousness of what he had said.
A few years earlier Tom had had some minor surgery on
his legs, and I thought that this must be something similar.
Uppermost in my mind was the thought that, no matter what
his illness might be, my son was home. I felt that now he
would get excellent medical care, which would make him
well again.

The following day Tom arrived in St. Louis. His own
words describe our meeting better than any words of mine
can: "I had to see my mother and explain to her in person
the truth of the cancer that I faced. Mother met me at the
airport and soon I was home again. From her strength I was
able to derive much. She had been through a great deal of
unhappiness in her life, and had a staunch way of taking all
this, though I knew it was so terrible for her. At Mass the
next morning, in the same Cathedral that I had known since
childhood, I prayed to the same God to Whom I had prayed
all around the world. I had some peace but little solace."
Late Sunday evening Tom returned to New York and on the

next afternoon, August 24, 1959, he entered Memorial Hospital on East 68th Street.

At the request of CBS Television and the American Cancer Society, my son consented to a TV documentary of his operation, in the interests of medicine and public education. Tom knew there was a great deal of misinformation and misapprehension about cancer, and once again he was performing his role as educator, except that this time he himself was the object-lesson.

On *Biography of a Cancer,* as the televised film was called, Tom said: "The very minute Americans hear the word cancer, they picture gloom, doom and death. This makes people crippled before they even get crippled ... Maybe, in a small way, people who watch this show and who know I've got this, will not fear the word 'cancer' as much as they have."

Interviewer Howard K. Smith asked him on TV what his feelings were about the operation. "Well, it's a perfectly natural reaction to have a certain amount of apprehension before you get carved on—doubly so if you're a doctor," he said. "But on the other hand I have a great deal of faith and confidence in the people who are taking care of me."

"Well, what about the future?" asked Mr. Smith.

"I plan to go back to Laos. I want to get another clinic going. I hope to get a small airplane from somebody and use this to set up a clinic in a village called Ban Houei Sai. I've got so much to do right now that I'm not particularly thinking about any length of time. Some people may say, 'Well, Dooley, you've got a year to go—you'd better hurry.' Or they may say, 'Dooley, you've got five years to go.' I don't know. I'm just going to live like I was told long ago—live as though you're going to die tomorrow. I'm not bleak about it, nor do I feel particularly blithe about it. I realize my case is serious, but I also realize that the doctors are doing a pretty tremendous job, and with the luck of the Irish and by the grace of God, I'll make it O.K."

On the morning of the principal operation, the priest came early to bring him Holy Communion. "After this," Tom wrote, "I had a few moments of thanksgiving and felt serener, safer, stronger. I was in His hands now, wholly, and in resignation. Peace of soul and body flooded over me, a deep, warm, quiet peace. I was ready."

On TV the masked surgeon looked up from Tom's chest and said: "I've felt a great deal of pity for this young guy. He has a malignant disease. He knows it. And he's been trying to act as though it didn't bother him in the slightest. This, for a physician, is a most trying and almost impossible feat. Today, for the first time, he admitted that he was beginning to be worried a little bit, and I told him I was very happy that he was appearing so normal."

Many hours after the operation Tom began to emerge from the haze of anesthesia. "When I was wheeled to my room," he wrote, "I remember seeing Mother, and her warm love gave me much confidence. Then came the slow recovering of consciousness, of focusing on objects in the room. I remember the tightness in my chest and the raw soreness in my legs. I knew that these were normal post-operative pains. I was determined to take no morphine shots for pain."

The operation was performed on August 27th. On Saturday the 30th Tom was wide awake, sitting up in bed. He was allowed visitors, and among the first was Clare Murphy of the Surgeon General's office. "On Saturday," wrote Clare, "I found him sitting up in bed, and on Sunday when I left he walked to the elevator with me. He said to the girl at the desk, 'Nurse, I'm checking out!' She looked startled, and when she saw the bathrobe and pajamas, she laughed. Sick or well, Tom Dooley was never dull."

Now the mail began to pour in from all around the world, wishing Tom good luck and the blessings of God. "I had no idea what a personal shock my cancer was to so many people all over the world," Tom wrote. "A lady in Ecuador said she was praying for me; Carmelite nuns in Texas offered up the litany; Hindu prayers were said in Delhi; from Korea some villagers sent me a lovely scroll with the Beatitudes in Korean; an elevator operator wrote that he heard conversations in which I was mentioned many times. What a wonderful way to learn that people are rooting for you—on elevators!"

The Womack children of Fort Worth composed new words to the tune "Hang Down Your Head, Tom Dooley," and sent them to Tom:

> *Lift up your heart, Tom Dooley,*
> *Your work will never die.*
> *You taught us to love our neighbor*
> *And not just to pass him by.*

> *We'll pray for you, Tom Dooley,*
> *Your cure and your patients' too.*

> *We'll send in our dimes and dollars*
> *For work that's left to do.*

> *Lift up your head, Tom Dooley,*
> *Lift up your head, don't cry,*
> *Lift up your head, Tom Dooley,*
> *'Cause you ain't agoin to die.*

Among the letters there was a long report from the team at Muong Sing. Dwight Davis wrote: "We are sure that you remember the man who used to come here with his little 12-year-old blind boy. Well, the man came back not long ago, bringing his blind son with him. He said he wanted to stay here with us for a while and try to kick the opium habit ... He does try to do some work and he really is slowing down on the *ya fin.*" The clinic had made a pet of a little blind gibbon, and the blind boy and the gibbon took to each other. "It was a tragic and yet beautiful thing to see the two of them playing together," wrote Dwight.

While Tom was in the hospital, he accepted advice which suggested separating Medico from the International Rescue Committee. It seemed to him that he was separating something direct, personal, and still small (Medico) from something larger. He thought then that Medico would go back to the simple beginnings he had always envisaged.

On September 4 Tom had a talk with his surgeon as the CBS cameras filmed the final scenes of *Biography of a Cancer.* The surgeon said:

"Tom, I have some good news for you. The report from the Pathology Department indicates that there is absolutely no evidence of this disease anywhere in the tissues that I removed in operation."

"If a primary cancer like this is cut out, as full and well as this has been cut out, and if everything comes out negative, then there's no sense in even thinking about living one year or two years or five years or ten years. I should just go ahead and continue living each day, is that it?"

"Just as you always have, Tom. I think that's always been your policy, hasn't it?"

Tom nodded as he replied: "Walt Whitman, I think, said that it's not important what you do with the *years* of your life, but it's very important how you use each *hour.* That's how I'll live."

On the eve of Labor Day Teresa Gallagher, Tom's devoted associate and our good friend, helped him move to the Waldorf. "We cleared out Room 910," Teresa wrote, "and stacked Tom's baggage and books on a couple of hand trucks. We came out of Memorial lugging two bronze busts by Leo Cherne—one of Dr. Schweitzer and the other of Lincoln. Tom had his arm in a black sling. He was very thin but he looked so much better than when he first went into the hospital. He seemed full of drive, alertness, determination, hope. There was no sign of illness."

A worldwide crusade of prayer for Tom's recovery had begun on the day he entered the hospital. Since it lasted twelve days, it happened to end on Labor Day, the day after he left Memorial. In St. Patrick's Cathedral, daily Mass was said for Tom's intention throughout this period at the altar of the Little Flower. Tom knew prayers were being said in convents, monasteries, churches and homes all over the world, so he decided to add his own prayers of thanksgiving. He tore over to St. Patrick's just in time for the final Mass of the series, and when the people present saw him entering the pew (he was not wearing his jacket because of the sling), there was amazement and delight at the sight of the man for whose recovery they were praying.

Teresa helped Tom get settled at the Waldorf, with the aid of another of our good friends, Ann Walsh. Soon after this Tom persuaded James E. McGurk of Metropolitan Life to give Teresa a three months' leave of absence to work for him at Medico.

The amount of energy which Tom expended in the months following his release from the hospital impressed everyone. One of the things which helped him to conserve his energy was the gift of a Soundscriber, or battery-run dictaphone, which Teresa and some of the people at Metropolitan Life got for him. He took it to Hawaii, where he worked on his last book, *The Night They Burned the Mountain*, and it accompanied him to Laos and everywhere else to the end.

In October Tom started a barnstorming and money-raising tour for Medico, with the superb help of Bob Copenhaver of the press department of Mutual of Omaha. Tom had learned from Dr. Charles Mayo, who headed the board of judges, that in November the $10,000 Criss Award from Mutual of Omaha was to go to him. He was so grateful for Bob Copenhaver's help on the tour that he asked Mr. V. J. Skutt, the president, if he could swap the award money for Bob's services. Of course, he got both. Mr. Monahan's account in *Before I Sleep* of the three-day fiesta in Omaha, when Tom received the Criss Award, is accurate in spirit and in detail. I had never seen Tom so sparkling and happy. He thoughtfully took time to introduce Emily Rhine and Esperanza Davis whose husbands, Earl and Dwight, were far off in Laos running the clinic at Muong Sing.

In St. Louis the Jaycees (Junior Chamber of Commerce), one of Tom's favorite groups, raised more than $18,000 for the airplane Tom had pleaded for while he was in Memorial Hospital. This was the evening when Tom brought together Prince Souphan of Laos and the Kingston Trio. He told us about it in one of his broadcasts over KMOX:

"When the Jaycees had that dinner in St. Louis, one of my guests was Prince Souphan of Laos, whose grandfather the King gave me the Order of a Million Elephants and the White Parasol. The Prince is 24 years old, but he looks 16 and he is enchanted with everything about America. Crawford King went to the airport to meet him and Pradith, who speaks excellent English, and Dr. Thonbphet. At the banquet, which was wonderful, they met everybody and had a good time, and around midnight we all said good-night and they went up to their suite.

"Then Bob Copenhaver and Crawfie King and I 'snuk' away. You know, I've been on this lecture tour giving an awful lot of speeches in an awful lot of cities and going to an awful lot of banquets, and I very seldom have a chance to get away and have a beer and relax and go to a movie. This particular night I wanted to do something, and Crawf and Bob and I ducked out at 12:30 and went over to the Chase Club to hear the Kingston Trio. I don't have to tell you the song that made the Kingston Trio great—'Hang Down Your Head, Tom Dooley.' Mother doesn't like the song; in fact, she had her phone number changed because of the song. I didn't like it at first, but it did much good for Medico and my kids, because it helped people to remember my name and send us donations.

"The Kingston Trio had done a service to Tom Dooley and Medico and my kids and I wanted to thank them. We went over to the Chase Club, and met them, and had a lot of fun talking. I told them about the little prince and how excited he was to be in St. Louis and they said, 'It's a shame we can't meet him,' and I said, 'Well, let's go.' So at three o'clock in the morning we went to the hotel, the royal party came into the living room in their pajamas, and I said, 'I have something for you.' And in came the Kingston Trio with banjo, guitar, bass fiddle and the works. Well, everybody was delighted. The Trio sang everything from *Mexicali Rose* to cowboy music, and the barefoot Prince in his pajamas was tapping his foot and clapping his hands with every beat, and thoroughly enjoying it."

When people ask me if I consider Tom's behavior at this period unusual, I reply that it is exactly as he behaved all his life whenever he was happy and in good spirits. This was fun for Tom, and it provided release for the tremendous energy he possessed. They are actions typical of a *young* man. Roger Straus, Tom's publisher, had an experience of this kind in the period immediately following Tom's operation.

"The Lotos Club of New York had a stag dinner for members and their guest in late September of 1959," Mr. Straus wrote, "and to my surprise Tom accepted their invitation to speak. I was rather worried, since he had not been out of the hospital very long. When he arrived at the club, I thought he looked well and had good color, although he was somewhat thinner. As I went to shake hands, he put out his left hand, and said, 'I'm still bandaged up and I have to be careful about my right side.' I noticed later, when he was speaking at the lectern, he leaned on his left arm as if to relieve pressure on his right side. However, he spoke so compellingly and persuasively about the situation in southeast Asia, his work in Laos, and his plans for Medico that I soon forgot about his health altogether. As he talked in his rapid and brisk manner, his audience listened with rapt attention. (Incidentally, one listener made out a check for one thousand dollars to Medico on the spot.) It was impossible to connect this brilliant and vital speaker with the cancer patient who had entered Memorial Hospital. He seemed more like the young Navy officer back from Viet Nam whom Jim Monahan of *Reader's Digest* sent to my office late in 1955 to discuss his first book.

"It was well after eleven when the dinner talk ended. I was worried about the drain on Tom's energy, and Bob Giroux, his editor, and I were anxious to get him back to the Waldorf at once. As we got in the cab, he leaned back and said, 'Do you know what I feel like doing? I'd like to go to

"21." ' And that's where we went. At '21' Tom wouldn't sit down, insisted on standing at the bar, and his humor and wit made him the liveliest member of the party. When we dropped him off at the Waldorf, he looked as fresh as when he arrived at the Lotos Club. Dr. Tom Dooley had some inner source of strength that made his thirty-odd years count for twice their span."

At the end of his speaking tour with Bob Copenhaver, Tom had made 49 speeches in 37 cities and raised almost one million dollars for Medico. Now he was ready to return to Laos.

On Christmas Day my son received a wonderful welcome as his plane landed at Muong Sing. He was greeted at the airport by Earl Rhine, Dwight Davis, the mayor, the chief of police, and a crowd of villagers. "Everything is just as I left it," he wrote. "There are 26 patients in the ward, and the clinic looks neat and clean—everything shipshape. The boys have done a magnificent job. Chai, Si and Oy and the others are still here, all except La who has been drafted into the army."

Earl Rhine thought Tom looked wonderful. "The same old Doc, thinner perhaps, and you could tell he was having trouble with that right arm from the way he held it. But his color was good and he was in the best of spirits." After dinner Tom passed out the presents he had brought—sweaters for the girls, colored shirts for Chai, Si and Oy, pencils, pocket combs and knives for the Lao students, and a fine stethoscope for the chief Lao nurse with her name spelled out in beads. Earl and Dwight presented Tom with a specially-made piano foot-rest, because there was a dip in the floor near the pedal about which Tom complained. There were also 160 individually wrapped gifts for the children of Muong Sing, who filed into the dining-room one by one to receive games, bags of marbles and modeling clay. Tom explained each gift as he presented it, usually ending up with, "Don't eat!"

Late that month the Gallup pole listed the world's ten most admired men, and my son was named along with Churchill, Eisenhower and John XXIII. On New Year's Day he wrote: "It's a wonderful honor to find I am the world's seventh most admired man, but it is equally frightening." He added: "I feel OK, but I definitely do not have the old bounce. This year, strangely enough, I haven't the slightest desire to ring out the old, ring in the new. All love to you, Mother."

On January 18 he wrote from Muong Sing: "I am here and working at the clinic. The plane is lovely indeed, so fast and smooth, and what a convenience to leave *when* I want. I see I am not the only one picking up accolades [late in 1959 I was chosen 'Mother of the Year']. Of course you know that you possess in large part *all* my medals, honors, degrees, decorations, and awards. Never forget that. My next letters will have to be short because it hurts me to type. All other mail I'll dictate on my machine to Teresa, who will send them from New York."

The day on which Tom wrote this letter marked the beginning of the last year of his life. I think he foresaw his final year in the dream he related near the end of *The Night They Burned the Mountain:*

"The month of my dream must have been May (Mary's month), the time of lilacs at my beloved Notre Dame. But in Laos May is a time when the season is driest. These are the nights that they burn the mountain. The mountain in my dream was burned, and now they were planting the new life into the near dead soil. I dreamed this clearly and when the blue turquoise of morning came, though perhaps neither ear could hear nor tongue could tell, I knew the meaning of my dream.

"From my hospital bed in New York, with the same white light of revelation I had known once several years before, I saw what I must do. After Communion that morning, Tuesday, the first of September, 1959, my God and my dream commanded me. I must, into the burnt soil of my personal mountain of sadness, plant the new seedlings of my life—I must continue to live. I must cultivate my fields of food, to feed those who cannot feed themselves.

"The concept came to me as strongly and as powerfully as if a peal of bronze bells proclaimed it. There was no more self-sadness, no darkness deep inside, no gritty annoyance at anyone or anything. No anger at God for my cancer, no hostility to anyone. I was out of the fog of confusion—standing under the clear light of duty.

"The jagged, ugly cancer scar went no deeper than my flesh. There was no cancer in my spirit. The Lord saw to that. I would keep my appetite for fruitful activity and for a high quality of life. Whatever time was left, whether it was a year or a decade, would be more than just a duration. I would continue to help the clots and clusters of withered and wretched in Asia to the utmost of my ability. The words of Camus rang through, 'In the midst of winter I suddenly found that there was in me an invincible summer.'

"Maybe I could now be tender in a better way. I was a member of the fellowship of those who bear the mark of pain."

six

promises to keep

The Lord is showing me that my time in Asia is up.

My son died on January 18, 1961. The number of things he managed to do in the last year of his life seem incredible to me now. To name only a few of them, there were the three trips to Asia and back, the publication of his last book, the establishment of the new hospital at Ban Houei Sai, medical work at the hospital and clinics at which he held sick-call, an audience with the Pope, two medical checkups at Memorial Hospital, his fund-raising speeches and lectures, the hundreds of letters he wrote, the radio broadcasts and TV appearances he made, and his efforts to effect changes in Medico which would bring it more in conformity with the concepts for which he founded it. As far as I could see, Tom not only did not relax the gruelling pace which he always set for himself, I believe he actually stepped it up.

Leo Cherne, his friend and counsellor, has made some interesting observations about Tom's sense of urgency. It was Leo Cherne to whom Tom often turned for advice. They had first met when Mr. Cherne, as chairman of the board of the International Rescue Committee, helped put Tom's first organized mission to Asia, Operation Laos, under their aegis. In a taped interview, Mr. Cherne spoke of the complexity of

Tom's character: "The initial impression of Tom took in his enormous energy, reflected in his incredible speed of speech. It was as though Tom lived always under the shadow of imminent death. Second, coupled with his energy there was an emphasis on the personal. Now how many ways are there of expressing the personal except by use of the words I, me, and my? It was only later, after knowing him for some time and seeing him in action again and again, that you came to realize this emphasis on the personal was what Tom's life was all about. His deep concern for other human beings—*personally*, not abstractly—was at the center of his character. That is why direct confrontation was so important to him—the laying on of hands, holding sick-call himself, the I-to-Thou. By this standard it would have been hypocrisy for him to speak of we, they, or our. As Tom saw it, the hands which rendered this kind of help had to be *my* hands, just as the pain or wound or sickness he treated was *my* pain (the patient's), not an abstraction. In describing Operation Laos, long before Medico, he borrowed the phrase, 'people to people,' but his concept was really even more personal than that—individual to individual.

"Another initial impression of Tom was that *he was always in a hurry*. After a while you came to learn that this urgency was the opposite of a superficial approach. It had a deep motivation: the life lost yesterday cannot be recaptured; the wound neglected today may mean a loss which cannot be restored tomorrow. Tom could not accept the older, more patient, and perhaps more sophisticated view that 'you do what you can.' It was just not possible for Tom to visualize himself or his purpose in these terms. He had none of the qualifying safeguards which protect a doctor against the erosion of pain. A doctor cannot be totally involved in the anguish of each patient. Again and again Tom admitted that he should not be, but he could not help it, he was.

"Tom never saw himself on a pedestal. He would come to me and say, tell me what I'm doing wrong, where am I making mistakes? This was not an egotist; an egotist neither makes mistakes nor wonders how to correct them. Often I would urge moderation, but you can't convince someone who is viewing Judgment Day that he should be moderate. A man who has vividly in mind a dying child, as Tom did, cannot be successfully urged to go slow. The warmest quality of all in Tom—and Dr. Schweitzer saw this—was precisely this quality of impatience and immoderation. This quality must have been Dr. Schweitzer's in 1914, when he first went to work in the hell of Africa. Had Tom lived to grow older, somehow he might have learned more moderation. I can only say that a moderated Tom Dooley would have been an urgent someone else."

Tom began the year by working at the Muong Sing clinic, where the two new replacements were being checked in prior to Earl's and Dwight's departure in March. Alan Rommel of Evansville, Indiana, and Tom Kirby, who spoke fluent French, were the new members of the team. Alan Rommel, who had had medical training as an Army corpsman, wrote that Tom "was really a very good doctor, and would rank with the best young general practitioners anywhere in the United States. He was practicing a better kind of medicine than the 'twentieth century' medicine that was practiced in the U.S. before World War II . . . Of course, the idea that Dr. Dooley was trying to get across to the American public was that you don't need white-tile operating rooms, stainless steel equipment, and air-conditioning in order to treat sick people living in the mud-huts of Asia. We didn't have any fancy stuff in Muong Sing. What we had was primitive but adequate. Our operating room may not have been as aseptic and spotless as those in the United States, but we didn't have any infections either.

"I was surprised by the daily case load. On a nice day we might get up to 150 or 160. . . The days were long, and we were all dog-tired by nightfall. After that first month I even got used to the sound of Dr. Dooley's voice dictating into that machine all night long."

During a visit to Cambodia in February, Tom met his old friends Patrica and John McCarthy of LaPorte, Indiana. John was attached to the U. S. Operations Mission and he and Pat drove to the Phnom Penh airport to meet Tom's plane, piloted by Jerry Euster. "His color was good, and he was in high spirits," Pat wrote, "but he was so thin! And when I saw that he had to use both hands to raise his coffee cup—somehow, that really tore my heart out. . . We flew to Kratie after lunch, and on the way we read the proofs of *The Night They Burned the Mountain.* As he finished each galley sheet, he would hand it to me to read. At one point I reached for the next sheet and found him staring out at the clouds, lines deeply etched on his face and pain in his eyes. At that moment all the happy, confident things he had been telling me about the great strides being made in cancer research and his chance of recovery went right out the window. I had a hard time holding back the tears."

Paul Hellmuth, lawyer, Notre Dame trustee and good friend of Tom's, visited Muong Sing in late February, when the new temporary clinic at Ban Houei Sai was in operation. This was the spot near which Tom had had his momentous fall just one year previously. He had chosen Ban Houei Sai because it was a good base from which to give medical service to people living in even more primitive and isolated conditions than those in Muong Sing. "I had the opportunity of seeing each morning the very thing I had come all this way to witness—Dr. Tom Dooley in action. I discovered that there were *two* Tom Dooleys, one entirely different from the other. The first, of course, was the dramatic Tom Dooley we saw on the lecture and fund-raising circuit. The other was the quiet, patient, dedicated Dr. Tom Dooley who had very obviously endeared himself to the simple people of this primitive community. . .

"One night in March, shortly before my departure I witnessed, completely unobserved, one little incident that helped to convince me of Tom Dooley's utter dedication to his people no matter how insignificant or hopeless they may have been.

"It had been a long, hard day, particularly for a soft Westerner like myself, and when I went to bed Tom Dooley was just settling down to his night's work on his dictating machine. I was awakened from a sound sleep by voices in the living-room. When I peeked out, I saw Dooley and Earl Rhine talking to a young man whom I recognized as the son of Wong, an old, emaciated Chinese who sold peanuts and Mekong whisky in a little road-level stand near the bazaar. Dooley had been treating old Wong's advanced case of tuberculosis. 'He's hopeless, of course,' Tom had said. 'All I can do is give him palliative treatment.'

"Now, from what I could hear of the conversation, old Wong was having another of his coughing spasms and was hemorrhaging badly. I heard Earl say: 'Doctor, I can handle this. There's no need for you to go at this hour of the morning.' Dooley replied rather angrily: 'Of course, I'm going! What are you guys trying to do—put me on the shelf?' Then he added, almost apologetically, as he checked through the contents of his bag, 'Okay, you can come along with me if you want to.'

"I looked at my watch and saw that it was after 3:00

A.M. 'Earl is right,' I thought... It was after five o'clock when they got back. Earl looked positively bushed, but Dooley looked fresh and untired except for the need of a shave.

"I said, 'That was old Wong, the Mekong whisky man, wasn't it?' 'Why, Paul! How did you know?' Tom seemed surprised that I had witnessed the incident, and pleased because I had recognized Wong's son. 'Yes, it was poor old Wong. I guess he's not long for this world. We gave him a shot, and he's no longer hemorrhaging. But we had to stick around for a while, because it sure looked like curtains for poor old Wong this time.'

"Sleepy-eyed Earl offered me some coffee, but I yawned and said I thought I would go back to bed for a while. Tom just went back to his dictating machine and took up where he had left off. I lay there in the next room, not wanting to sleep, but reminding myself that, whatever it was I had come to Laos looking for, I had found it—beyond any doubt. No one could ever make me doubt the sincerity of Tom Dooley, the physician and the man."

On March 30th, the day on which Earl Rhine and Dwight Davis were to leave the hospital which they had served so well for eighteen months, the King himself arrived in the village. They thought it was a state visit to the governor, showed surprise when Tom led them to the place of honor, and were flabbergasted when he told them they were to be decorated. The governor, who preceded them, went on his knees to make the Lao *sathoo*—hands raised, with fingertips touching the face, head slightly bowed. Dwight, who was next, started to kneel, but the King said: "Stand up, lad." Dwight and Earl then received the Order of the Million Elephants and the White Parasol, the beautiful decoration which Tom had received from the King over a year before. The King spoke gratefully, and said: "You have brought to us the real heart of America, and we shall never forget you." Tom had promised Emily and Esperanza at the Criss Award ceremony in Omaha that he would get Earl and Dwight back home by April 1st. At the airport he bade them farewell: "Goodbye and God bless you and your families."

Tom was soon due back in the United States for a checkup in Memorial Hospital, and he was worried because the Medico administration in New York had not yet found a fully qualified doctor as replacement for him at Muong Sing. In Bangkok he met Dr. Hautmann, a gentle Viennese, sixty years of age, who had done much medical missionary work in Indonesia. Tom was happy to make arrangements with him to direct the hospital temporarily. In April Tom went to Viet Nam to visit the new Medico project at Quang Ngai, where the young Vietnamese, Dr. Sau Baa, was already working.

On his return trip to New York Tom stopped first in Africa, to meet Dr. Mungai Njoroge, a native of Kenya who had trained in the United States and was in charge of the Chania Clinic near Nairobi. "Dr. Dooley . . . was impatient to get his physical checkup in New York over with because he felt he was wasting a lot of valuable time," wrote Dr. Njoroge. "To my mind he had no doubt whatsoever that he would be dead within a year. He did not show any doubt, fear or hesitancy about what had to be done during his remaining months. In Nairobi he was entertained at a number of parties, and when he talked of his work and even of his own illness, he did so in a way that made guests envy him rather than pity him. . . I told him that the joint work he and I were doing would continue in Africa so long as the spirit of our agreement remained. Tom Dooley was one of the best friends that I ever had."

My son's next stop was Rome. He felt very much at home in the General House of the Oblates of Mary Immaculate, which he called "my Mother-house." It was there, in September, 1957, at a time when I was also able to join him in the Eternal City, that Tom was given the rare privilege of being made an Honorary Oblate. On this occasion the Father General of the Order presented him with the Oblate Cross, which he always cherished. He not only took the Cross back with him to Muong Sing on his last trip to Asia in the fall of 1960, but he requested that it be placed on his coffin. His tombstone in Calvary Cemetery outside St. Louis bears a replica of the Oblate Cross.

The Oblates of Mary Immaculate have an interesting history. They were founded in 1816 by Charles Joseph Eugène de Mazenod, who in 1832 became Bishop of Marseilles. The life-work of the Oblates is the service of the poor. Today they number 7,300 missionaries working in thirty different countries in most difficult missions among the poorest of the poor all over the world. Father Matt Menger, whom Tom met in Laos, is the Oblate Father who offered the requiem Mass for Tom in Vientiane described by Norman Cousins in his *Saturday Review* article after my son's death.

In Our Lady's month of May, Tom experienced one of the

high points in his life. An audience with the Holy Father had been arranged by the Oblate Fathers in Rome. After Tom's death their magazine, *Oblate Missions*, published in Ottawa under their Provincial Director Rev. Joseph R. Birch, O.M.I., made this comment:

"There was a facet of Dr. Dooley's character which the press tried but never quite succeeded in capturing. They failed because Dooley did not want them to succeed. Although he was a frequent and even daily communicant, he considered his spiritual life out of bounds to the press. He would say, 'The only thing that bothers me is that people keep trying to make me into a St. Francis. It's got so that I can't walk into a bar and have a beer.' There was nothing phoney or pharasaical about his religion.

"When he was in Rome to visit his 'Mother-house,' en route to America for a cancer check-up, he showed the deep and child-like devotion he had to the Blessed Mother. He liked to visit the church of St. Susanna, where there is a statue of the Madonna before which he liked to pray. His first morning in Rome he spent at the foot of the statue, reading his correspondence. 'Was that a sin?' he teased. For him it was just as natural as reading letters in his mother's parlor in St. Louis."

Tom was thrilled as he stood face to face with the Holy Father in one of the throne-rooms in the Vatican. Pope John XXIII knew a great deal about Tom's work, and spoke to him in French in a friendly, paternal, and considerate way. Tom had brought with him a great many rosaries and medals for the Pope's blessing, and these the Holy Father blessed. Then, as Tom later told me, an unusual thing happened. At the completion of the audience, the Pope returned to his private apartments and all the guests began to leave. Tom started to go out with his Oblate hosts, when suddenly one of the *monsignori* came after them. The Holy Father, he said, had got back to his desk, sat down, and had a second thought. He opened the desk drawer, took out all the rosaries and medals in it, blessed them especially for Tom, and asked that they be given to Dr. Dooley before he left. My son was deeply moved by this unusual gesture. He turned to the Oblate Father and said: "I think we'll go into St. Peter's. I want to say a word of thanks to Our Blessed Lady at the foot of the Pieta." In the great basilica, in the chapel where the Pieta rests, Tom knelt and prayed his thanks for the wonderful graces he had received.

Soon Tom was in Memorial Hospital in New York, undergoing a series of tests. It was there that he met Dr. Carl Wiedermann, the hard-working young physician who was to take charge of the hospital at Ban Houei Sai after working with Tom at Quang Ngai. Dr. Wiedermann met his death tragically in June, 1962 from an accidental gunshot wound. Before his first meeting with Tom at Memorial was over, Dr. Wiedermann said: "Tom, what is the truth about your health?"

"Do you ask me as a friend or as a doctor?" Tom countered.

"I am just asking out of curiosity. I am going to work with you and I want to know what the score is."

Tom replied: "Carl, I think this thing is metastasizing to my lungs, and probably to my bones. I'm pretty sure I haven't got more than eight or ten months to live." Dr. Wiedermann stated that Tom said it with such simplicity that it left him speechless.

After addressing the annual dinner of the Medical Society of the State of New York, Tom returned to the familiar environs of South Bend, Indiana to receive an honorary degree from his Alma Mater which had not, you will recall, awarded him a bachelor's degree. President Dwight D. Eisenhower, at the luncheon for honored guests prior to the ceremonies, asked Father Hesburgh: "Where's Dr. Tom Dooley? I want to meet him and have a talk." Tom was therefore given a seat beside the President and had a marvelous opportunity to tell him about his plans and hopes for Medico. One of the after-effects of this Commencement Day ceremony was that my son Malcolm got a ride back east in the Presidential plane, which led his daughter Maureen (who hadn't progressed very far with Presidents in school) to boast to her playmates: "My daddy flew in a plane with President George Washington."

En route in July to Laos again, Tom was fortunate in having the piloting services and companionship of his old Navy friend, Ted Werner. In Vientiane on August 9 there was a *coup d'état*. Captain Kong Le bravely occupied the capitol while officials were attending the cremation ceremonies for the late King. Ted at once dashed out to the airport and flew to Bangkok. Tom was in Muong Sing, and Ted knew that, once the rebels seized the plane, that would be the last they would ever see of it. It was with great difficulty that Ted was able to get out of Bangkok and rejoin Tom. When he did, Tom asked him to fly right back to Bangkok, where much-needed supplies for Medico's overseas installations were being held up. A mere $65,000 worth of Thailand duties on these supplies seemed to be the cause, so Tom went into action. When he learned that only the King (who was away) could waive these duties, he obtained an audience with Marshal Sarit, the Prime Minister. "I had a tough time selling him," Tom wrote, "but finally he agreed that the humanitarian concepts of Medico were above war and politics." The embargoed supplies were released without the payment of $65,000 in duties. Tom had surmounted the first hurdle.

Muong Sing and Ban Houei Sai were both desperately in need of pharmaceuticals. Now that the supplies were freed in Bangkok, the problem was how to get them into war-torn northern Laos. Tom had a plan, which through hard work on the parts of Tom Kirby and Terry Cotter, and the help of airplane fuel which Tom managed to provide—no one ever learned how—went off without a hitch. According to Tom Regan, who followed the whole supply problem from New York: "After that, the boys called Tom 'Old Smuggler.' It was an incredible maneuver for anyone to bring off so successfully, but I think it was downright heroic for a man as sick as Tom must have been at that time."

My son then returned to New York to undergo his second series of tests at Memorial Hospital between October 7th and 29th. On the latter date, he reported: "No extension of the cancer was found. I have put on a few pounds, and I feel great." If he was comparatively well physically, he was very gloomy about the one thing nearest to his heart—Medico. On October 15th a board meeting of Medico was held, at which Tom was elected vice chairman of the board. This was his wish, for Tom was determined to have an administrative voice in the affairs of the organization. He was greatly disappointed over the failure of the New York office to *follow through* on his plans more effectively after he left the country and went back to Asia.

He put it all very frankly in a letter circulated to all the team members around the world on October 28th, prior to his own departure for Laos:

"The visit to New York was most productive. . . . Things were produced, that is all I care about. I was elected vice chairman of the board. As you know, in the past I have only been a 'moral' voice in Medico, with no legal corporate power, but now I have powers second only to the chairman. I intend to utilize this power forcefully. We have a bit of a supply problem, but this can be worked out. . . . We have a marked decline in donations when I am not present in America. We have received nothing in the way of corporation or foundation gifts. This also will be remedied. It is unfortunate that I have to inform you that we have no more doctors or corpsmen available for the various Medico teams. . ."

It is only fair that the people who supported Medico so faithfully because of Tom should know the full story of the disappointment which he felt in these final months. He was caught in a tragic dilemma, because just at the moment when he felt that administrative reform was needed, he was fatally ill. That abundant and copious energy which he had been able to call upon at every moment of his life, and which he had always expended so freely and almost thoughtlessly, failed him now when he felt he had most need of it.

My son explained his concept of Medico to the American public over and over again—in his books, in speeches, in letters, in press conferences, in TV and radio interviews, in conversation. It is clearly stated in the chapter he entitled "The Start of Medico" in *The Night They Burned the Mountain:*

The simplicity of Medico's program is this: we actually believe that we can win the friendship of people only by working beside them, on equal terms, humans to humans, towards goals that they understand and seek themselves. Medico is a person-to-person, heart-to-heart program. There is no more personal relationship than that of a doctor and his patient. In Nam Tha . . . we tried to show, with love, that we understood the responsibility of those who have towards those who have not.

Now this is a very personal concept, and obviously there are some who do not agree with it. But a great many Americans not only agreed with it, they got excited about it, and were happy to learn that there was a young man in their midst who still had ideals, and was willing to stand up and speak about them, and what's more *act* on them. At a time of cynicism, selfishness and materialism, my son said: "Half of the people on the face of the earth tonight will go to bed just a little hungry. *This is the half with whom I live.*" That is the message which people heard, understood, and responded to so whole-heartedly. I would not have established the Thomas A. Dooley Foundation if the organization which he himself had brought into being had really carried on his work.

One of the last workers in the field with whom Tom was able to spend some time was Dr. Alex Zlatanos. This was in early December, 1960, after Tom was wearing the back brace which he needed to support the disintegrating vertebrae. He always referred to this brace as the "Iron Maiden." Tom arrived at Bangkok from Hong Kong, where he had been fitted for the brace, and Dr. Zlatanos noticed that it severely restricted his movements getting off the plane. The first thing Tom asked him about was the operation on a woman patient at the Muong Sing hospital. A long neglected abscess had left a hole in her cheek, and she had begged Tom to do something about it.

When Dr. Zlatanos told him that the surgery had been successful, Tom said: "Thank God. You know I promised that poor woman that we would do something for her, and now we've done it. I don't know how to thank you, Alex."

"Then I knew," wrote Dr. Zlatanos, "why I was sent to Laos. To Tom Dooley 'promises to keep' was more than a line in a poem . . . Despite his condition, he talked about his plans to visit the other teams, to spend Christmas in Muong Sing, and return to the States for another coast-to-coast fundraising tour. Then I saw his overwhelming sadness, and I knew that his real agony came not primarily from his physical condition but from an awareness that it would never permit him to do all the things he had to do."

"On December 16th Tom went to Cambodia, to the hospital at Kratie. He spent a day there, ate almost nothing, and took pain-killing drugs. Dr. Zlatanos noted that physically he was breaking down fast, though he continued to drive himself desperately. Tom wanted to remain and assist in the delivery of Dr. Rosenbloom's wife, Edith, whose baby was due that day, but his plane came while she was still in the operating room.

"The last I saw of him," reported Dr. Zlatanos, "was when he peeked into the room and waved goodbye to us. When I looked up at him, he frowned and shook his head and pointed to the draped figure on the table as if to say: 'Doctor, remember who you are and the high duty you are about to perform.' There was a momentary silence in the Kratie operating room as Tom Dooley walked out of our lives forever. But in that same moment the silence was broken by a loud wail, and Arlen Rosenbloom's son was born, reminding all of us of the Divine Wisdom of life and death."

In Saigon Tom bade a tearful farewell to Madame Ngai,

whom he had met so long ago as a Navy doctor in those days in Viet Nam which changed and shaped his whole life. He also spent four sad days with Pat and John McCarthy, his close friends from early youth. At the airport Pat was horrified because when she went ahead to clear his passport and luggage, while he filled out papers, the official told her Tom's visa had expired and he could not leave. Pat asked to see the director, who alone could straighten matters out, but he was away at lunch. It was now time to board the plane.

"I began to get frantic," wrote Pat. "Just then Tom walked in through the gate. The customs man took one look at him, wearing his ghastly brace and obviously in agony, and picked up his stamp and marked the visa. Not another word was said."

On December 23 Father John Boucher of the Holy Redeemer Church in Bangkok went to the Erawan Hotel in response to Tom's phone call. He found Tom lying on the floor on a mattress, with the telephone beside him. He explained that his back hurt him too much to use the bed, and that he had called because he wanted to make sure that he would receive Holy Communion on Christmas day. Realizing how sick Tom was, Father Boucher said:

"Tom, I don't want to alarm you, but I think it might be wise for me to give you Extreme Unction. It might help you."

After receiving the sacrament, Tom seemed entirely relaxed and at peace. Next morning Father Boucher gave him Holy Communion, and Tom asked if he could have a spot in the choir loft for midnight Mass that night. Though the arrangements were made, Tom was too ill to make it. On Christmas morning Father Boucher brought Holy Communion to the hotel room: "This time I found Tom deeply depressed and in extreme pain. 'Pax huic domui,' I prayed and arranged the Blessed Sacrament on the small table. Then, disregarding the rubrics, I turned to him and said, 'Merry Christmas, Tom.' He tried to smile, but I could see there was something bothering him, so I waited for him to speak.

" 'You wished me a Merry Christmas, Father. I can't help thinking that this is my last. And it's not a very merry one, is it? Not a very merry one at all, and yet somehow I feel resigned and peaceful. If this is the way God wants it to be, this is the way I want it, too.' He paused a moment. 'Sorry I couldn't make midnight Mass, Father. Last night was a pretty bad one.'

"I tried to say a few words of assurance, then I gave him Communion. But his words stuck in my mind. Here was a young man in the prime of life, at the peak of his career, saying a thing like that. A couple of thousand years ago a Man of the same age spoke almost the same words in the Garden of Gethsemane: 'Father, if it be Thy Will let this Chalice pass from me. Nevertheless not my will but Thine be done.'

"As I gave him Communion, Tom cried softly. The rosary was still in his hand. He seemed to be never without that rosary. After a few moments of silent prayer he held out his hand to me. 'I'm leaving tonight for New York. So long, Father, and thanks for everything. Remember me in your prayers, please.'

"I stayed on a few minutes to pray with him, then we started chatting, although it was obvious that conversation was a real effort for him, and I had no intention of remaining more than a moment. This is when a very strange thing happened.

"For some reason I mentioned the word 'Medico' and all of a sudden Tom sat up, his eyes brightened and for the next four or five minutes he became a changed man. This was the old Tom Dooley, with all his youth and enthusiasm and machine-gun chatter. This was Tom Dooley the crusader, face alive, pain forgotten, eloquent, determined, convincing.

"I sat there amazed. He told me all about Medico, as though I had never heard of it before. He talked about its beginnings, progress, present state, and his dreams for its future. He even told me about the stations he had yet to visit on this tour. 'I've got to keep them going, Father. It's important that I go to them. Perhaps, somehow, God will let me do it.'

"Then suddenly he stopped talking, sank back on the pillow and a grimace of pain came over his face, and tears moistened his eyes. After a moment of silence I knew it was time to leave. I gave him my blessing and walked out of the room. But those few minutes left an unforgettable impression on me. I thought to myself: how dedicated can a person become? This man was not only dedicated, he lived and breathed his dedication. He was dedication personified. This is what gave him his true greatness, and Dr. Tom Dooley was truly a great man."

Ted Werner made the arrangements for Tom to leave for New York via Pan American on Christmas night. When they got to the plane. Tom asked Ted not to take his arm going aboard; he wanted to make it on his own, if possible, and he did. Ted saw him to the double seat he had reserved, and Tom shook hands saying: "Goodbye, Ted, and thanks for everything. God bless you." Ted watched as the big plane taxied to the runway. When it took off, my son departed for the last time from a part of the world and a people he loved.

Two days later he entered Memorial Hospital. On January 18, 1961, at 9:45 in the evening, only a few moments after the priest, in concluding the last rites, leaned over and whispered in his ear, "Son, go now and meet thy God," my son died.

seven

the thomas a. dooley foundation

The sick have claims upon us, the well; the hungry upon the well-fed; the poor upon the rich; the suffering on those without pain.

And his work goes on.

On September 15, 1961 in San Francisco I announced the establishment of the Thomas A. Dooley Foundation, Inc., a publicly supported organization which would be non-sectarian, non-profit, and non-governmental. The Foundation was established to carry on the ideals and the work of my son. In all the programs emphasis is on a person-to-person and self-help basis—the Tom Dooley concept.

Those who worked closely with Tom, and understood his ideals, joined with me in setting up the Foundation—such people as Doctors Verne Chaney, Emmanuel Voulgaropoulos, William Van Valin, Charles Webster, Omar Fareed and the late Carl Wiedermann. On our board and on our national and foreign advisory councils are such friends and old associates as Eugene Burdick, Admiral Arleigh Burke, Dr. Melvin Casberg, William Lederer, Leo Cherne, Travis L. Fletcher, Erica Anderson and Teresa E. Gallagher.

180

In November, 1960—two months before he died—my son had promised the Dalai Lama of Tibet two mobile health units for use among the helpless Tibetan refugees in northern India. This fine and gentle people, whose country has never in its history known war and whose religion abhors killing, live in misery and wretchedness because Communist genocidal policies—including sterilization and castration—have made them flee Tibet in terror. This outrage against humanity is one about which my son felt most strongly. He, who supplied Medico with so much, gave his word that help would come, but this was a promise that Medico, after his death, seemed unable to keep.

On January 17, 1962—Tom's birthday—the Foundation presented the two units to the Dalai Lama. One was donated by the Monterey Peninsula chapter of the Foundation, the other by the Chicago chapter. Both mobile units were equipped through the generosity of the Long Island chapter. To man the units, the Foundation is fortunate in having Dr. S. A. Nallathambi in charge. He is aided by Sonam Dondhup, a Tibetan nurse; two drivers, Tashi and Lobsangi; and a cook, Panditije. Laboratory facilities were set up by the Carr Foundation of Los Angeles, headed by Dr. Omar Fareed. The Indian Government cooperated through the Central Relief Committee, whose chairman is Acharya J. B. Kripalani. Dr. Melvin Casberg, now at Christian Medical College, Ludhiana, India was most helpful in setting up the program.

Help with dignity is the Foundation's guiding principle. No luxurious and costly "American type" hospitals or clinics are being established. The aim is to help the local people to establish their own basic care centers, and to train them to operate these centers for their own people. That is why the Foundation can operate at a fraction of the cost incurred by other institutions with similar humanitarian aims but different concepts and different approaches.

At Ban Houei Sai in Laos the Foundation is continuing to carry on the hospital which Tom set up. In the summer of 1962 young Reggie Gordon, who had worked with Tom and Al Harris and the late Dr. Wiedermann at Quang Ngai, Viet Nam, flew to Laos to serve as surgical technician with Al Harris at Ban Houei Sai under the direction of Dr. Judson Lloyd.

I feel that the Foundation is fortunate in having Dr. Verne Chaney as its executive director. He has become a dedicated successor to my son. A veteran of the Korean war, in which he served as a battle surgeon, he left a chest surgery practice in prosperous Monterey, California, to work among the sick and hungry of Asia.

"These Asian people need help today," Dr. Chaney has said. "They are sick today. We want to give them the kind of help they need today, not five years from now. I'm sure our country is loaded with people feeling the Tom Dooley urge. Most of them can't give a lifetime or even a couple of years, with family and other obligations, but there are many who can spare two, three or four months for our kind of work. These are the people I want to reach."

Dr. Chaney points to the nursery school in northern India as evidence of effective non-medical work in Asia. Two Pan Am airline stewardesses, Marleane Thompson and Marge Burgey, took leave from their jobs for three months to run the nursery for 300 Tibetan children. The nursery was set up by Gyolo Thondrup, brother of the Dalai Lama.

The Foundation's present plans call for the establishment of 25 chapters throughout the United States, and the formation of the Tom Dooley Youth Corps, to encourage youngsters—as Tom always did—to take part in this wonderful movement, was announced in April, 1962. National headquarters have been established at 442 Post Street, San Francisco, California.

Teresa E. Gallagher, who contributed such a moving account of my son's last days and hours to *Before I Sleep*, recently wrote a tribute in the form of a letter to Tom, from which I quote: "Your friends all over are trying to take care of the unfinished business you worried about so much ... We don't really feel you are too far away because so many doors are opening for us, and so many things you wanted done are being done. The hospitals in Laos are needed now more than ever. The vans you wanted so much for the victims of the communists in Tibet are now in service, covering an area of 300 miles and spreading compassion as they travel. Ban Houei Sai is back in operation, and the Laos government wants us to open up Nam Tha. (How you worked to set up Nam Tha!) The chapters you wanted throughout the United States are being formed, the subway advertisements of the Foundation are now to be seen. We are still begging, as you did, but we haven't all your talents. And so, Dr. Tom, each of us will do our bit to keep your candle lighted. The kids you loved so much here in America are going to do the best job of all."

And so his work goes on.

At the White House on June 7, 1962 the President made the presentation of the Congressional Medal.

I was accompanied by Malcolm and Gay and their three boys, Malcolm Jr., Michael, and Thomas Anthony Dooley IV. (Maureen was unfortunately kept home by chicken-pox.) My friends, Lucille Selsor, Clare Murphy, Bob Copenhaver, Joseph Jones, and Robert Giroux were also present. Miss Eva Adams, Director of the Mint which designed and cast the medal, attended. Among the members of Congress present were Senators Hubert Humphrey, Stuart Symington, Claiborne Pell, John A. Carroll and Edward V. Long; Congresswoman Leonor K. Sullivan, and Congressmen Hugh Carey, Frank M. Karsten, and Henry Reuss.

President Kennedy, in presenting the medal, said: "I take great pleasure on behalf of the Congress and the country in presenting the Dr. Thomas A. Dooley Medal to Mrs. Dooley and members of the Dooley family. This is an extraordinary action by the Congress which takes place only on the rarest occasions, when a medal representing the strongest feelings of the American people is struck and presented.

"I think it is most appropriate in this case. All of us have been impressed by the extraordinary example of Dr. Dooley, who went to the farthest reaches of this earth in order to serve people. The letter he wrote when he set up his last hospital indicated his strong feeling of service. It typified the best of our country. In presenting this medal to you, Mrs. Dooley, we want you to know how appreciative we are to him for the example he has set to all of us, and the impression he has given to the world of the compassion of Americans."

The front of the medal bears my son's head in semi-profile, while the verso shows him standing in a doctor's coat, holding a baby, surrounded by four children in native costumes. Behind is a map of the Pacific; Laos and southeast Asia are on the left, and the western coast of the United States on the right. Around the rim are these words:

"IN RECOGNITION OF THE PUBLIC SERVICE TO ALLEVIATE SUFFERING AMONG PEOPLE OF THE WORLD."

epilogue: letter to a young doctor*

*Village of Muong Sing
Kingdom of Laos*

Dear Bart:

It is far past midnight. I am sitting at the table in my house at Muong Sing, high in the foothills of the Himalayas in northern Laos. The kerosene pressure lamps overhead are hissing at me, and the wind is lashing down my valley. It whips the palm and frangipani. All the earth on this sad cut of the world seems flooded in the monsoon rains. This is the season of the crashing violence of the tropical storm. The crickets, frogs, and wilder jungle animals screech and scream. The high Lao night land is not calm.

But I feel very calm in writing to you. I feel as though I have just met you outside the medical school auditorium. May I thrust my hand out and say, "Congratulations, Bart. Congratulations on your graduation from medical school. Congratulations on being a doctor." But along with my congratulations, I also want to inject into your mind some thoughts to mull over during your coming year of internship.

Four years of medical school are behind you. "What is past is prologue." You have been given much by parents and teachers. Use it wisely, for others. You have worked hard and learned a good deal, but because you are out of the stress of doing does not mean that you are yet in the peace of the done. You will never be.

As a doctor, you have a tremendous potential. There are a lot of glorious things ahead of you, if you choose to

---

* At the time of his death, Tom was working on a book which he had entitled *The Night of the Same Day*. He planned to include his "Letter to a Young Doctor" as a chapter; it was the only chapter which he completed.

184

choose them. I know this very well, though only six years ahead of you in time of practice and age of life.

Know that this passing and precarious time in history will demand much of you. It will maroon the hesitant, but inspire the brave. Stand up and shout, "This is my time and my place in this time!" And seek that place. The state of total gratification is for cows, possibly for birds, not for man. Seek greater things than the material.

Do not aim for just a certain socio-economic position in society. Seek something beyond the split-level ranch house and the two-car garage. Become supremely aware of and intimately involved in the great issues of your day. You have the potential for great deeds, and today demands deeds. Human deeds. Principles enunciated and hopes expressed are not enough. Remember this.

You are a doctor. The proud state of being a doctor is a joyful thing. There is a lot more to you than just the knowledge of bugs and drugs. All the information you have acquired has certainly distilled itself into certain beliefs. Your beliefs may be scattered, rough and unclassified, but you do have them. You are well trained. Your hands are keen, your mind incisive, your sensitivity deep, your vision well honed. You are aware of the sadness of mankind. You know the physiognomy of pain and, accordingly, the quality of mercy. You know the power of drugs and understand the importance of the "patient who has a sickness" rather than the "sickness that is in the patient." You have a capability to know the pain and glory of other men.

You possess more than knowledge of the healing art. You can do more than laboratory experiments and herniorrhaphies. The greatest attribute of you is that indispensable and essential aspect of your human spirit. Learn how to utilize the fiber and core of your heart.

There is a great deal more to living than just existing. Believing is a fine thing, but placing those beliefs into execution is the real test of strength. The state of being a doctor is a happy one, a lofty one, and one filled with tremendous potential for good. You commit a sin of omission if you do not utilize all the power that is in you. Seek a way to practice your art of medicine, utilizing all the deepest powers of your belief. As a doctor, you must be a part of your time. Isolation from and indifference to world affairs are completely past and over. You can no longer be just a doctor or just a researcher or just a teacher. All men have claims on man. And to the man with special talents, this is a special *claim. This is your challenge. It is required that man take part in the actions and passions of his time at the peril of being judged not to have lived at all. You are qualified not only to take part in, but perhaps to lead in the actions of a segment of the world today. A doctor's job is to cure sometimes, to relieve often, and to comfort always.*

You must utilize, along with your medical talents, the powers of your spirit and heart. This will help to buttress up the fragile peace of the world.

Bart, you've a year's internship ahead of you. And after that, the choice of a residency for specialty training or private practice. I know you have been plagued with some indecision, "Shall I be a specialist with years and years of more training, or shall I go into private practice now?"

I am going to presume that you will choose the life of a general practitioner. There is a place in the world for specialists (speaketh the young G.P.), but this battered, beaten world of ours needs a few more country doctors in even a few more countries and villages, too.

As a general practitioner, where will you practice? There is a need for you every place. But the world is all lopsided in its distribution of doctors. Almost all corners of America have available doctors. With veterans' benefits, Social Security, labor union programs, industrial group health plans, and all the others, there is hardly a citizen who cannot find medical attention if he is willing to make some little effort.

I live in Laos. This valley, prior to our Medico hospital, had nothing but black magic, necromancy, witchcraft, clay images, sorcery and betel juice. The villagers wallowed in monkey's blood, cobwebs, tigers' teeth and incantations. They never had much hope, much less help. Today, the people of Muong Sing have good medicine, compassionate help, training and a fine little 25-bed hospital. Twentieth century.

You know the world's statistics. The Congo. 13,000,000 people and not one native doctor. South Viet Nam, 11,000,-000 people, about 180 doctors. Cambodia, 5,000,000 people, seven doctors. Laos, 3,000,000 people, one Lao doctor. Other nations' statistics are equally staggering.

Though this is sometimes called "the age of the shrug," I do not believe you would say, as some do, "So what, it's not my problem." You know, Bart, you and I are the heirs of all ages. We have the great legacies of music, art, literature and our own medicine. We have been born and raised in freedom. We have justice, law and equality. But we have overlooked the uglier side of our inheritance. We have also the legacy of hatred, bred by careless men before us. We have the legacy of abuse, degradation, and the inhumanity of men blinded by prejudice, ignorance and personal spleen. To people like you and me, richer in educational opportunities than many, this is a special legacy, and a challenge. To accept the ugly as well as the beautiful and to answer this challenge is a privilege and a responsibility. Accept it without fear.

Bart, I personally believe that the unique aspect of this challenge to young doctors demands that we invest some of our lives in the practice of medicine in foreign fields. I say "Some," not a lifetime. This is not expected of us. But we can give a year or two. It can be part of the maturation of a man, the metamorphosis of a doctor.

You went through college, medical school, clerkship; internship lies ahead, maybe residency, and then . . . come to the developing nations of the world for a while. Bring your gadgets, and the armamentarium of drugs, to be sure, but most of all bring your human spirit. Bring your youthful enthusiasm, your drive, your energy, your dedication to help the sick. Bring your wonderful spontaneity, your belief in the good and the right. Bring along a sense of humor, don't forget it; you'll certainly need it when the roof leaks, the patients eat all the pills the first dosage, and the witch doctors put cow dung over your sterile compresses. Bring also a few cents' worth of the spirit of adventure that our founding fathers possessed. Spend some time in valleys like Muong Sing. Invest some of your life to answer personally the challenge of today, your legacy, your heritage.

It is more difficult for other professions to enter and work in a foreign country. Citizens and governments are suspicious —as they are even a bit suspicious of the doctor. (There are some who are not yet convinced that I am not an agent of the FBI or a Jesuit-in-disguise.) But your M.D. diploma does open many doors. You will be allowed to come to these underdeveloped areas and build your small hospital. Splash some of the warmth and goodness of your human spirit on people who heretofore have known little of this element in the Western man. My villagers' lives were just one great groan of agony before the Medico hospital was built. They knew only Western men bent on colonizing them, and perhaps exploiting what little they had.

Your medicine will have a twofold effect. You will find

that just by being a doctor with qualities of the human heart, you will help to unify men. Simple humanity makes the primitive lands of Asia and Africa important to every American. Simple self-interest makes it vital.

You are probably thinking, "Tom, hate to sound this way, but what's in it for me? We are all a little selfish, you know." Right you are, Bart. Perhaps we should be a bit wary of the man who is completely unselfish. There is a great deal "in it" for you. By investing a portion of your life for work here, by depositing a year or two of your time you will take back with you into private practice a great sense of accomplishment, coupled with a vast human experience. Your accomplishment will be beyond the narrow confines of continent and custom. Your accomplishments will be on a wider scope; along the broad horizons of peace for the whole world. You will always know that you have given a fragment of your life for the good of many.

All men yearn to lose themselves in something greater than themselves. You will have done this, and will have helped to achieve that unquenchable promise that someday all men of all races will learn to live together in peace. I do not believe this fulfillment is achievable in private practice.

You've always been a bit of a cynic. I imagine you are quietly snarling, "Okay, Tom, you've made your point, but to give up a year or two for a spiritual thing called 'fulfillment,' don't know 'bout that."

I can only remind you that the history of mankind constantly repeats the exclamation that the only way man can achieve his own happiness is to strive for the happiness of others. And you reply, "Ugh, Dooley's murky mysticism again." History also proves, Bart, that men rarely learn from the teachings of history, but must learn for themselves. Come to Asia. Learn.

There are programs in the world with which you could work ... These will pay you enough to keep you out of debt (though perhaps not much more). They will handle the mechanics of medical procurement and supply. Free next year, Bart?

Today demands a deeper emphasis on the brotherhood of man. All professions must seek ways to do this. For the doctor it is not a difficult thing. It is in the root of the tree of a doctor to understand and believe in brotherhood. This concept was not so important in the times of our fathers. It is now. The Brotherhood of Man exists as definitely as does the Fatherhood of God. And we must not forget it.

I do not believe "brotherhood" is a sentimental, mushy-mouthed hyperglycemic thing. It is a potent, mighty force to bring men together as men. We are not as actively engaged in solidifying this idea as we should be. Doctors know the alikeness of all men. The world does not need another union of white men, or of American men, or of Dutch men, or of Negro men. Or more fragmentation of peoples into endless exclusivisms. Brotherhood should be a force to unite men—as men.

Patriotism is not enough, either. Nations must belong to a larger world, with a wider horizon than that of any single country. Countries working together, each giving something to the other—this is part of brotherhood. Asia and Africa need picks and shovels, bulldozers and syringes to remove the high cliffs of poverty, injustice and sickness. You as a doctor have those syringes. We must do what we can, as individuals, to help other individuals.

We young Americans must take the drama of our freedoms (from disease as well as from tyranny) that we have received from the past and project it into the future. For other men. We who have it must help those who do not have it.

The kerosene is running out of the lamps and they are sputtering and flickering. Dooley needs to hit the sack, so I'll stop the letter just now and continue it tomorrow.

A full day has passed since I began this letter to you. At clinic this morning we had 78 patients. Everything from a blazing malaria to a man who brought his donkey, requesting that we suture up a laceration in its flank. We gave the malaria patient chloroquine, and sutured the laceration in the donkey's posterior with chromic catgut, size 2 (tough ass).

Some children had diarrheas, eye inflammations, and one had a case of head lice. My American corpsmen pulled some teeth (dentistry is not for me). The kids howled just like they do in America. The old gals complained about having to wait in line, just like they do in America. A few of the older gents wanted some "vigor pills," just like . . . well, anyway. There are no really deep differences between people. I have spent six years of my life among different men, and always I find the similarities outweigh the differences. Each life is infinitely precious as a life. Everywhere.

To recapitulate what I've written, Bart, I believe that as a young doctor, as soon as you finish your internship, you should spend a year or two in lands such as Laos. You should utilize your profession and your heart as a cable to bind men together. Danger cements men; why can't other forces be used? Many tools must be implemented to destroy the false walls that separate us. Medicine is one. Medicine when enveloped in that indispensable element of the human spirit. Kindness and gentleness are daily instruments of the doctor, more than of other professions. Kindness and gentleness can be potent weapons to fight against the anger of the world.

The world is made up of persons. Internationality is only a conglomeration of individuals. All individuals yearn for something human. This flings a special challenge to you as there is no more intimate person-to-person relationship than that of the doctor and his patient. Bring the talents of your degree, and the spirituality of your heart, to distant valleys like mine. And take back with you a rich, rich reward.

Dedicate some of your life to others. Your dedication will not be a sacrifice. It will be an exhilarating experience because it is intense effort applied towards a meaningful end.

So along with my congratulations on your graduation I send my wish that you will utilize yourself as a force of unity in the fragile peace of today. And that you will know the happiness that comes of serving others who have nothing.

Sincere best wishes always,

TOM

The work which Dr. Dooley has done has struck a loud responsive chord among Americans. He has appealed to what Lincoln called "the better angels of our nature"— our compassion and our generous concern for our fellow-man.　　　　　　　　　　　　　　　　　　—HENRY CABOT LODGE.

My dear Thanh Mo America: Before I go back to Laos, I want to be something that will help my people. I am not thinking to be big shot like king. I think it is time for us to turn our head up. . . . I learned new words every day in school, but could not find a word thanks for your great help. As long as I am still alive, I will remember you.

Your truthly,
NGOAN

I tried to assure him that in his 34 years he had done what very few have done in the allotted Scriptural lifetime.　　　　　　　　　　　　　　　　—FRANCIS CARDINAL SPELLMAN.

Dooley was not just a doctor. He was an educator. And he knew the success of an educator was to be measured by his ability to teach others how to pass their knowledge along. According to such a yardstick, Dooley may well have been one of the most useful teachers of his time.
　　　　　　　　　　　　　　　　—NORMAN COUSINS.

Young healer of souls and bodies, with invincible summer in his heart, moved by and moving under the law of love . . .
　　　　　　　　　　—ST. MARY'S COLLEGE CITATION.

Dr. Tom Dooley is already a fabulous figure in the suffering, anguished heart of the world. His life, so brief, and yet so complete, is an epic that transcends the lines of faith, for Tom Dooley found his great inspiration in Schweitzer, a Protestant, though he was a devoted son of his own faith . . . I knew this man.

—DR. DANIEL POLING.

You are a credit to our country. As long as the United States has Tom Dooleys doing the kind of work that you, Baker, Kessey, Shepard and the others have done, the Republic will be in good and safe hands.

—SENATOR MIKE MANSFIELD.

This is an extraordinary action by the Congress, which takes place only on the rarest occasions, when a medal representing the strongest feelings of the American people is struck and presented. I think it is most appropriate in this case . . . —PRESIDENT JOHN F. KENNEDY.

In Recognition of the Public Service to Alleviate Suffering among People of the World. . .

—CONGRESSIONAL MEDAL.

The cancer went no deeper than my flesh. There was no cancer in my spirit. —DR. TOM DOOLEY.

Reporter: "What do you get out of this deal, Dooley?"
Dr. Dooley: "Plenty. My life is more worthwhile."